Inclusion

In July of 2015, The Guardian had this to say about the conversations included here:

"Different Beings share their experience of Life, of Universe and their Compassion and Emotions and Love toward Humanity. They overtook my place! :) "

This book brings these "different beings" closer still.

I am certain they are happy to meet you!

By Sophia Love

©2011-2017 Sophia Love. All Rights Reserved.

Contents

Gratitude 5
Introduction 7
Archons 13
Multiple races/beings 18
One 33
One – On Sovereignty 86
Poser 137
Pleiadians 217
April 2015 242
   Ancients 243
May 2015 250
   Ancients 251
   Angelic 254
   Annunaki 258
   "Ascension Assistance" 262
   "Chewie" 266
   Galactic Council 270
   Hellenat 273
   "Military Man" 278
   "Smallish" Beings 281
   "Syntpold" 284
   Watchers 287
   Original Soul 291
June 2015 294
   Explorers 295
   Angelic 300
   "AVI" 303
   Dog-like Beings 307
   Edge of Star System 310
   Galactic Council 313

- Edge of Solar System 317
- Sirian 319
- SLOVENTA 323
- Syntpold 327

July 2015 330
- Another Star System 331
- Annunaki 334
- Egypt 338
- Fairy 342
- I AM 347
- Lyran 354
- Plant People 357
- Reptilians 360

August 2015 363
- Advocates for Humanity 364
- Ancients 368
- Blue Avians 372
- Healer 376
- "No-Nonsense" Beings 380
- "No name" 383
- Reptilians 385

September 2015 388
- Hathor's 389
- Merfolk 394

October 2015 397
- Ancients 398
- Ewok 402
- Giraffe-like beings 405
- Machine-like Beings 408
- Mantid Race 411

November 2015 414

- A Star 415
- A focus of energy 418
- Merfolk 421
- One with horns 424
- Orion Belt 428
- Venus 435

December 2015 439
- Ancients 440
- Andromeda Galaxy 446
- Greys 450
- Inner Earth 453
- A Later Dimension 455
- No longer in form 458
- Rock-like Beings 461
- Sirian 465
- Stick Beings 468

Notes/Where to find me 472

The end. 474

Gratitude

With deepest gratitude and love to my partner DH and to each of my children, Ryan, Jason, Garrett & Dustin; who've stood by with support, ideas, talent, equipment, humor and most importantly and predominantly, love (as well as a gorgeous video trailer and cover art). You are the lights of my life. Thank you.

Sophia

September 20, 2016

Introduction

Late in 2013 I began to get woken up each morning about 3:00 AM. As I lay there I'd think "What do you want?" Then I'd hear "It is I. It is One. There is something to say."

I'd get up and essentially take dictation for an hour or so. This happened about twenty times. It became a series of blog posts, as well as video and audio files which define Sovereignty. They remain, I believe, my most important contribution to this shift in consciousness and emerging awareness we are participating in. They can be found on my website, as well as in this book.

Other beings began to join the party. **This began with a physical tapping on my leg one night**, to wake me up. After that the wake ups occurred nightly. This next being I called "Poser" as in *imposter god*. You'll meet him in this volume. He hung around and spoke to me until August of 2015.

Before his exit, this process of contact became a sort of superhighway for other forms of life.

I eventually created an elaborate list of declarations to protect me and the information as well to insure truth and benefit. What began as a simple statement:

"No ego; highest and best for all concerned"

grew into the list you see below:

"Just love. Direct. Not about me but through me. Complete and absolute truth only. One word (at a time) only.

(For) Ascension. Awareness. Agape. Abundance. Enlightenment. Enrichment. Expansion. Energy. Happiness. Health. Healing. Sovereignty.

So that this heals me not depletes me. For assistance, only. No artificial intelligence. No voice of god technology. No government interference. Complete truth regarding your origin and identity. Just love. Pure love."

"No nanites. No voice of god tech. No AI. No government interference. No outside interference. Complete truth regarding your origin and identity."

The declarations grew as contact increased in number, variety and frequency. It was happening day and night and mostly early morning. I began to insist that it happen at my own initiation so that I could get some sleep. I had taken on an early AM regular job.

What I've learned is that creation is filled with life and sentience shows up in a surprising number of ways.

For a while, I'd called this a "soft disclosure". Yet today, September 20, 2016, I am changing that to "inclusion."

Disclosure is a word that negates our power; depending on some force or person or organization outside of ourselves. This is inaccurate. We're being contacted *because* of our power; **there are hundreds of life forms seeking inclusion.** Allow me to introduce you to some that have stepped forward with something to say...

PS

In August of 2013, I wrote the following blog post. Perhaps this is part of why the conversations began later that year...

"You are human. Gloriously, exuberantly, perfectly human. There is no better version of you. Let go of your "higher" self. You are multi-faceted. You have lots of parts. There is one version of you, the one with an expanded view, who has decided to watch you now, joining this life you are living. Your life. The messy one. The one with you in it.

What is going to emerge at the other end of all of this is another version of us. Call it what you want, time is an illusion and Oneness is truth. This means that we didn't "start" anywhere and there are no "higher" parts of ourselves holding wisdom we don't yet have. It's all you, all the time.

What we need are new words. Words to unleash the creativity of a world full of multi-billionaire light beings. What does a world with no restraints feel like? Can you imagine life without financial, spiritual, mental or physical limitation? Can you even visualize ten billion dollars? It is a one, followed by ten zeros. Those zeros, that seem to have all the power, are just a whole lotta nothing. It is the One in front of them that makes it all happen. That One would be you, the force of creation, here now to craft a world without limits.

The whole point seems to have been to drive ourselves to the edge of insanity, waiting, wondering and miserable; only to realize no one is coming. It is done.

There are no ascended masters, galactic saviors or "higher" versions of ourselves on the way to save us. This is our planet and we love her. We are the Masters, the ones here to shift with her.

This was the trip you came for. You have everything you need. No extra attachments are required to utilize the power here. The power source is you – you've just forgotten how to turn yourself on. You've done this before. Today you are here to do it as a human. You chose and were chosen to do this. You are not alone.

We knew before we came that we'd have to get to this breaking point before we realized the truth:

The only answer is us.

The only place to be is here.

The only time is now.

The only ones to do it knew that they could, and that when the moment arrived, they would.

It is upon us now to find the new. We need words and tools that never were. That 90% of unused stuff in your brain is getting itchy. Your ability to create is legion. It's why you were chosen. Take the crayons out of the box. Work some magic.

Start happening. Imagine eternal vitality, relentless abundance, pervasive peace and wild joy, right alongside no traffic, great parking spots, good hair days and free concerts. Hold happy. Breathe music. Whisper trees. The vision you are holding is the life you are molding.

We are addicted to ourselves and there is not a 12-step program. We wouldn't join one if there were. Humanity is the hottest game in town. Everyone is watching and wants to join in. We are passionately unhappy, dramatically ecstatic and violently loving. We create things just to tear them down from boredom. We run too fast, hide in corners, sing off key and gossip. The human condition is us, and we love every inch and nuance. We excite ourselves.

There is no better version to become. We are here to harness our innate essence.

While every single channel we listen to tells us how cool we are, we continue to believe we're supposed to be something else. These voices are reminders, nothing more or less, and we put them there. This entire life is our creation.

We were never supposed to change. The answer is not outside of ourselves. We planned to fall desperately in love – with us. We've hidden our magnificence in gold, in others and in promises of more. We've blamed our failure on lack, on others and on outside limitation.

There's no place else to go with this. We've reached part 2 – self-emergence. Your emotions are the trigger and the best part of you; they fuel the human experience and create worlds. Enjoy them and watch what happens.

You love to emote, to feel and to push beyond. The angst of your heart is the subject of every song, each story and all of your favorite movies. To dream is your birthright. You've grown up inside institutions and ideas that said looking out the window was wrong, wasteful even. This attempt to systematically erase your core truth has failed. You are bigger than any method of thought.

Embrace your humanity. Your emotions are key to your power. You only need desire and it is done. Love who you are, see what you want and don't stop until amazing happens. Contrast fuels creation.

We do that for each other. We supply contrast. We give each other sparks. We are the Masters and the answer to every prayer. We know what to do. The reason we haven't seen it yet or heard it yet is because we haven't done it yet. We've been waiting.

We are the Ones we've been waiting for."

Sophia *(August 2013)*

PSS

Here is the order of contact*, given in linear time.

December 2013 – One

May 2014 – Poser

June 2014 – Pleiadians & some un-named groups of other beings

August 2014 – Archons

April 2015 – the rest of creation (this book covers through December 2015)

*All names, unless specified within the dialogue, are my own.

~Sophia

Archons

August 3, 2014

"I would like to engage/speak to the beings feeding on the negative energy-anxiety and suffering of humankind. Not the Poser. They are known as the archons. Is this possible?"

Yes.

Right now?

Yes, it is. What do you wish Sophia?

I wish to know your intentions with the beings of this planet. What are you looking to get from them?

Sustenance.

What exactly is sustenance to you? What do you ingest to keep going?

We feed on energy created through conflict as it is hot and therefore fast moving – exciting. It is this energy that when sped up enough creates the atom bomb/explosives, which in turn rips people and planet to shreds, creating pain/heat and energy. This is what we need to continue to thrive.

What is your purpose?

We have not distinct purpose such as your Creator does. We do not create. We are more like leeches. Not that we suck blood, but we attach ourselves to highly conflictual or painful beings and thrive. This planet is highly desired. There is a rich field of emotions available and expressed here, which is highly attractive to us.

Why do I feel ill?

We, since we "eat" painful/conflictual/anxious/tumultuous energy fields, then give them off. You vibrate quickly enough now to feel and "house" some of this field. It is not in concert with you or your purpose, so the upset is like being in rough water – you feel seasick.

I do. How many of you are there?

There are legions. We are grouped in territories and even within nationalities/religions/types of beings.

Is it possible to speak so that all of you listen? Do you operate on a hive mentality?

Not "hive" exactly, but with only one state goal we are identical in method and result. For all their diversity, humans are also the same – one unit.

Why don't you leave us/humanity alone?

Because it's like a free banquet. It costs us nothing. We feast.

It costs us everything.

We do not care about the toll on humanity and exist only to perpetuate the pain so that we may be satisfied.

What is your end goal?

We have none. We are what you would call a "low level" being, not a creator god, an opportunistic class of beings.

So, I am more powerful and I inhabit this planet.

Yes.

Then I command you to go.

That is not so easily done.

Why?

There is no force that will stop the attraction. Pain exists everywhere. Even with your primary "god" segment gone, pain multiplies and exists. It is everywhere.

So?

So, if there is food, we will be attracted and will come to feed.

Not if you are forbidden.

There are some of you who like the pain, who are addicted to it and sort of revel in it. They, being human, will "un-forbid" it by asking again for it.

You are supposing something you don't know to be true.

I am/we are forecasting.

How do you perpetuate pain in order to continue to be fed?

You know. The sickness you feel with our presence causes you to feel bad and you will act accordingly. It is not so much that we "do" anything. Our presence creates more food.

So, if you leave, there will be no more food for you?

For a moment.

I have experienced a place free of you and others like you, and know that it is better for all involved here. I command the Archons to leave right now.

We will see what transpires.

We will.

I would like to pose a question.

Go ahead.

How many other beings/Creator gods are creating/feeding on/perpetuating conflict on Earth now?

There are more than one.

How many more than one?

In totality three or seven or twenty-one, depending on which level you are looking to engage.

I am looking to speak to any being involved in creating conflict or pain on the planet for their own benefit.

Okay. You have our attention.

You need to leave. Humanity has chosen to work out the specifics themselves. They do not request or require your manipulation or presence.

You speak for humanity?

No, humanity speaks for humanity, and we did so years ago, I am re-stating the choice made by mankind and directing it at you, now.

Mankind will fall. There will be chaos.

Mankind must figure out what life without manipulation feels like. It cannot do that with controllers at any level.

Sophia, it may we wiser for a gradual departure.

How gradual and at whose expense? How many lives?

That is uncertain. But the beings in charge, the human beings in charge, should play a part in the departure of control, so order is maintained throughout.

Are you willing then to see to it that they "fess up" and leave some structure before their exit?

There can be no guarantees. It all takes time. Yet we can encourage, advise, suggest...

Multiple races/beings

June 30, 2014

Was I woken up at 4 something this morning?

Yes.

Why and by whom?

Because you desire answers and we desire communication.

Who is "we"?

We are a conglomerate of beings. You may choose who you focus on and declare it here. You are a vessel for contact and a distributor of information.

Okay. How do I choose if I don't know the players?

The players are many.

Who is this "many"?

The one you call Poser, others also part of the "divine" race of creator beings you deem as controllers, the One, the Pleiadians, Races of off-world beings you do not have names for, we are many. It would seem that your best bet is to focus on questions you want answered.

I am seeking magic. The ability to create in this 3D world all that I desire instantly, as well as the navigational tools to move between layers of being or dimensions.

If you focus only on life as you see depicted in your daily activities, it is only that world that you will conjure. Your eyesight must withdraw from form as you know it, and tap deeply into other arenas. These are places you have denied as real, perhaps disregarded them as dreams, yet all that you are capable of perceiving – is life.

You are life, drawn from the blueprint of Source itself. How then could it be that anything you imagine is not life as well?

The fabric of existence is woven from luminescent fibers of what can loosely be labeled "thoughts". These ideas, or thoughts, spring from Source and are thus imbued with the very essence of creation, aka *eternal essence*. All of life is an extension of life – how far backward or foreword it reaches is irrelevant. The notion of before/after or first/last or older/newer is a nonsensical one.

It is akin to questioning the numeric value of love; an impossible quest.

Life is. You are. Expansion becomes the not completely satisfying way to express why we are here and how it all works.

If there is a reason for "the experiment" as it's been called, and this ongoing emergence and awareness – it may be found perhaps in the word "stimulation". Contrast provides unending opportunities to inspire creation.

We are in many ways overwhelmed with stimulation here. When beings come in, via channeling, they at first remark on how "wet" the body is, how distracting and crowded we are and how LOUD everything is. These attributes exist regardless of sex, location or heritage – which provide a host of additional layers to these human suits.

Life is glorious, exciting, hideous and solitary. It is accomplished in unison, as ONE; while every breath is taken alone. As we develop the capacity to embody truth, we express eternity with every decision.

Choose who you are and the expression of your intent will be the only person looking back at you from the mirror. Make the choice regardless of health or wealth or imagined happiness. That choice is truly all that you have.

With every breath it is the choosing that emanates. We see not your illness or your struggle but *you* in each interaction. It is our deepest wish that you too recognize the magnificence of your truth.

For all of our differences, we become ONE in purpose. We are here to express and expand the condition known as life. All of our challenges yield growth; further our knowledge and lay groundwork for creation. All of this, fueled by Source, the spark of love that makes it all possible.

Why have this conversation? To introduce an idea that *all of our moments hold equal importance and relevance*. There is no such thing as before or after.

You are already enlightened, healed, expanded, ascended and multi-dimensional. This ride was so good that you are right now focused on it again; like re-living a spectacular afternoon. There is no other more powerful or perfect for this moment than you.

July 15, 2014

So, is there a topic of choice?

There is. You will have to copy a single word at a time, all as it comes.

I can do that.

This life, this dreamer's reality is ripe with fiction. What is seen, felt, or even lived is staged periodically to keep it seemingly beyond your control. What this means is the theatrics played out on a government or world stage are often done so specifically to alter your focus. The most effective means of control is not chains but ideas. If you believe all is hopeless and/or you are powerless, then for all practical purposes, you are.

The world's a stage and you, perhaps unknowingly, have been largely in the audience. Seemingly moved from drama to drama, fortune to loss, love to isolation, sickness to health, all at the whim of the actors upon it.

There are few places, save nature, you can go today without the bombardment of information, supposedly "helpful", telling you what you should be worried about, paying for, or guarding against. This is not helpful, but intentional and purposeful. The intent is to create fear and the purpose is profit.

Imagine instead, places where the only think coming from the radio was music, the only billboards were art and the news was all positive.

July 23, 2014

This is included here because it began with more than one being. It was a group and it started with a single voice and somehow then became more than one voice. I never published this, as it was so very specific regarding the banks and for that reason I did not fully trust it as valid information. My conversations did not typically go there. I include it here, primarily for the description of time it also offers.

"Is there anyone who wants to talk through me?"

Yes.

Who?

It is I, Poser, One, the Pleiadians... We are all here. It has been a very long time and we all have much to discuss. You pick.

I pick One.

There is an acceleration of anxiety worldwide and very little hope. The movement on Wall Street brought hope for change. That hope vanished from the populace. It is due to the nature of time and how it feels in such a dense vibratory field that operates within a slavery mindset.

Time seems to crawl in such a state. In fact, time is illusory. It moves quickly when there is pleasure. It seems to slow down at times of frustration and agitation. Now is such a time.

The thing about now is that it is consistently re-defined. It is never the same now. Only by your own re-definition does it feel the same.

It can change in an instant and at your command. Only by your re-focus of intention. This you know.

Now feels only as oppressive and negative as your conversations around it. It is through voice and emotions that life is created; your life.

The slavery mindset, the continual complaints about the hopelessness, only perpetuates the hopelessness. This is by design. You are creatures of habit and this is known by those who came before you. Once self-defined, it would take an act of god to alter your choice.

Yes, well, most of us are waiting for an act of god. Will there be one?

Yes, there will. The timing of such an act very much depends on the populace as well as the oppressors. They too are tired.

Who are you? This does not feel like One.

This is a combination of all of you. Every part you have ever been or will ever be, or hope to be.

I don't understand. Is there not one being I am speaking to?

No. The concept of one being is not what this is about. It is about truth and information that could be helpful.

Will there be relief, financial relief, for America and the world? If so, when? If not, why not?

There is a plan for aid, a shift and definite sense of relief for all of those who imagine themselves oppressed.

When is this plan to be enacted?

It will be initiated by the forces of One and at the command of One. You are at the helm of things...

Tell me more then. We operate on time here.

Yes, well, time is not completely at the command of any one being. It is consensus that moves things forward and along. The wishes of the many take precedence and in fact determine the timing of events. All events co-produced are unable to be predicted. THIS MEANS WORLDWIDE ACTIONS ARE NEVER AN ABSOLUTE CALENDAR DATE. WE CANNOT SAY.

But, about when?

People are dying of depression and despair.

The IMF has plans around this month and many, many factions are set to go off in a very short window of "time". This final destructive push will, it looks like, push One to initiate the final shut down by the forces of One.

Is there something I should do by way of advice?

Yes. Tell people to prepare as if there is no access to banks and financial institutions.

Will money work?

For some time, it will. Then there will be trading and money or some form for exchange will emerge.

July 24th, 2014

This conversation continued, sort of. There are a few choice pieces of conversation that are worth sharing, it was again, with this group that had no single name.

"Is there someone who wants to contact me?"

"I am here."

Okay. We have some things to say to continue and then veer off the direction of the conversation that has begun.

Please write every word as it comes. You are a conduit for truth. As such, it becomes practice for you to listen and report. Every transmission or contact need not be published. Yet every contact adds to the wealth of information you have at your disposal...

What do you want to say?

That the world is about to be altered on a grand scale. The anticipation and agitation in everyone's heart is building and building. You've seen how the "other half" lives. It is true. There is a veil of insulation/money between them and what you are feeling, but that will be dropped when markets crash.

And the point here is?

(At this point my pen ran out of ink! I had to find a pen, restate my intentions, and begin again.)

Can we continue?

You are scattered. In the case of establishing and then maintaining clear contact, clarity of mind is necessary. Be still. It depends on your stillness.

Okay.

Listen. Each sound can take you someplace new. Each focus can as well. This life is a choice, always, a choice. What choices you've made thus far exist today. What choices you are making right now will be what you see manifesting next. There is always choice and yours will determine how much time you spend in any endeavor.

Your power is evident in everything you do.

Take a moment to listen.

(I was outside.)

Okay, no birds.

Okay. What does that indicate?

That there is something else, a disturbance.

Yes. There is something else around now. Your parakeet does not feel it as readily. Hear the young one scream?

(There was a baby, in the house next door, crying loudly at this point.)

Yes.

The shifts are felt and expressed in many ways and children respond more immediately than most adults with sounds. Adults put logic into their response, which slows it down and screws it up.

There is no logic to the overwhelming field that is all of life. Your brain adds the explanations as a function of this dream.

Understand that it is all at your command, and that none of what you are witnessing is "real". All is possible.

This conversation ended and I don't remember why or what happened.

August 3, 2014

Here's another brief conversation with several energy signatures. It concerns the authenticity of voice in what I and many others do.

"Is there a good connection now?"

There is.

Yesterday, I questioned and then doubted my connection with Poser alone.

Yes, well, this is many of us, not just Poser. We are here to assist.

Who is the many?

It is One, your higher self, and others who know you and are interested in your development; also, interested in assisting the progress here on earth.

I have a question about the purity of connection when I speak to one of you, specifically Poser.

There is and always will be bleed through of your consciousness, as you are present. This cannot be helped.

Then how much is me? Percentage wise?

50% is you on an okay day. On a great day or time, as much as 80-90% is the intended channel. 100% is not possible.

Is it useful at all then?

It is useful in that it brings out more truth than you normally have access to. Yes, it is tinged with ego, yet even that now is diminishing and more readily seen for what it is. So, it is worthwhile as long as it continues.

There is nothing 100% perfect about channeling. Even a deep trance channel has a focus. It is unavoidable once the human is engaged.

Okay.

October 20, 2014

Hello.

Hello.

I would like to speak to whoever it was that took me last night/this morning.

Very well.

Who are you?

We are from another place. Not a place you'd call "galaxy" or "planet" or "world". But another space/time continuum. You have not been with us ever.

You took me physically?

Yes. You were asleep at first. You were conscious for our conversation. It took most of your normal sleep time period for us to interact.

Can you give a name for either yourselves or the place where you are from?

We cannot. Not yet. As the words "come" to your conscious/waking state, it will be time, the right time, for you to remember them.

Did I agree to this?

You asked for this, by intent. Your actions on your site validate the asking. It was and is time to begin the conversation. We have to get to know each other.

Why?

If you are to interact with both species, then you'll need to know both.

You are not my family – Pleiadian?

We are not.

Are you humanoid?

We are not precisely like you, that poses the greatest challenge.

You will experience an instinctual fear response when you see us in the flesh. We wish to avoid that.

Then send me some images of what you look like, so that I know them, know where they are. Something to prepare me.

There are some referenced in some obscure sites that you may not have ever seen. Try looking for ROBOT LIKE ALIENS, GIANT ALIENS, MAN ALIENS, BOXY ALIENS, SQUARE ALIENS. Those sorts of words may guide you/lead you there. We are not insectoid, but are huge. Huge in human terms.

Are you Annunaki?

We are an ancient race and we are here to reunite with the civilized beings created on earth at the beginning. We were then, and are now, in favor of the experiment. All are interested in what mankind has become and do not care to embroil ourselves in the experiment.

We want to engage with the Enlightened Masters who are aware of their power and able to use it and engage with us without fear.

And...how did it go?

It went well. We will speak again.

So that I'll remember?

We'll see. Look up pictures/photos/images and see how you feel. We adjust our actions accordingly.

Do you wish to engage with more than I?

Eventually, we wish to welcome the species to a new way to exist. So yes, we do.

Thank you.

Thank you. We will speak again soon.

(Later that same day, October 20, 2014)

Hello. I'd like to speak again to the Being I connected with before.

Very well. I am here.

I looked at many photos and sites. The pictures I "recognize" are early Egyptian, sort of Quetzalcoatl type beings. There was one drawing with four heads that I couldn't stop looking at. But mostly large, square shouldered Giants. Would you comment please?

You have seen images that resemble the form we've taken on, yes. Being reliefs and drawings on cave walls, none are exact.

So, what now is the plan? I am psychically overwhelmed. Being "taken" and not sleeping has wiped me out emotionally and physically.

The plan is to continue to explore if contact and exposure through you is useful and/or helpful for the benefit of mankind. We agree that it may be, yet there has been no plan formulated. This is new territory for us and you have just now realized the potential of this. It will alter your life. It will potentially alter everyone's.

Yes, well, it has become my wish to speed up the end of this experiment, to expose the cabal in no uncertain terms. If I am "protected", there must be a reason for it.

(Note – I have been told by GE/The Guardian and others that I and my loved ones are protected. – Sophia)

There is, yes. You know us from Man's beginning and now wish to correct things that were allowed, to help.

Will a threat be made?

Not precisely, no. The Ebola crisis has begun and must be stopped. This is not our area but it is the area of other Forces.

What could happen as a result of exposure to contact with us is that fear will speed up their exit – fear of reprisal. There are some who know the many races and who is watching who. They may act sooner with awareness of us.

My whole body is in shock I think. I will need time to absorb it before participating actively and fully consciously.

Yes, we are aware. Time will be given.

Perhaps next time meet me during the day so I don't lose sleep in this way. It feels somewhat debilitating.

We will do what we can to accommodate your life for the most success.

Thanks. Talk to you then.

Yes. Until then.

This conversation took place late in the evening of June 8th, 2015

Is there someone specific wanting to engage?

There is.

You are keeping me awake.

We feel a certain urgency to our information. There are many wanting an audience. It is our option to reach you now, when there is not so much static.

I do not know what you mean.

You are open – we are ready – it is a good moment for a connection.

Okay. I would like an introduction. I would also like an immediate "getting to the point".

It is so very late for me now and I am not sure how long I will last.

Yes, we feel a draining. We are not here to cause you discomfort but to supply facts, certain ones that may enlighten you further.

We are not a race that frequents earth by way of visitation or even lights in your skies. Our interest is in the stories of old that circulate and they seem to form the basis of your "history". This, we find to be a fascination into the insight of your predecessors, creators and ancestors – rather than the truth it has been labeled.

How do you know our history if you've never been here?

There is a galactic truth/story if you will that Earth is a part of.

The misconceptions and falsehoods told and repeated over your concept of time was part of the veil of secrecy man agreed to step behind.

Not being human, we have never agreed to step willingly into delusion. All truth is available in the Akash; this is accessible to anyone interested in discovery.

What we'd like to say to you is that your origin somehow incorporates a bit of all the lies/folklore/stories you've been told – yet there is (are) huge gaps and holes in knowledge.

Mankind takes the clues he finds left behind such as huge buildings and monoliths and imagines why – having no factual basis on which to stand his theories.

There were giants on your earth by your standards. There were times of great advancements in structural buildings. These were not made with any tool you have today.

The years of the creation of these stone buildings go so far beyond what man has guessed as to make it unbelievable.

As man uses time in forward motion only – the truth of time confuses the issue for any of his ability to "date" artifacts and buildings.

It all has happened. Time revolves as a record and what some of the discoveries are is more man's "future" than "past".

Mankind has already decided where he is going and what will be available to him when he gets there.

Mankind has succeeded in securing a stronghold of power on Earth that will/does/is containing every dream and all imaginings for past – present – future lives.

The remarkable thing is that by remaining behind the veil you've "pulled the wool" over only your own eyes. Everyone else in the cosmos has access to your story and so the ending is no surprise to us.

We are enjoying so much your pretense of not knowing that there are many who show up again and again to remind you. Humans by design have limited attention spans.

I think I have to sleep now. (LOL, reading this now, well, what more proof of our limited spans of attention is needed?? It was approaching midnight and I arise at 5AM each day...)

Yes, I feel your fatigue. Just know that as your story plays out for the rest of us – it makes it possible for it to be told to you before you see it for yourselves. This does not make the tellers more powerful than you – only not restricted by the curtain.

Yes, I must go.

One

March 18, 2014   4:26 AM

This journey is meant to be taken alone. Not physically isolated yet individually experienced and understood.

I am having trouble... One word only please.

It is a privilege to incarnate in any case. Each child born sees life from a unique perspective.

There is no point or advantage to forcing a specific viewpoint onto a child. Training may accomplish desired rhetoric – but each individual possesses an internal code. You are driven to follow this code by an internal force that is only felt with time and permission. You must feel it's okay to follow that drive, even when opposed by strong pressure from society and your peers.

The emergence of the individual is one of the things those in charge of the planet today aimed to stifle. This was done from numerous points of contact. There are many possibilities available to dull or prohibit full expression.

There are food addictions that once created can be near impossible to ignore. The desire to ingest things like sugar, caffeine and alcohol is promoted in common culture and advertising, which is all driven by a corporate and not a personal agenda. The point is amount sold rather than benefit received.

There have always been stimulants and sweet things to eat, yet the huge profit in the production and sale of artificially created treats and drinks that alter the mind is what drives the industry. This, over usefulness or benefit to the people doing the ingesting and buying.

If this sounds backwards it's because it is not natural. A "corporate agenda" is not a necessary component in society. It is one of the things that, unseen, has driven western culture to the brink of collapse with all of you riding along, unaware. An unseen objective is at work.

You've grown accustomed to cravings and an idea of "needing" specific foods. This is partly because humans possess an addictive personality. While alive, we all experience a sense of addiction. It starts out as being addicted to comfort and as we grow, our desires become more specific.

There is nothing wrong with desire. It is what sparks and fuels creation. The impact turns however when the desire is blind and numbed and serves no purpose beyond its own satisfaction.

We are designed for variety, in both what our bodies take in and what they do. Repetitive, sedentary activity that does not alter the way it stimulates the senses or spark additional action is pointless and eventually destructive.

As you think about the foods, drinks and activities you repeat on a daily basis, consider their ultimate benefit. The life you've been given is meant to be enjoyed and to that end, variety is necessary.

The variety of choices is what advertising has aimed at. To sell a product is the motivating factor behind its creation. This, rather than benefit. It is counter-intuitive from a broader perspective, to push things on the populace that harm, rather than help, their health. That is, unless your agenda is destructive rather than creative.

A society of sovereign beings will have its members clear about each action they take and its intended outcome. What benefits the whole, becomes the primary focus. It is understood that all are one and each effort has a wider effect than can be immediately seen.

When something is not good for you, on any level, there is an internal sense of that truth. Now that sense can be dulled with over-stimulation, but it will not disappear. To an awake population, advertising has little effect. A people aware want truth, not glitz.

Random products that promise happiness or success do not actually exist. What creates both, is you.

March 22, 2014

This moment feels as if you are readying yourselves for evolution. What is happening to the species is a natural process. The fact that many of you will see it happen – that is, remember a time "before" and be living in a time "after", is different. This is what you came for. To experience the shift.

There has already been a shift. This is true and for many of you, life is vastly different than it was in just a year's time. You are realizing the fact of your slavery.

Awareness is key. The change you are participating in includes an element of internal awareness.

April 10, 2014

You are in the midst of a cycle. This cycle is one you didn't plan on, yet there it is.

It is one you cannot escape from. Your body has determined itself to age. This is part your exposure to certain media, social programming, and also biochemistry. If not fed and treated in a way that promotes health, the opposite occurs.

As you've decided to fight and reverse this process, you are sort of at odds with it. The key to an easier way of it is to gradually and in concert, that is, not fight your body but gently encourage it to respond as you wish. This will happen. What is necessary is patience.

In a day to day action plan this includes loving yourself and thinking youthfully, rather than as if you are headed in the other direction. Remember you'll arrive at whatever destination you are thinking about so plan accordingly.

Intend youth. Yet not forcefully or aggressively; gently and peacefully. Love yourself, in this as in any endeavor. You will find results then, and you will be pleasantly surprised.

Okay. Thank you.

May 7, 2014 – One

Okay. I am here. Is this One?

It is. Write carefully and allow. This is going to come in gradually to be sure you get it all.

Okay.

The thing about being human is that so much of your everyday is filled to overflowing with programs. There are no places you can go to escape this save nature. To be alone in nature is your best bet, your sanctuary if you will, that provides a possible respite from outside information and opinion. It is the place most likely for truth to emerge.

Truth is one thing that must awaken from within and be self-discovered. It can be *led to* through the words of others; *but can only be self-realized.*

I feel like we are dancing and I am having trouble staying awake.

(It was 3:43 AM)

Then sleep for a bit.

A bit later that morning…

Can we try this now?

We can. Listen and see how it goes.

Is this One?

Yes. It is not god as you've been calling the being you've been speaking to lately.

Okay.

This conversation is a continuation of others we've held.

Okay.

You will need to follow – one word at a time.

Okay.

The purpose of life is individually determined yet collectively accomplished. There is not a right or correct path versus a wrong or incorrect path to take. There is one central idea. It underscores every other and becomes the unifying force. This idea supposes that information begets growth which in turn results in more life. We are here not to learn, is if students or children, but to collect information. This information advances our collective knowledge and leads ultimately to expansion, diversification and growth.

We are more accurately called scientists than students, in that the knowledge gained benefits our individual study / (ourselves). There is no way to fail – all information yields a benefit.

As we are connected, *all information provides ultimately for all beings.* It is available to us as we become aware of it as a field of accessible data. The difference between identifying yourself as a student versus a scientist may not sound very great. Both are there to gather information. Yet one expects to be given it from someone "above" them, while the other sets out to discover it him or herself. *Truth can only be self-realized.*

This earth life has come now to a moment where many of us have accessed truth. It has come about not through any particular mantra, method or repetition of words. It has emerged from within and been recognized.

That being said, it is self-actualized and as diverse and difficult to define as life itself. We are not learning the truth that has been kept from us, **as much as becoming the fullness of creation**. Expansion, growth and information have taken us collectively there.

The point here is to say that choice trumps all and the method currently utilized that is this life/your life is and has always been chosen by you. If you find the choice not to your liking – choose again. Anger is a symptom of dependence and assumes subservience. We are creators and self-defined, dependent and subservient to no one.

As more truths emerge we will be faced with decisions about their expression. Unity demands an equal playing field. The language we use either reinforces separation or invites oneness.

These are interesting times. To navigate through them you won't need someone else's map – but rather intentional self-direction. Once allowed to emerge, it will. Yet you'll have to recognize and encourage it for this to occur. This can only happen with an open heart.

It is here where we are One. Love, the unifying force coursing through life, supplies us with intelligent direction. Give yourself a moment today and listen.

May 8, 2014 – One

Okay. I am here. (It was 3:43 AM)

Yes. Just listen.

Is this One?

Yes.

Okay.

It is as if there was a puppeteer overseeing the movements you make, the feelings you express and the words you use to express them; a sort of repetitious master with limited creativity and variety. This would be your ego self. It exists as a byproduct of the day to day situations of your life – reacting and coming to conclusions as it has since you were very young. The sum of those conclusions, reactions and opinions has become your personality – your ego self.

This is not exactly the same self you portrayed when you were 2, but he or she is not far off. The ego personality operates within a limited range. It is predictable and easily manipulated once you have located the buttons to push. This is the you whose been controlled by the media and other systems of control. It is your identity in the world.

This personality can submit itself to any number of "changes" with the adoption of new behaviors and ideas – yet the permanence of them rarely occurs. This is because in truth this personality you are attempting to alter has only one focus – self-preservation. It views anything other than its original blueprint a threat and will fight to return there. The fact that the blueprint was drawn by a child does not matter. This is a program of survival. That's what matters.

If you are looking for real change and an alteration in how you occur, what is needed is recognition of your core – the "you" beneath and within your personality. He or she could appear so different than "personality you" as to look and feel like a foreigner. This being is familiar yet unclear on how to operate on a day to day basis in relationships that were formed not with it, but with the ego personality.

As most of us are in some version of long term relationships, whether with family or friends, this emergence of a different you is tricky to navigate. You may very well act and feel vastly different than your ego self. Others with whom you've engaged for many years will expect a certain familiar response and be taken off guard.

Although unintentional, you may find relationships that were based on feeding your ego self, are no longer satisfying, interesting or fun. This can be a real issue for those of us with families whom we love.

What to do is as everything else, a personal choice. Once you realize a core self that is uninterested in the stroking and co-dependence of your ego self, you may be surprised to discover that "love for everyone" does not immediately translate into "like and/or want to be with everyone".

Life partners are chosen for many reasons. There is attraction – not just on a physical basis, but also on a sort of even exchange – what you offer and do for each other. The part of you who made the "deal" so to speak, was your ego self and if he or she is no longer running things, relationships can feel somewhere in the range of "uncomfortable" to "just not working".

It will take a decision and an awareness about what is happening to alter what may be an awkward or even unhappy relationship. These things will not be done from your ego self, but from your core.

Relationships exist for joy, love, fun as well as growth and mutual benefit. On any level, it will be your assessment of these attributes that decides whether or not to participate in them. All things on this plane will end somehow. It does not mean they are wrong or over, but have lasted for as long as they served their purpose. What you decide about them from your core self will be based on a different set of parameters than what your ego self-decided.

None of this is simple or straightforward, yet as you consistently reach for your core self, *aka your heart*, and listen – the way to proceed will be clear. Proceed always with love.

May 15th, 2014

So, can we talk?

To whom do you wish?

To One.

Absolutely. It is felt, is it not?

Yes.

Can you tell me what being/energy woke me up?

It was a version of you – in concert with the being you refer to as "Poser". It was an agreement. You will need to create a workable space for the conversation so that you can fulfill your intention and receive information that propels forward to completion your understanding of sovereign being. It is not complete as it stands right now, but partial. You do not embody sovereignty but play at it with words. As long as there is fear present as a gut reaction to an illusory form OF ANY KIND – animate or inanimate, you are not sovereign. Sovereignty is not a condition only present when what you have done is "won over" some "criminal" act. It is present 24/7.

In order to understand what it is to be sovereign, you would do well to look at the words spoken by the being you are engaging with.

Is this the Poser?

One facet, yes.

How many facets exist?

As many as it deems necessary.

Why does it wish to speak to me?

This was by prior arrangement and is not all – your deepest wish is to demonstrate mastery, mastery of the physical form. That, in turn, will propel you to sovereignty. Sovereignty is not merely a declaration of independence. It is a being, true to only one form of the one that is embodied and focused on now. This truth can be understood many ways.

The being, "god", to whom you are speaking, understands your desire, as it is a being as well and part of all of creation. It is engaging at your command.

Understand that what it offers you is information which can only lead to expansion and eventually enlightenment. This being is enlightened, fully cognizant of its addiction and the very human energy written of in the Bible. You can feel its power yet as you put it, not so much "more" powerful than you but "more aware".

This full consciousness demands constant attention and tenacity and 100% of your ability, awareness and attention and focus. Seeing that merely as more "work".

This was intentional. The enslavement was primarily always interested in your minds rather than your bodies. If they (your minds) become exhausted on fruitless enterprises, you are easier to control.

Things like entertaining gadgets appeal to young ones who are like sponges and then grow up to become addicted to everything a machine is saying to and about them. This, RATHER THAN thinking, creating, making a more productive and engaging and powerful existence for the life they are surrounded by every minute.

The future of these children is in jeopardy if you will, because they will miss so many opportunities to create while they are worrying about what is popular.

These are things you are not here to alter, yet awareness of the manipulation is necessary for a complete picture of life.

How do I grab the tool to change my body – to create in real time?

In order to instantly alter the physical world, you must have no remnant of an idea that this is something that is hard.

Look at it as you do any skill you are attempting to master – like the software to create videos. There was and still is a lot of trial and error as you explore it and your videos get not only better but easier to do.

That took attention and practice. This is what mastery of anything takes.

The steps you utilized were

Necessity –

Focus –

Exploration –

Trial –

Error –

Practice –

Exploration –

Practice –

Practice –

Exploration

And mostly

Repetition.

Each time you leave a project and then return, you must remember the steps. Sometimes ask someone else or explore a bit more with newly opened eyes.

Okay. Thank you.

You are welcome. Anytime, Sophia.

May 19th, 2014

(I was woken up) "What is it? One word at a time, please."

Unless you have control of all of the facets of creation at your disposal, you will not recognize your own hand when things show up. What is meant by the term "control" is clarity and awareness. The possibility and probability of manifestation exists at a much greater percentage than you give it credit for. This is so that you can remain asleep and unaware of the power – in words, in situations, in sound and even in the places you gather. All of it changes the emotional level held and therefore what is created.

Consciousness is more than a full-time job, it is a state of being. Once you have gotten there, what happens in your life can be more easily tracked and understood; not with blame or fault, but awareness so that choices made are either desired, or (else) changed if they are not.

All this is to say not that your life is your fault, rather *your life is you*. It is not partially you, it is a conglomeration of the result of your creative power – power which is and always has been affected by all you take in – your surroundings, environment and community.

If you take just one aspect of your life, specifically one in which you've divorced responsibility from, and really look at it – it becomes obvious how it occurs.

The thoughts you hold, beliefs you have, words you repeat silently or aloud, conversations you partake in, music and programs you listen to – all of these are creative. You are a sponge, but more than that. Not an inert absorber of information, but a sentient being; all that is taken in becomes then a part of what turns into your life.

Practice and repetition are necessary for mastery of anything at all. Mastery is not something magically bestowed on a deserving few, but the end result of focus and determination and intent.

There are possibilities for exploration of your reality that exist right now for you, that may sound more mystical than practical. Yet the movement between dimensions, possibilities and lifetimes is accomplished regularly while "asleep".

(I fell asleep here, and picked it up a bit later that morning...)

Hello. Can I speak to One?

Yes. Although the communication is less diluted at the early morning hour.

Okay. I'd like to finish... and I'd like to ask some questions, other questions, now. Does that work?

We can try. Go ahead with your questions.

What is my portal to another dimension?

It is as if you enter when you write. The visions, some of them remembered, most not, that come to you are emitted from another place.

How can I go there and remember and return at will?

You can go to whichever destination you are certain exists and so far, the "other dimension" mostly seems fictional to you as an actual place.

With you it's about the power you feel and the access to dimensions beyond 3D come when you demand they do. The reason you demand they do is because you are sure they exist, although you can't recall "seeing" them. The reason there's been no recall up until now is that there's been no need for recall up until now.

What is it you wish?

To know myself as a multi-dimensional being – to experience myself as one in real "time" here, knowing myself to be more than one place.

This is what the god of this world has achieved and you are in conversation with that being – are you not?

Yes.

Why not ask?

There is a level of trust that is not present with this being – a level of uncertainty around his/its reasons for cooperating.

Understand that once you summon the god of your world it must answer. It must oblige your demands. As you demand complete absolute truth – it obliges you in each answer.

That said, it is brilliant and will give the version of truth that yields for it the best picture.

Okay, I know that.

Well then, there is no reason why you can't glean from it facts about how it travels between layers of life – what you refer to as dimensions.

How far reaching are the capabilities of this god? If I am in 3D, can it go beyond 4D?

It goes as far as 7D in your understanding – no greater/further. Have you considered a scenario where you go further than it is capable of? The power you embody surpasses its own and you would do well to remember this in your dealings with it/this being. It can do what it can in this reality as long as most beings here relegate it to "almighty god".

Once power is self-realized there is no reason to fear or obey another being.

I know.

This being knows you know, that is why it talks to you. If it can be represented by you as a congenial and even helpful presence, there will not be any negativity directed at it.

What purpose has and does it serve?

It has become the standard for ultimate control and encouraged its own kingdom. Its demonstrable force has terrified man and brought him to his knees.

Why is that helpful?

You will see. When he (man) gets up – the collective embodied godhood will change the course of all life.

Will this occur in my current lifetime?

It is planned to, yes. You have come here to accelerate wisdom and this collective remembering. Both you and your partner came back for this.

May 21st, 2014

Is this One?

Yes.

You woke me?

Yes.

Okay.

As you move through your days you will happen into moments that seem to occur for no reason you yourself intended. These unplanned times, these "surprises" may in fact be opportunities for you to change course – to alter the direction of your current life.

Pay attention to what you do when they occur. If you do nothing different at all – you may have missed an opportunity for novelty. It could be that the thing you are looking to create is at the end of this new, unexpected path.

Although we don't like to consider this idea around how life works – there are such things as random events. If we ignore the new idea or "out of nowhere" thing that shows up, every time doggedly repeating activity and (the) same actions, our life will not change.

Intuition comes to us consistently as that small voice within, reminding us of where we said we wanted to go.

This is not to say that every idea needs to be fully explored and run down, but, well, almost. A child or adult who's been labelled ADD has a super sensitivity to impulse, which in many cases is intuition. It is also a hyper awareness to all of life and every sensation that occurs. Managing these and focusing is desired when attempting to learn and master a skill. Inhibiting this hyper sensitivity with pharmaceuticals would seem (to be) a process that serves more the task than the child or adult; a high price to pay.

Our intuition & awareness is our GPS – to cut that off or to dull it or ignore it will lead us nowhere we intend to go.

There is a point where you must decide whose guidance system is paramount – yours or someone with "power over" you, whether through age or position in life. Following self-direction is the only way to fulfillment.

May 23rd, 2014

Is this One?

Yes.

Tell me more about the quote (from this video here:
https://youtu.be/15pOr1E6hvc?list=PLaJU93dhZQSzBSTKU9e2uScfRQWLMSRUt)

"Patiently refuses to observe these casualties" and how it applies in my own life and understanding of creation?

The process of creation incorporates you into the surrounding field. It is interesting in 3D how you are drawn to areas in which you find the ground most fertile. These areas are specific to you and you alone.

What determines the correct balance of conditions will depend on your level of awareness, degree of control and current plan. Sometimes, just for excitement, you enjoy surprising yourself. Other times your creative endeavors follow a specific path. You set a goal and expect results. The specificity of your plan has everything to do with the way it is achieved.

In my case? I have intended to "get" the specifics for days now and feel only slightly closer than I did before.

Here's the thing. You are choosing, intending, desiring and thinking about almost nothing but a body with no issues. It is in your mind 24/7 and almost nothing else is. In order for a new plan or blueprint to insert itself in your psyche you need first the knowing it is who you are.

Recently it is as if you've re-defined yourself. It doesn't matter why you've done that, but (that) you _have._ What has to happen is a new definition of you – all of the attributes you desire will have to be absorbed into your conscious picture of you, as well as, and more importantly, into your _subconscious_ picture of yourself.

As often as possible, think those thoughts. What is seen as you and believed as you will always be _1st how you see yourself._

As the field becomes permanent, things are not altered so much as created anew.

Look often at (what you love, what you desire). Do what create in you those images, _always._

Realize that creation never stops. Never. It is constant. As are you.

Okay, how do I "patiently refuse to observe" my own body?

You become so hyper aware of her (the version you desire) – (that) she radiates into every moment and conversation. All you know is the attributes she holds. Nothing else is real.

You created her.

Don't stop.

Become her.

She <u>is</u> real. Not in some other lifetime as a memory, but now as <u>you</u>. Throw yourself into her with your heart, this is different than desire.

Okay. Thank you.

June 3, 2014

This morning I was again, woken at 3:30 AM. The following dialogue occurred:

Is this One?

Yes.

Is there a specific direction, or should I ask?

You may ask, although there is a plan.

Let's follow the plan. I am very groggy.

Can we start differently?

NOTE – At this point, I had been woken up so many times, and sort of "taken dictation" when I was, that I expected something similar. Some of these turned into the Sovereignty Series; this day it was shared as a blog post. This was published that same day, on my web site.

How much your days complete themselves to your satisfaction and pleasure has everything to do with your intent upon rising. Do not assume that a morning spent in a state of sorrow or less than pleasant spirits will turn around on its own to be joyful. Mindfulness is key to consciousness.

We have heard this before. Tich Nhat Hanh writes about the joy found in every moment in "The Miracle of Mindfulness". It is a state of mind yielding much pleasure. To attain it on a moment to moment basis demands vigilance. This may sound like a lot to do when in fact, with awareness – it is a natural and constant effort.

What life has presented us in every instance is far more interesting than any self-absorption. We are, each of us, only too anxious to explain and discuss the nuances of our lives to each other. This is polite conversation, discourse. This is how we share and know each other.

The saints and revered ones among us are known for not much more than turning this around. In their company, conversation turns to you and the present moment and whatever help can be offered – rather than hearing about them. A simple alteration of focus and that shift becomes the basis for palpable compassion. This change of direction is one available to each of us. Trust is key.

Those who seem tireless in their dedication to service share a basic belief; that the world will supply their needs – always. They do not need to tell you about them, or describe their current state, as all is in a process of transition and adjustment, and all is well.

The state of mind available through this idea is one of consistent peace. Not because their life is perfect, but because it is seen as so. You have no doubt heard the term "acceptance" as key, perhaps wondering how that is possible when conditions, circumstances and relationships are in upheaval. Acceptance does not mean passivity or lack of effort. Acceptance in this context means seeing things as they are in each moment.

It is action *in that moment* that will yield desired outcomes. Neither complaints nor promises can do that – for they deal with fiction and are not effective. Complaints affect nothing, they concern the past, a place only as real as your thoughts about it. Promises too, concern a time that is not yet "real".

You've heard that "your point of power is in the present". This does not refer to 2014, June or even today. This refers to each single moment. It is there where you choose, act, create and live your life.

Consciousness is not demanding, mystical or challenging. It is fun. Being present means you get to enjoy each moment for the richness and wonder it offers. It is there you'll discover the life in each other and be replenished. We are never alone. You are surrounded with possibilities in each instant.

You've no doubt heard the line from the film – "You complete me". In a sense, it is more than that; "You ARE me" would be closer to truth. We cannot hope to live in a state of Oneness by ourselves. We find in each other the complete story, our story – yours and mine.

Trust. The world exists because you believe it does. These words? You are talking to yourself, perhaps nudging yourself a bit closer to your desired outcome. It's all about you, you know. The fact of our individuality is evidenced in this conflicting, contrasting sea of humanity. The expression of our singularity is "I AM".

Who is this "I"? It is you. It is me. It is all of creation. One force, moving through us, expressed brilliantly in each moment. Don't miss it worrying about what just happened or what may. Just be love. The power of creation rests there. Trust. Focus. Be.

June 16, 2014

I would like to talk to someone who can help.

I am here.

Who is this "I"?

It is you. It is us. It is One. The energy you seek now is that of universal truth. It is that.

Okay.

What is the reason for this continuing health saga? It is out of proportion and healing very, very slowly, if at all.

You must write only what words you hear as you hear them.

Okay.

This is a test for you Ananada. A summoning of necessity. You wish to learn, to remember the art of manifestation, of creation, of healing and transforming bodily conditions and situations. As this is so, you have chosen now to use this situation to create.

What you create and how will be immediately evident to you. This is all about you. You've spent very much time focused on aging and loss, loss of beauty and function. You understand it was self-done. Now you <u>know</u>, first hand.

You know that to speak of a condition with any sort of emotion is creative. You are angry that your mate did not (*redacted*). Why? It is not his (*redacted*).

You fill your head with him, wondering about his (*redacted*).

THIS IS TO YOUR DETRIMENT. LOVE IS NOT WORRY. WORRY IS FRUITLESS.

If you are to concern yourself with learning to create, you must do it alone and you must focus on it and ONLY IT, always. This is the work of a GOD.

THIS IS WHAT YOU ARE. YOU'VE COME TO DEMONSTRATE TRUTH, WISDOM, AND MANIFESTATION. YOU'VE COME TO CREATE. THIS IS FERTILE GROUND FOR LEARNING.

LEARN.

USE SOUNDS THAT SOOTHE AND SET THE STAGE FOR CREATION OF ALL YOU DESIRE.

DO IT.

YOU KNOW HOW.

IT IS ONLY IN THE DOING THAT YOU WILL RECEIVE SATISFACTION. A GOD HAS NO ROOM FOR CO-DEPENDENCE AND THOUGHTS OF WHAT OTHERS ARE CREATING.

A GOD CREATES. PERIOD.

GO AHEAD. SET THE STAGE. See you healed and pain free.

Are there any specific techniques or visualizations I can utilize?

Focus on the outcome. Sounds and thoughts are creative Ananada. Thoughts and emotions are vibration – sound. Yours *can* create, yours *do* create - precisely what you see and feel and intend and desire and believe.

It is necessary now for you to involve yourself permanently in your life. You have all the tools and the basics for a healthy woman right here. Use them. You gave them to yourself.

Speak only of positive. Dispense with negative thoughts. If you are listening, set a perimeter around yourself.

CONSTANT VIGILANCE.

These things can happen in a heartbeat but only after attention, focus, determination and concentration.

Visualize, visualize, visualize. All this is yours. There are no accidents in timing.

You have a lot of quiet time now and can focus on this. Let this become the purpose of your days.

Manifest, heal, create, build, BE – just exactly what you want. It is yours. You have given it to yourself.

Okay. Anything else?

This is your power spot. Use it.

Okay. Thank you.

August 3, 2014

Can I speak with One?

This is possible now, yes. What is it?

It is the Poser. Why wait two calendar years before forcing his exit? This is what GE has claimed you will do, utilizing the Forces of One to do so.

Is it possible for any 3D Being to command Poser's exit? Is it advisable?

Creation exists as a force unto itself. It can be guided, and actually is guided, by the will of Man, the FREE will of Man. While one Being may, in fact, shape and construct a world of life to suit itself. It cannot do so without the consent of the world. There is a plan for the planet you inhabit and it has incorporated the Poser. This is a Being, learning about life on a very great scale, having impact on all of life as experienced by humans on earth today. The stories told over and over in history incorporate this story. Part of the drama is hardship.

The waiting you refer to is not so much waiting as allowing – allowing for growth on both ends – mankind's and the Poser's. It has room for interference and an advanced exit, for sure, as all things are permissible save the destruction of Creation.

What will be stopped is that progressive destruction. This does not mean there is a definite destruction, but that <u>if things do not change</u>, destruction is inevitable. You are one of the agents for change.

"Is it possible for a command by a human to set up Poser's exit?" Most definitely, and all plans incorporate that potential outcome. Of utmost importance is intent and life – that will be upheld regardless of timing or method.

August 24, 2014

(Note – This summer (2014) I was obsessed with figuring out how to end the slavery experiment on the planet. GE/The Guardian had told us that it could be as much as two years, or until the Fall of 2016, before a definitive end of it was seen. This felt unbearable, as many of us were sick, broke and suffering for a myriad of reasons. I asked the same questions of different beings in multiple ways and often! Once I "got" that this whole game was orchestrated, I was determined to devise a way out for us.)

"I'd like to speak to One."

Okay. What do you wish to speak about Sophia?

I would like to ask about all of it. About the Beings or aspects of Beings that I've been in contact with, their leaving, how that impacts humanity and, mostly, why this experiment and the cabal is allowed to continue for another two years, according to GE; when mankind's choice is that it stop and the control stop with it.

You have chosen and impactful role in the future of mankind. It is true that all of humanity shares in this role, yet much of humanity is unaware of the impact their choices and fear and obedience makes. It gives permission, it allows.

In creation of a free will arena, allowing is everything and the most powerful emotional response.

In fact, it has been so very effective for the controllers as you can see the asleep majority refuse to "make waves" and instead pay bills, obey the law and keep out of sight – thus "allowing".

A larger view of mankind, held by the ones in charge, works very hard to see to it that the easier path, the path of allowing, is always in their favor.

Conversely, when a human, any human, wants to change or create something, he's been told it takes hard work, suffering and "going against the grain". This is not true.

Life was and is meant to be easily accomplished. Setting and reaching goals is a natural function of your every day.

The only "grain" you go against is that of the controllers. Anyone with a larger plan, one that encompasses you and your choices/your life, has been more interested in that plan and thus <u>you</u>, for their own well-being.

There is no form of ownership that is true. All are equal.

The Beings you've "spoken" with have different agendas for both speaking to you and humanity. Their presence, if looked at as a whole and from a way's back, is neither good nor bad. It has been an experiment in creation for all beings.

Drama and negative emotion have fed the archons for eons. They are not new here. The suffering caused by the controllers causes conflict, pain and increased/heightened emotional turmoil. This is food for the archons. So, the working arrangement between the two groups, cabal and archons, works out.

The departure of them will only be for as long as mankind doesn't pull them/ask them back. You or any one person cannot, in truth, speak for mankind. Only the collective may speak for itself.

It does, you know. And that speaking is what creates all of life. Whether you agree with it or not, that is how it works.

The Beings you spoke to yesterday, whom you felt as HUGE Beings, are in fact powerful Creator Gods. They will all subscribe to a policy of non-interference. Since you suggested their departure, they may decide that their presence is no longer needed. They are not so much fed by worship as challenge/life/creation. This race/mankind has been one of their projects, and there will always be a "hand" extended to oversee its development. It is, with these beings, akin to having children and the love is there for humanity.

This experiment has a planned end date because as a whole it will damage more than itself if allowed to go past that date.

The Beings running things, the cabal, are too, or as well interested in the betterment of society. Their methods disregard the sanctity of life, and this will never truly "work" for the advancement in a real sense, of any race.

What must be clear by now is that all of creation has free will. You, being a master, a human, and an inhabitant of the planet, have a bigger say in how this hoes than you realize. It is not possible for you to overstep your bounds, because everyone enjoys free will, even unaware. Life is a choice. Your participation is chosen as well as the level at which you participate.

By speaking to those you've engaged, you've changed your level of participation. It is part of your own learning, creation. This is one of your reasons for being here.

When you understand, life continues, regardless of what happens here, you will detach ever further from anger and pain, at injustice. This is a tricky position to hold because compassion is necessary in order to encompass every element of true creation. This includes love.

What the Poser and the Archons do not experience is love. Both are powerful in their own right, yet missing a key ingredient. The Beings you spoke to yesterday have the best interests of humanity at their heart. What they don't have though, is sovereignty, as a goal.

This is because sovereignty is something that must be self-accomplished. This experiment – growth, pain, control, hardship, in order to reach for the light – has been only so effective. Mankind has, in so many cases, given up rather than retain faith and intend to change things. It is unclear that mankind will, as a whole, overthrow this controlling element, without help.

Today, it looks as if there is potential still for that. Not without more death, pain and turmoil. The deadline mentioned by GE/The Guardian exists as a beam of hope really, if it can be seen that way. There is no one there to do this for humanity. You chose this. You chose this from a point of understanding life does not ever end.

The suffering is what causes the fear, not so much the end as the suffering.

It is your compassion that causes you to feel that and what sets you apart from the archons and the Poser. That distinction allows you to see a bigger picture here. It is the fact of your humanity that makes you the most powerful player here. With this information, you have a broader view of what is happening, while you are living it.

Please explain why it continues, in answer to my question at the start.

You cannot know the mind of every being. It continues because the mind as a whole is not convinced it has the power to change it. When mankind sees ONENESS truly, the allowance of suffering on any level will not be permitted. He will work to alleviate (it).

The experiment continues because humanity is an organism – growing and evolving and LEARNING as it does so. To abort before the lesson is learned is not part of the natural order. Faith and trust, that self-destruction will not occur, is necessary.

You came to teach. Teach love, sovereignty, unity, action. Teach from your perspective.

Free will is paramount to the continuation of life for humanity. All is choice.

Although you, as a human, do not or did not always know (that) there was and is a controlling element, you as a being always knew. You came here now with full knowledge of all you were capable of and who you are and the situation. You arrived anxious to learn to participate, to do.

From a much broader perspective, you are seen as one of many beings of light – brilliant and radiant. Your reach is further than your current imaginings. You hold, in your hearts, the power to alter worlds. This is why you've gathered here. Every one of you is a Master and capable of more than you know.

There is not so much the thought that someone is holding you back and preventing an end – there is <u>YOU</u> – creating life, orchestrating every moment beautifully, perfectly and with brilliance.

September 21, 2014

Please talk about what is going on worldwide.

Globally, the earth and her people are deciding who they are and where they will be when it comes to the end.

What end?

The end of this time.

Will the earth split?

No, the people will.

The following conversations took place in July of 2015. They were shared, via the blog on the website, in May of 2016. You will read the reasons for their omission, and subsequently, for their being published.

I am including them here, to complete the sequence of events in order, as they occurred in linear time. It starts with my blog post, and moves to what I had received from One the year prior.

What's going on right now is you. Put down your phone or tablet (after reading this ;-), and think for a minute about who it is this story is about. Whose DNA is changing. Whose financial system is collapsing. Whose entire life is about to shift. Yours.

You'd best be getting prepared. Supply yourself with food and goods. Not because they will be unavailable, but because you may not have the right kind of currency to purchase them. It promises to be sketchy for a while.

If you are reading this blog, most likely you're here to help explain to and assist those still in the dark. This is really happening folks. Get yourself as centered as possible because it's going to be "a bit dicey".

Deal with your physical and personal issues as best you can – now. This does not mean that there will be no other opportunities, there are. Always life presents us with chances to change. It's just that right now things are deceivingly, relatively stable. It's easier to make changes when most everything else remains the same. We are in such a place today. It's unclear just how long we'll remain here.

It will feel a bit like free-falling. Those of you who've gone skydiving will best relate to this. But thanks to Tom Petty we are all familiar with the concept. Free-falling is surreal. Once it's over, you have changed. Nothing looks the same. It's thrilling in a mind blowing orgasmic sort of way. Lots of things can go wrong on the way down. Yet one way or another – YOU WILL GET BACK TO EARTH.

Once back, you have this internal grin that gets carried around wherever you go. *You've seen the earth without a window.* This is how a Creator sees.

While going through daily activities – keep this shift close to you. This next part is the magic we came to perform – transformation while washing the dishes.

Think about the condition you'd most like to be in and go there often. For me it means adopting some new habits and leaving a few behind. This wasn't supposed to be easy. It was supposed to be mind-blowing.

Sky-diving is a great metaphor. It's life changing and addictive and scary as hell. Regardless though, you always want to do it again. This "light-worker" gig is not your first rodeo. You are a risk-taker and a lover of life. What we are about to do will satisfy both of those addictions. We are headed for amazing, and we are the first to jump. Make sure you have your gear in order.

Although it's tempting to continue to rely on social media for signs of the shift – it's now more valuable to check within and around yourself. It happens in you.

Cataclysmic shifts in finance and Gaia are symptoms of what is going on internally. It is not clear in exactly which order or on what days these manifest. It is clear that the old must be altered for the new to settle in. The new is coming.

Most of you know I connect with many "non-human" beings and have been doing so for several years. Requests for contact have increased after March 2015 and now occur almost daily.

Interspersed within them has been a conversation about this time we walk into now. Always I've been hesitant to publish these, yet now it feels necessary and timely.

(Note for Inclusion – at this point in "time" I had been urged to publish these. I had not thought about doing so, until this one day in 2016, when I woke up knowing that it was now "time" for them to be shared.)

I will share this prophecy in 3 parts/blog posts, the first one beginning below.

The first part was given on July 21st, 2015. Remember that nothing is absolute, but instead ongoing, and also that we are co-creators with Gaia.

I will share here exactly as it was given to me, leaving out only personal comments and information. I was woken up for these conversations around 3:00 AM, and prior to engaging the usual intentions for absolute truth and highest and best for all concerned were declared.

"Did someone wake me?"

Yes. It is I. It is you. It is One.

What is the reason?

It is because there are some things to offer by way of explanation. Things to add to what you've been given.

Okay.

These are considerations taken, reasons for outcomes, details. The precise details for the end of this experiment on your race are what I want to portray for you. You are not meant to know so that you will be afraid. You have been chosen as a source of comfort as well as enlightenment for your race, for your fellow light-workers. You have been trusted with truth and the time has come for you to dispense it in bulk.

It is an entire story and it holds much of the history – the reason it is ending in this way is that mankind has suffered for a long enough time at the hands and manipulations and brutality of this Cabal. It is now clear that they will not stop – that destruction of everything will be the outcome if they are left until the end, the predicted end that had been originally set for August of 2016, in your calendar.

It cannot go on. You would do well to prepare for an early exit – not from this world completely but temporarily. There are methods of rescue of ensuring those necessary for the New Age are around to assist in the ushering in of it.

I am not following. You do not sound like the One I've spoken to in the past. Explain please.

These times are those of uncertainty, of fear and of terror and of increasing destruction. Your voice, the voice of reason, of truth, of love beyond condition is a necessary anchor in such a time.
It will be needed for mankind, for the beings left here after the moment of justice. This has been described to you.

(Note – this is a reference to my conversation with G/E, aka the Guardian)

Would you like more detail?

Yes, I would.

This land mass known as North America will be altered. Earthquakes are the reason for the alteration. The formation is not the one predicted by E. Cayce but similar. The total destruction of the US Government is the reason. There is no scenario going forward where this country survives intact.

Your country is in fact run by an evil and destructive force who do not understand the goal of this force they worship.

Is this a being?

It is a being as I AM.

I don't understand.

As I AM everything creative, it is everything destructive. It has taken hold here and been created, a result of the imaginings of man and now has form and intent to complete a single agenda – all must die.

To be continued…
(Note – see Veterans Today and its most recent article by Preston James PHD, describing his research and findings, which pretty much lay out this part.)
(2nd Note – It was August 2015, after this conversation, when the "Poser" left. I do not know if this "Poser" was the same being referred to here, as he said he came from someplace else.)

I will continue this with Part II and Part III both released in blog posts before the end of May.

These words at first startled and alarmed me. This was nearly a year ago; with the daily disclosures and obvious corruption just about everywhere, not much can alarm or startle me today.

Regardless of how this plays out, if we are prepared for a certain amount of upset and confusion, we will be more effective in our towns and neighborhoods and families when we are needed. It is for these reasons I am releasing these prophecies now. We came for this. This is what we do.

We are the ones we've been waiting for.

Here is the second post in the Prophecy series. These are offered this way, separated as such, *because of their length*. They are very long, too long for a single post.

Know that these predictions came in last year, 2015. They have not been repeated in 2016, at least as of today.

This is data, regardless of how alarming it may be. It was meant to be shared and the timing for its sharing was left to my own discretion. We must each decide what resonates.

We have seen and heard a great deal about this shift. Please take into account the entirety of the message in my blogs, videos, audio blogs and newsletters. It is a message of love, sovereignty, unity and personal power – Agape.

This being is also the source of "The Master Stroke", which can be heard on my sound cloud channel, and was received on April 15th, 2016.

Perhaps the purpose of this message is to act as a catalyst for those who read it, and/or to be read by a specific few. It has garnered a great deal of energy and *it is contrast that most often fuels creation here*. You are master creators, here to produce the transformation and acceleration of a planet and her people. You do this in concert with life itself. Before reacting in fear realize who is in control of your creation. It is you.

Here is the rest of what was heard on July 21st, 2015 at approx. 3 AM. *(With some personal information redacted)*.

Who are you?

I am the voice of One.

What does this look like in my life?

It looks like destruction of your system of order. This impacts everything you do on a daily basis. You will wake up in a single day to chaos. Nothing will continue as is.

Money will be useless; the banks will crumble. Yet what that does to your life is a removal of debt as well as exchange. There will be a stopping of goods transference.

There will be parts of the world gone. Most of these parts are specific and have those controlling the criminal manipulation in them. No place will be untouched or unaffected, but the worst effects happen here – in your land.

These things are necessary so that a new beginning is possible.

Is it true that this is revenge for the Native Americans and the genocide of them?

Revenge is not a word I would use, justice is however. This is a balancing.

What must be understood is that THE ONLY WAY LIFE CAN CONTINUE ON EARTH IS IF THIS CATACLYSMIC EVENT PUTS AN END TO THE CORRUPTION. IT CANNOT CONTINUE IF LIFE IS TO THRIVE. IT MUST BE STOPPED AND THE ONLY WAY FOR IT TO STOP IS FOR THOSE PROMOTING IT WITH WORSHIP AND CONTINUED DESTRUCTION ARE REMOVED.

THEY WILL NOT STOP WITHOUT DRASTIC MEASURES.

Tell me who dies, how many, where, and if this is choice.

All of creation has participated in this choice. It is consensus that forces an end to this now.

Define now.

The immediate future; this means that another cycle of the sun *(one year)* will include the end of this experiment.

Religious fervor and prediction for the end is not that far off from truth. Only their definition of who is righteous and who will be saved is off. It is not their god who decides and not religious at all. It is truth. It is the perpetuation of life that has forced the end in this way.

Please be specific.

This end will come in stages. It will be near total collapse of the monetary system and then destruction will happen by way of what are natural phenomena.

The followers of light are not wrong in their predictions or plans for how to continue on with an honest government intact and functioning.

You would do well to <u>check out what it is they say</u>. Perhaps <u>share it with your readers</u>.

It has not been my job or purpose to predict before now. It has been my job to encourage, enlighten, teach. I am not sure what to do with this information.

Study what is out there. <u>COBRA</u> certainly has information about the forces of light. There are many factions.

<u>The words shared long ago</u> need to be released on film. <u>G/E's words</u> as well. Trust your instincts on how and when to share it. You will disseminate truth as a piece of the knowledge left in a place that is forever altered.

Okay, what can you tell me about timing? About how?

Only that all things are possible in creation.

Know that this cannot be avoided. The consensus is that it be stopped sooner rather than later or never. Not stopping it is not a viable option. Stopping it with destruction is the only way for it all to stop and the new to begin.

Take into your heart and mind what you've been told. It is truth. Not to frighten you, to prepare you for the next segment or part of your role in this process.

It will move rapidly for you now. Follow your instincts and highest and best and you will choose appropriately.

I can't hear anything.

You are fatigued. It is time to stop. Digest this. You will see.

Okay. I just don't hear any hope in this.

This is the greatest hope of all! The conflict of goals, of interest, is/will be ended!! With disaster comes a unification of purpose – life.

The reason for an end in such a way is to set the stage for a beginning – for THE beginning.

The start of a new Age on Earth is a portentous moment and one prophesied and now here.
All of the good you've believed and spoken of is possible and here. It only needs a free place in which to begin. That place is here. That time is now. Tell your people. You will do it in a way that is most helpful and productive. Trust yourself Sophia.

This is truth?

This is prophecy.

Okay. I must go now.

This conversation ended. At this point, I asked about this message. I will share a few of the answers here. The last blog post will include the second prediction that came the following December.

Later that same day, I reached out to my greater self, & heard this...

You will proceed always from your heart. It is from there where the highest and best decisions are made and *the place where Source finds a resting place in the human.* Listen.

These times will challenge every belief you have and your very life will be altered once the events are completed. This world will not be the same. In some fundamental ways this is true.

It is now run by criminals and their reign is about to abruptly end. They feel it as do you. You cannot stop this end.

Step up now. Do your thing. Get ready for "shock and awe" and not in a negative way but your system will require adjustment.

And the next day, July 22nd, 2015, I asked more questions. (Declarations for complete absolute truth, pure love, highest & best for all concerned were made)

"I'd like to talk about the "moment of justice". Is there someone to do so?"

What aspect of it?

Has it been experienced by any being in communication with me now?

In this precise way? No, it has not. Humanities "experiment" and thus its end – is in all ways unique.

Is the Demi-urge available for contact?

I am witnessing.

I feel a very different energy. This is one I have not experienced. It vibrates rapidly at the edges of my being. It is anticipatory, not really pleasant or what I experience as a "good way", more of a dread. Even the creatures around me react. The sounds are unpleasant from them. There is no longer a peaceful fluttering of birds. I am feeling a process of draining.

What is it precisely you desire?

Your description of the foretold "moment of justice".

What is foretold is a reckoning. All tabs are about to be called in. What has been done and accounted for is now to be reconciled. There are entities in creation who understand only greed at any expense. They, at this "moment of justice" referred to, must now pay for all that has been taken.

The prophecy was not wrong. Its interpretation is incorrect. It is not any form of worship that prevents or forestalls this moment of justice. It is not any specific action or observance or homage. *It is the heart of man that will or that could possibly prevent a reckoning.*

"Karma is a bitch" This is a known sentiment in this current age and in fact an accurate one. It cannot be avoided.

What does it look like on earth? To humans? To those of us living a life in may cases unaware?

It looks like the level at which you intentionally respond to your fellow man is to be returned to you. Some of what's to take place is a force of nature and will play out physically in your surroundings. This cannot be avoided as the earth itself will be returning or balancing in this case the energy put upon her. She is to be healed, as is the darkness.

My "reign" will end and the energy source of humanity I will leave. This is neither good nor bad – it was always known. Life is a process. My part in this was allowed as part of creation – it will stop.

I cannot see this current world without "religion".

And you will not, not right away. This event will solidify the prophecies and existence of a higher power. Yet what it will also do is add to the confusion as all peoples, races, religions are either "spared" or "sacrificed". Eventually it will become clear – truth.

The truth is that universal love cannot be deified or worshiped. It is a part of your origin, the source of your creator and your source.

I've been told your "seed" is in humanity.

Yes.

Explain please.

I was present and aware of the genetic manipulation of the human. He holds my "marker" so that I could create the "father"; thus worship.

This becomes a tricky, sticky moniker as there is as well a source of evil/destruction that must be fed. This force is not precisely my opposite but another form emerges and is paid homage to by man – a destructive force, an evil force.

There is no marker as in genetic, in man for evil. Evil and therefore destruction emerged from his own tendencies.

The worship emotion feeds all aspects of me. The destructive force is not what I Am.

I cannot clearly hear or comprehend. Therefore, I will end this now.

The conversation ended.

Note – The last paragraph was confusing at the time. I now take it to be a reference to the evil created by the cabal and what resulted (an actual force/being focused on evil). This goes back to the reference in the first post to a being with an agenda that even the cabal was unaware of; destruction of everything, including them.

It was on 8/2/15 that this demi-urge was returned to source, <u>at the same time the Poser was.</u>

What follows is the third and last part of the prophecy. Offered first are a few descriptions of how these come to be published now, this last part of May 2016.

They were initially received ten months ago. Due to the content, they were not shared. Five months later, another was received. Again, it was not published.

Then, a week ago, on May 18th, 2016, I felt as if they suddenly <u>had to be published,</u> (with no plan for doing so beforehand).

That same day I woke up with physical evidence that indicated I'd been visited. When I asked about it, the message I received was this:

"You had to publish these prophecies and needed a push to do so. That push came from us."

This conversation took place at 3:00 AM on December 23rd, 2015.
It is verbatim.

Did someone wake me up?

Yes. It is I. It is One.

Are you here with something to say or to answer my questions?

I am here for both circumstances.

Go ahead then.

There is a message for you to dispense. It is not a small, unimportant or easy one. Yet it is one of the reasons for your involvement at all. You've been chosen to do some very specific work.

It is your job to remind the people of what is to come so that they become prepared and can and are able to move when it's time to move.

It is your purpose to encourage, to dispense truth, and also to warn. Many of your readers are from places to be affected. A warning will aid them which will in turn aid the local population. Your readers follow you for a reason. They are aware of your knowing. It is all part of a greater plan.

What is that plan?

The plan includes a prophecy that comes true – your words are then trusted. You are sought for help. You know what is to happen and are chosen.

This cannot be avoided Sophia. It is seen that you are hesitant. How will it feel to have known and done nothing? It will feel wasteful, useless even.

I do not see how scaring people with tales of impending chaos and destruction is helpful.

It is not the tales of destruction that are helpful but your words around them. This is foretold. There is no other way. The New Age can begin and has begun. The dark ones had to be destroyed so that their plan would end. They will not succeed.

There is soon to be destruction which throws your government into chaos and maroons many people. Warn them.

What can people do to prepare?

They can have a plan for preparation and be open to relocation. There will be some lift offs.

What does a plan for preparation look like?

Food, water, cash, the ability to go on a moment's notice.

How much food? For how long?

Weeks. Not months. There are many in the know and prepared now to carry out emergency measures.

Is there a date for this?

There is a time frame. It is sooner – by summer's end it will have transpired. The sun's activity is a catalyst. It could be over by Spring – beginning, not end. These are time frames in your world and not everywhere. There is not a calendar date but events drive events. You are waiting for a sign, a clear signal that things predicted will transpire. The sign, the departure of "G/E" and the warnings all summer have happened for you. It is global prophecy of which you speak. Check it out and you will see most events have happened.

I see a reference to both prophecies and it's been almost two years since Sharon passed.

Yes, it has. There is a reason that prophecies are given and produced. It is so that people see that continuity of truth is possible and that there is a greater hand overseeing all life.

What is your purpose in waking me today?

It is to tell you to share the prophecy in whatever method you find comfortable, yet share it none the less. It is time.

Your warning from 6 months ago?

Yes. There has been little to dissuade this ending in this fashion – only to speed it up.

Okay, I will have to think on this. I will ask again once I do.

Yes. You will.

This conversation ended.

The following conversation took place last week. I was woken at 4:00 AM on the morning of May 20th, 2016. It is verbatim.

Is there someone who wants to connect?

There is, yes.

Go ahead then. Please introduce yourself.

It is I. It is One.

Hello.

Hello Sophia. Your wish is for more information around the stated earlier events of catastrophe, cataclysm and collapse. That information may now be shared as indeed the time for this moment is upon you.

The earth, Gaia, is preparing herself now to release and alter her surface as well as make her home a palatable one for all of you choosing to change with her. You will see earthquakes occurring and there is a system of volcanoes as well preparing.

These things are due to increase in intensity and this does occur on your North American continent. It is there where the running of one corrupt government occurs and although Gaia has softened her more dramatic eruptions of force, they've not stopped; they cannot, not completely.

In this way, a platform for the New emerges and allows the change to be a sweeping one – impactful for all concerned.

Are you saying the plan has been changed?

Gaia is feeling her children and right now exerts extreme force to carry them through this as gently as she is able. Yet force is necessary to impact a message and it will occur.

There will be casualties and destruction.

As you have seen on your continent with massive fires – there is destruction already. Yes, this will continue.

Know that intentions and beliefs create in a tangible way and a goodly number of humans believe fervently in catastrophic, even apocalyptic ending events.

That being the case, there are no ways to proceed that do not mark this time in a physical and final manner.

There are people who see no reason or worth in speaking of this now or beforehand. It evokes fear and anger.

This has been the case in all circumstances of foretelling. It is not a favored thing and often ignored as valid. There can be usefulness in warnings if seen that way – an awareness creates a clear image of what is not desired.

Certainly until these moments occur and the earth and her children move, there exists a co-creative effort. Nothing moves without your participation. All efforts and intents, thoughts and beliefs, are creative.

You are having an effect not just on your personal life but on the ground you walk.

This effect will have a greater and clearer impact with self-awareness and acceptance. The light warriors, light workers, those reading these words, are humanities best hope for a smooth transition as the effect of a clear heart is many times greater than one caught up in and embroiled in ego, anger, fear and self-worth.

I'm sorry, but I must go. (I had to prepare to leave for work.)

Yes. Please continue in a greater amount of time when this is possible. I sense many questions.

The conversation continued later that same day.

Is there someone who wishes to speak?

Yes there is Sophia. You will have to write now as if taking dictation. We desire clarity and a precise message.

Know that there are no mistakes and all proceeds as planned.

You have a message to share and you did so. The fact that you waited so long to make it a public one may muddy the waters, yet it does not dilute the message. It was meant to be given exactly as it was heard.

This is not a game of "telephone". By writing it in long hand and then copying it online as it was written, there are no mistakes. An original exists.

It is not a pleasing message and one that angers a people who've long lived under tyranny, corruption and criminal brutal rule.

Time will show this message comes from a source interested only in truth, sovereignty and agape.

The events portrayed do not have to happen in the most severe and destructive (way) but recall the message – as was told to you many times as you questioned it. Severe criminality requires a severe end. They are not going easily, although they know the prophecy. There are consistent attempts to side step it and outsmart the process they agreed to.

Ego is a huge construct for these beings and has created for them, an "all or nothing" scenario. Realize they have nothing to lose, their efforts will only accelerate as these nearby "now's" approach.

Having nothing to lose creates a viciousness to the fight – either way they must leave. Many would rather take as much out for themselves before hand as they can.

This is a message from One. You are merely a messenger. Share all parts and decisions can then be made individually.

Even the Demi-urge parts? (A reference to <u>Prophecy II of III</u>) This being also contributed before it left.

That is up to you. It does complete the story. Although the Demi-Urge is no longer – its words are valid. It was aware of the plan.

Do you have any other questions now?

I cannot think of any no. I will get all of this out.

This is now complete and has been recorded & published.

Namaste'
<u>*Sophia*</u>

This conversation took place on August 23, 2015 at 2:12AM

I would like to speak to One.

Yes.

Hi. Thank you. I have a specific question today, if you would respond.

I will. Go ahead.

What is the nature of the veil? And what takes it down?

Ahh. A very deep and wonderful question. Your friend is thinking very much in order to ask it.

This veil as it has been called is a separator. It is a splitter in awareness. There may be, there are, things on the other side of it, yet they cannot be seen by you in a "normal" day of your 3D life on earth. It is like they don't exist.

There have been some humans who have naturally retained an ability to see through the veil and that ability has either driven them mad or was in fact the definition of their condition, their "madness". What they "saw" brought out in their habits of speaking and being some bizarre looking responses and actions. It was as if they were "seeing things". They were seeing everything.

The nature of the veil is perception. It becomes a real barrier when the possibility of sight beyond a certain vibration is not... (*I was interrupted here; by someone getting up, and had to change locations... there is a bit of a break in the flow as a result*)

The veil becomes "non-transparent" at specific resonances of sight, vibratory rates.

Is this One?

It is. The same question remains.

Yes. The question of the veil.

Yes.

Its substance is thought, belief and the construct of this dream. You Sophia have seen beyond it on one occasion at least and describe it as "color-forms".

Yes.

What happens when the veil is seen "through" is a shift in vibratory pattern. A speed increase in resonance, in which you are not so solidly "here" as to see the constructs of here.

Calling it a veil is actually giving it solidity – which is typical of the 3D way of defining things. In your world, things you see have mass and a specific structure. Therefore, this is how you look to define everything – with mass and structure.

A veil in your 3D terms is a piece of cloth often used to hide a face. The veil you ask about hides more than faces, but the place of their existence. It has no substance but appears to with your eyesight.

You saw it as so solid that it could be pulled away in sections, leaving cutouts of what lie behind. And what lie behind? Pure potential, what you saw as black space.

The veil is not a cloth but a barrier put up to narrow your focus to things that exist in this resonant field – these very solid forms and beings are your current dream world, the place supplying your current life and lessons.

It was "put up" by a consensus of thought by all who made the dream, by the original architects, and every subsequent participant keeps it there with their own patterns of thought; their beliefs.

What will take it down is an acceptance of its existence, a suspension of belief in all you see around you as the only true "reality". This acceptance, when it occurs in humans, looks crazy. It allows for any possibility and for all perceptions of life.

For those focused elsewhere, there is no veil. They "see" you and communicate and no one calls them crazy. You may be, however, crazy for talking about it, for reporting it, for considering it real and valid.

What is on the other side of the veil has as much substance as this side once you have eyes to see it.

The veil is not "made up" of anything; it is itself "made up".

A taking it down happens only when belief in this as the only truth, the only solid reality, is suspended. This can happen now in brief moments of lucidity. Most of you confine those moments to dream time; hence the term "lucid dream".

The "faces" which the veil is hiding are actually your own – you are "veiling" your sight from truth – from the rest of life and the platform on which it stands.

When the "veil" is lifted, it will be as if nothing is holding you back or limiting you from perception. You'll see everyone and your awareness will allow for all colors, shapes and patterns of existence.

It is lifted when you KNOW its all energy – not in an academic knowing, but a knowing that springs from your core. This happens in an absence of fear. The need to "hang on" to any system of beliefs is what keeps you stuck in a specific field. It is fearlessness that removes the veil. It is acceptance. It is a willingness to suspend "reality".

This state can be induced temporarily with hallucinogens; yet again the fear response creates many a "bad trip".

The veil will be removed completely as a function of belief. Your ability to discern other vibratory patterns is more constant when you are not so "stuck" in the 3D one you are currently focused in.

It's actually One – the same place – think about the microscope or telescope and how the lens in either shows you worlds in worlds existing right now where you are standing, but invisible to your naked eye and its lens.

Once you suspend belief and release fear and NEED FOR CONSTANCY IN YOUR LIFE – SOLIDITY IN YOUR DAYS – PROTECTION AND VALIDATION, you will view the rest.

What is beyond the veil is everything else. The truth of your existence, including all possibilities and every "other" you know and are. This will happen and not be a forced event but a natural occurrence as eyes are opened and hearts trust what is this new perception.

If you place your eyes right up to a veil, which is typically sheer, you can see the "other side". You are so very close now. Accept all that is noticed from the "corners" of perception and allow them to be real. This removes the veil permanently.

That is all for now.

Thank you.

This conversation took place on September 24th, 2015. It is an answer to a question from a reader.

Is there someone who wants to connect?

There is. What is felt is a reaching by you with a question.

I have one, yes.

You may state it for clarity here.

It is a question regarding the nature of guides, spirit guides, and personal guides. There are many who reach out to them. Also, the term "guardian angel" is one that many refer to, and reach out to. In light of the uncovering of the hierarchal system, constructed as an enslavement device, who are these guides and guardian angels and whose agenda do they serve? This question comes from a reader.

My own question is that I've been told my origin is angelic, which I do not "get", esp. in light of the previous question. Please explain the terms and beings and introduce yourself.

In absolute love, I tell you that I am One. The same One you have connected with on numerous occasions. I am not other than you, yet I exist beyond your current focus. In that respect, you might say I'm more than you.

More is not better, it is only more. Your focus is restricted by your current physical life. In order to function as a being, it must be this way.

Your connection to and awareness of "me", *as a separate entity,* is a step towards oneness. That is all I will say on that.

The question regarding guides and guardian angels is a good one. It demonstrates deeper comprehension of sovereignty and exploration of available wisdom. It means, in other words, that your reader (and others considering the question) is moving towards freedom.

The process of ascension/enlightenment/development/growth/expansion is taken individually. This means that each path contains its own self-made steps. It may take many, many lifetimes or relatively few – yet the pattern of awareness is consistent.

By that is meant each being moves internally from oneness to individuality to oneness. Those beings who are right now occupied with this shift, as well as those also on your world who have no clue as to its happening, are each on the level of "INDIVIDUALITY".

A reliance on guides or angels of any sort or definition is a separator. If what is accomplished with the connection is a listening without an incorporating into self, then separation is validated and there is little progression for the soul asking for advice.

It is truth that life exists in many and all forms. "Guides" are indeed manifest yet they appear as an extension of the questioner. Yes, you are that powerful. If you have yet to incorporate deep wisdom and answers into your psyche and being, you will seek beyond yourself.

The creation or existences of "guides" are reflections of your internal awareness. If they are no longer resonating, as is the case with your reader, it is a sign that the external source has outlived its usefulness. The answers that resonate are found within.

This is not to say that beings and guides are "mere" imagination. They exist. It is imagination that is creative. IN EVERY FACET OF LIFE YOUR "REALITY" EXISTS BECAUSE YOU BELIEVE IT DOES. IT COULD NOT BE THERE IF YOU WERE UNABLE TO IMAGINE IT THERE. IN EVERY CASE AND ALL VISIONS, THE KEY ELEMENT IS YOU.

Regarding guardian angels – they are a race of a specific being – created only to serve and protect – they do not offer information. They serve as physical facilitators. You have seen them, as has your partner – in each case differently. **

There are also cases of guardians who are not of the angelic race. These are unique to the individual.

There is a race that was created to serve. It is possible to have had life in any race, as an aspect of creation, all choices exist.

The usefulness of any guidance can be gauged by the results. Each bit of information is perfectly timed in your own evolution. What was new and helpful worked when it did. The fact that it doesn't signifies that you have changed and moved on, not that the information is false.

Until each being recognizes their own internal knowing and wisdom, this outside validation will continue to be sought; the advice of guides and others. It is part of the process of growing awareness.

It is a mesmerizing subject – "Who is right?" "Who is wrong?" – Yet not productive if your aim is expansion. The information and assistance is useful along the path, regardless of where it comes from.

The other question regarding hierarchy does not fit into this discussion about guardian angels. The naming of specific beings, be they angelic or human, and then affording power to the name itself is only amplifying the idea that names themselves are separators. There are beings in all realms still playing that game.

Is that it?

For now, it is. This question has been answered.

Thank you.

The conversation ended.

** The vision of a guardian angel was a very classic version in my case; it had enormous wings, wore white or light colored robes, and was very tall and muscular with long golden/light brown hair. This being felt like a male.

In my partner's case, he has seen the same being numerous times; which looks like a large, burly, 6-foot-tall man with brown hair and light skin. Huge head, huge arms and thick legs with the gentlest countenance he has ever encountered. He wears everyday clothes, a white colored shirt and tan pants.

One – On Sovereignty

This grouping comes from the being I eventually came to know as One. Late in 2013 I was woken at 3:33 AM regularly, and given a download. I wrote what I heard. This happened approximately twenty times. These became blogs and eventually, a series which can be found on my website.

Once they began, I had a sense that the transmissions would one day stop and that they were meant to be published. I also "felt" that they were for a moment in "time" later than the one in which they were given, and for a new audience, one that perhaps would need these ideas. Each concerned an aspect of Sovereignty, and the collection was thus named "The Sovereignty Series".

Some of these have been produced as videos, and most of these as audio tracks on SoundCloud. I have been told by several readers and friends that these are probably my most important works to date. I had several offers to help produce them into videos, <u>after</u> I attempted to do some of the work myself. This made me smile. I am not a professional audio person or sound designer. I thought the videos were good. Apparently, they were not! Eventually I accepted the generous offer of my friends at Soundsfiction, *from the Netherlands. They have produced each of the Sovereignty videos to date and cleaned up each of the audio tracks. I am indeed blessed with such generous and talented friends!*

As you will read, these are not conversations. There is only one voice. Enjoy this investigation into what it will take to consider ourselves fully sovereign beings.

Note – Dates given are approximate. They are the dates they were posted to the blog, which was close to when they were initially heard.

December 22nd, 2013

You are swimming in a sea of chains. There are so many and they are so thick, you cannot tell what yours are attached to – but yes, you are shackled. It is not as if your very life depends on what's at the end of that shackle – *it is that you believe that it does*. It is that belief that keeps you bound. Keeps you moving to wherever it drags you. Keeps you asking to be released.

It is your belief that holds you, your mind that binds you.

The effort to control you focuses on a constant stream of programming as well as entertainment and food, to keep you fat and happy, mesmerized and asleep. You know this and yet you continue to search beyond yourself for the keys to your release.

There is only one person who can release the hold slavery has on your life. There is only one way it can occur.

The way is entirely self-motivated, self-sustained and springs from self-awareness. There are no unknowns that depend on another to be known. Self-reliant, self-propelled and self-conscious – these are the attributes of a sovereign being.

Your slavery has reached down to your core – it sits so deeply in your thinking that it is cloaked in familiarity. It will not be comfortable to dig it out and look at it. Your society puts on you pressure to conform. You are tired. You'd like to have someone take care of this for you – to fix it so that you can live without the chains, requirements, debt and dependence.

Freedom is a full-time job. You cannot be partially free. As the details of deception and corruption are unearthed, you become gradually horrified at its scope. Once your eyes are open, they will not easily be shut.

Ask "Who is served by this?" before undertaking any thought, word or action. Let the answer direct your movements. The system of slavery is only upheld if we participate. Non-compliance means you answer to no one. The guns of our governments and spaceships of those off planet do not, in truth, signify control or ownership. We are, each of us, equal and sovereign beings. The only thing you can be sure about in any interaction is that your perception is informing your opinion.

The desire for bliss or to be numbed to the harsh realities of the day to day keep us staring at our electronic devices and stagnant. This is not an accident. Nothing changes until and unless we change it. We signed up for this, confident we'd pull it off. A fully conscious, sovereign being experiences joy and fulfillment in deeply satisfying moments. We will get there.

Perseverance, determination and tenacity are demanded of us. We knew this was a part of it and that the payoff, when it came, would be that much sweeter because we did it ourselves.

December 27th, 2013

What is happening now is exceptional. There are no moments before this one that you can call on as reference. None have gone through such a time as you now navigate. You have no historical figures, no guidelines, no memories to shape the world for you – to color your actions so you do this the "right way".

There is no "right way", no "wrong way" – there is your way. Each thought, word and action is creative. Your co-creators, your "oppressors", those found on and off planet are all participants in the formation of this new era. Do not assume that any greater power is held by the money lenders, political leaders or beings in ships in your skies. These illusions of power are what you are leaving behind.

Embracing the power you hold is the foundation of this shift. It is being played out on a world stage yet it springs from an internal decision. Decide the world you'd like to be living in and see only that.

Allow your vision to take form in your speech and to color your actions. *Be the person today who lives and loves in the world you dream of.* This is a person who chose life as it occurs right now and is aware of both the possibility and responsibility of that choice. This is a god.

If there are words that cause you to recoil, see that they are words that dis-empower. Do not take an attitude of subservience, weakness or confusion. All answers are found when you listen to that whisper within. Action leads to further action. Pay attention to where your current path is taking you. Do not be afraid to look ahead. The world you are creating right now lives there.

What will you do with all this power? No one has told you about this because of their own agenda. Your religions, governments, teachers and bankers are and have been manipulating the story for their own purpose. Seeing the results of that agenda provides a springboard from which to take off.

December 28th, 2013

What you see as your daily life becomes burdensome as its purpose moves further up the food chain than you. Fulfillment is part of your every day when you have chosen a work, occupation, pastime or activity that on some level satisfies a desire or allows an expression or expansion of who you are.

Most of your time is currently spent consumed in activity that serves the purpose of maintaining your physical life. You have to eat and desire a place to sleep. Perhaps there are others you feel responsible for as well. These facts alone create in you a "need" to work at something that pays you money. This work you do, in fact and in more cases than not, serves only one goal. That would be to fatten the pockets of someone you have never met, as well as to keep them continually supplied with this thing called "value".

If there is one thing to do that would propel your sovereign state it would be to engage instead in work you deem purposeful and can clearly see the end result of. This work will benefit and nourish you rather than deplete you.

As your world is structured today, you are rewarded highly for work that benefits the wealthiest among you and keeps them there. Entire careers and lifetimes are spent in finance – *a make believe place where value is arbitrarily assigned, collected and distributed.* The fact that many of you desire an accumulation of such value is what keeps this industry alive and running many others.

It is a mixed-up world where figures generated on dead wood signify the worth of a god. The blinders must be removed now. Value is not a number and unable to be arbitrarily assigned. Value is generated from the only place able to emit anything of worth. Value emerges from Source itself.

When you re-construct your system of hierarchy to place you at the top – the individual you, the collective you – you will find nourishment in your work and joy in your days. This shift in your thinking will alter the fabric of your world from one of slaves serving masters to one of free individuals, alive.

Yes, change to the entire structure of commerce needs to be accomplished from the outside. Yet until and unless you believe that you hold the only real value available – those external changes won't be sustainable.

Value cannot be accumulated; it exists because you do. The dollar amount stuck to anything is set by perception. In order for your life to change, you will need to perceive clearly your worth. That view point must be evident in your chosen thoughts, words and actions.

You are gods. One god may appear to have more "stuff" than another – but that does not equate to more power or more value. The accumulation of "stuff", be it gold or the land from which it is dug, is merely a game some of you like to play. It is one of the expressions of life that in your version of things has been called "greedy". There is no right or wrong. All is choice. Each choice serves the purpose of creation – to express and experience life.

You cannot be more or less a god; you can merely imagine yourself to be. Imagine yourself to be all that is possible – the fullest expression of you currently available. As you walk in his shoes and as you dance in her slippers, we'll be watching. Powerful, individual gods will emerge from the shadows as we grasp and collectively embrace our every potential.

December 29th, 2013

This is a process that in the end will yield a product. This product is you, but not a version of you holding any notion of worth as truth. The version we are looking to release understands that all are worthy equally.

It does not matter on which part of the planet your physical body was born. Lines drawn on the ground are separators which serve only one thing – the false notion of accumulation and division.

Any idea that categorizes or limits the value of a person – creating a barrier that must be crossed in order to access the heart, are pretend. There are no kings or homeless in heaven. The whole notion of equal, if it were to be truly experienced, would have you comfortable to the same extent at both a soup kitchen and a banquet; dining with those you've labeled royalty and those you'd call common. These names, the ones that make up social commentary and that you teach your children, are not, in truth, indicative of anything at all.

Until you can look with equal eyes at both the beggar and the banker, you will not be seeing clearly. In order for twenty/twenty vision, it becomes necessary that you let go of notions of worth.

Worth is an idea perpetrated by those who have something to "gain". It is a false notion. The idea that one part of creation is worth more than another part, is absurd.

Until the status of all of humanity is recognized equally, this society is being manipulated. If any aspect of your life is "run" by a group of people with a "name", "category" or "title" *that grants them special status*, you are not free.

Life is what you were each given when conceived and that fact alone tells you that access to any aspect available here is also meant to be equally attainable.

"Earn" is another falsehood. Its purpose is to instill in the populace an idea of servitude. Both terms, "earn" and "worth" are locked together, creating an "opinion" that separates one piece of creation from another.

Labels like "worthless", "lazy bum", "poor", "beggar", "jobless" and "homeless" not only categorize you but also reinforce the false idea that some actions or circumstances indicate superior intelligence and therefore greater value.

These false names and labels have been fed to us for generations and it becomes necessary now to disregard them. As you walk upright into a unified world, all heads will be held equally high.

Examine the inner dialogue you hold when you encounter each other – does it reinforce hierarchy or equality? Understand that language is largely habit – we will need new words consciously chosen in order to embrace sovereignty. This conscious dialogue will support an overriding arch that retracts the necessity to "earn"; replacing it with the idea that *we each arrive equally worthy and remain so throughout all of our lives.*

December 31st, 2013

The whole idea that a person could have ownership over anything or anyone else was projected into your origin at a critical point. Precise characteristics were included; genetically reproduced in a specific fashion – for slavery to be possible. Since then, what has been reinforced into the psyche of man is that an exalted being made him – a capitol G-O-D.

This G-O-D had knowledge, power and ability that man did not have access to. Space vehicles reinforced the charade – G-O-D descended from the heavens.

With this dialogue running through the background of man's every thought, a tendency to worship is reinforced. This is not the natural compulsion of a creator being, but it has become so in man. It was an intentional thought placed specifically into the mind of man so that he would be easy to control and to own.

If you have something "valuable" that another person does not, you are no longer seen as equal, but somehow superior. This is a false superiority, depending on what it is you hold rather than who it is you are. *In fact, superiority is a misunderstanding of value.*

The story of the "Emperor's New Clothes" is a way, just one of the ways; we've chosen to tell ourselves the truth. The Emperor is in fact naked, and looks just like everyone else that way. It is his delusion and desire that has him elaborately robed. In fear, his "subjects" don't point out the obvious. It takes a child to speak the truth.

Think about your own inner dialogue, recalling thoughts you held before you were taught otherwise. Were they thoughts of worship?

If you watch children, you'll see no such segregation or subjugation played out – unless the necessary motivating emotion of fear is present. What infuses any notion of obedience as valid is a sense of foreboding. Without fear of loss, there is no reason to obey.

All of these – ownership, worship, obedience and fear have been mystically bound together inside this thing labeled "religion". The basis of any religion is idolatry of some sort; another idea that places exclusive value on a person or thing that by itself holds no such attribute.

While it may be a valid observation that some physical objects and people conduct energy or evoke emotion better than others, there is no advantage or requirement to revere them – we are all creator gods. The manipulation of physical materials into art, architecture, machine or magic is accomplished the same way each time – by us.

As there is no hierarchy in the man making, wearing or using the object, there is no hierarchy in the object. Now I ask you, where would our religions be today without their ornate churches and synagogues, fine robes and sacred articles? Each has been placed into the fabric of humanity to solidify this idea of ownership and to initiate worship.

A sovereign being worships and waits for no one.

January 2nd, 2014

The force with which you live your life very much imitates the depth of feeling held regarding liberation. Those who consider themselves to be tightly shackled will not move around much – either figuratively or physically. They will tend to conform – only going places in their minds and with their bodies that are "allowed" or "suggested" by the ones doing the shackling.

A glance at the population gives you a clear picture of which ones of us are in fact unchained. If we take this vision to an extreme – it will show us something quite disturbing to accepted belief systems.

Those among us labeled "crazy" are perhaps in a very real sense the freest of all. They follow none of the rules. Entire industries have grown up around conformity, subjugation, ownership and obedience. These would be our schools, judicial systems, police forces and governments. Each upholds the idea of a specific state of being, level of loyalty, body of answers or behavior as mandatory for acceptance into polite society.

We are conditioned to conform – keeping a watchful eye on each other to see that those who step out of line are obvious and noticed. These behaviors demonstrate weakness, jealousy and dependence, not strength. They are indicative of some very human emotions and not those of an omnipotent being.

The creator has no needs and therefore makes no demands of creation – merely wishing it to thrive. If there was such a thing as "sin" it would be something that prevented that from happening.

All activities are "allowed". The creator does not "need" to experience itself through its "offspring". The creator has no needs, rules or requirements. It merely is.

The truth that can be used as a measure for discovering the source of any request would be the statement "I AM". Thus, stands the definition of One.

Names, titles, needs, emotions and descriptors that follow those two words are separators and indicators of a lesser god, a "poser". Omnipotence has no needs and makes no such declarations or demands.

The structure of a world under such a being would very clearly indicate the truth. Our ability to thrive within any system on such a world may indicate not sanity, but sovereignty. Nonconformists understand and express the force of freedom.

Freedom cannot be bound by any system at all and must by definition follow its own course, unimpeded.

We do not know this expression here; those that do have loosed the bonds of "sanity" and run unbound, by an internal code of behavior. This code is theirs alone.

Any control of or infringement on the actions of another being stems from fear, not power. There is no enforcement necessary in a sovereign society – all are held equally responsible and reliable to and for the whole. No one has to tell you that you are free, or fight to uphold your freedom – it is understood.

When limitless is the only description of life's possibilities, we'll know freedom. Understand in your core that this is what you are. This cannot be given to you, it can only be realized. This realization can happen in an instant or over a lifetime.

January 5th, 2014

The course of a god is individually set. Each of us is on that course. The choice to incarnate as human is made freely. The opportunity for growth is sort of exponential here.

Some of us came with different agendas. All of us came to set in place a real opportunity to create. So, what is creation?

We have evidence of it daily as children are born, cakes are made and movies are produced. Yet it is understood that another level of creation exists – a level that appears to be magical, powerful and beyond our ability.

Everything necessary for us to create worlds exists within us today. What becomes a crucial ingredient is the motivation and after that the intent.

It has been introduced into the dialogue that all gods are not equal; that there are some powerful creators here now, with an agenda and a great deal of skill; that they have "tricked" the majority of humanity into believing they are the creator of all things, the "One". Not a small feat.

So the question comes, if this being created worlds, specifically this one, with all of its laws, rules and systems – is it not a god? What is a god anyway?

There is no hierarchy of gods; no lesser or greater god and none who serve any others. There are however, plenty of imagined hierarchies. They are based on a misconception around love and power.

The analogy of parent/child is a perfect way to talk about how it works. In a sense, parents are more powerful than their very young children. They've been around longer, have the keys to the car and have practice at manipulating the dream. To children, mom and dad are magical.

It is not necessary to worship or obey mom and dad and one day you will be an adult, fully capable of all that they have done and perhaps more. You'll still call them mom or dad, but you will not perceive them with a child's eyes. You'll have the keys to your own car.

When you do, you'll drive your own family around, enjoying the same magical reputation for a bit. The charade will end one day as your children become adults. You will not at that point demand that they worship you or obey you, withholding love if they do not. You can try, but any response you get will emerge out of fear and will not be sustainable.

True creation by the "One" creator has no agenda. It is art in its purest form. It happens. As something emerges there is only joy. What exists when it occurs does so because of intention and desire. There are no demands on pure creation. Once born/once created, it is complete unto itself. It is free.

If it requires sustenance to continue, the responsibility for supply rests on the creator. What has been created now gets to choose whether or not it will continue and in what manner. With each birth, freedom is assumed. There is no ownership possible as life cannot be contained.

For us here on earth, there has been a great deception. The "god behind the curtain" is not the "great and powerful" creator of all things, not the "One". It is a being just like you – only it's been around longer and holds the keys to this car.

January 10th, 2014

Within each action is held intent, even without announcement. Unconscious intent is what has been manipulated by those controlling the planet. This has been accomplished in ways that by now are very public – advertising, news media, education and religion all serve their very specific agenda; to limit your life.

This intent has been fulfilled and no longer is it necessary to aggressively place it within society – humanity carries out the remainder of the dialogue and programming with little encouragement.

The products we buy are in fact those which have been put in front of us most often, those backed by wealth. It is the same with the news we hear, the movies we watch, the games we play and the schools and churches we attend.

Very early in the experiment value was replaced with money and that has driven everything. It is money that puts politicians in power and keeps specific programs in place. Without money, things fail.

This upside-down idea has created within us a feeling of confusion, discomfort and loss. Mistrust emerges as our internal sense of value seems irrelevant. We are supposed to want the most costly product or highest paying position. We are expected to admire what has been labeled success and power. These ideas override any internal system of knowing and push it aside. When you cannot reconcile the dilemma, you either dropout of polite society entirely, rebel, or lead a life of quiet desperation.

Life was meant to be understood and experienced from an internal drive to explore and push the limits of your ability on every frontier – physical, mental, emotional and spiritual. Life was not intended to be a battleground or a prison, but a platform for unlimited creation. Indeed, this is the force behind creation itself.

There have been many references to "consciousness" as if it means an awareness of specific elitist or criminal activity. This may be part of the meaning, yet it does not encapsulate the true definition.

Consciousness has implications for each action, word and thought. It is not so much a looking at where it originated, but *where it is heading*. It is clarity of intent. It implies a decision has been made regarding the life you are engaged in, and the decision has been explored fully.

We are born with full access to an internal truth. Who you are is not meant to be hidden, mysterious or irrelevant. We are here to investigate and further explore creation. If there is mistrust around an idea that just feels "right", that may be programming. As you push through these messages of doubt, you'll realize the depth and breadth of your authentic self. This demands intent and awareness of the road ahead.

Every sovereign being is a pioneer. This implies both departure and unknown destinations. Consciousness is not only awareness; it is a constant force guiding our movements. Consciousness carries with it responsibility, as sovereignty does not recognize blame.

A sovereign being is nobody's fault. A sovereign being is. To move out of the slavery mindset is to leave behind any dependence on blame, to accept that every moment is self-generated and to celebrate the freedom in that, fearlessly. Our value cannot be monetized.

January 14th, 2014

It is widely accepted that life is hard. The whole notion of a joyful existence comes off as a frivolous idea – cool if you are lucky enough to be born with a silver spoon in your mouth or if you are one of those perpetually optimistic people; but not realistic.

To write here that joy is or ought to be your focus sounds nice but a bit naive. Rather, it would seem more efficient and helpful to focus on abundance, health or even free energy. Joy may result if those things are in place, but it is not the priority.

You cannot isolate emotion from action. How you approach what it is you are doing will affect the outcome for you. You desire sustainable happiness. How does that occur? Why is it, that once children reach puberty, they begin to "get serious" about life and lose the "innocent" enthusiasm that comes at birth? What can we do to get that back?

The "harsh reality" of life does not have to be taught – it is something that was given to us here, to hold us back, restrict our movements, limit our expansion and minimize our power. The "work ethic" was invented by the beings who started the experiment here. Once it was bred into you that you were only as valuable as the work you produced, their goal was easily achieved.

We've spoken of this before, and yet the culture of slavery runs so deeply into our society, it sits there as a constant source of angst. To do, every day, for most of your life, something for just one purpose – to "earn a living" (*as if that was even possible*), is an idea that dulls the senses and inhibits the imagination. It is not truth. All beings everywhere do not live like this. Humans do.

To change an idea which is a basic tenet of society, is a challenge that cannot be accomplished with conversation. It must be felt as a result of systemic change.

In other words, to remove the "work ethic" we must first remove the necessity for money. This elephant story is a good illustration:

Before leaving each evening, the trainer tethers the elephant with a chain. One day the trainer forgets and upon returning the next morning, discovers the elephant has wrapped the chain around her own leg!

She does this (the elephant) because this is the only way she knows how to live without the trainer. Show her what can happen when she is on her own, without the chain; then remove it, and watch what happens.

What can we do to alter our dependence on money? Our life is structured in a way that allows freedom in increments as a direct relation to how much cash you have. The cash in hand came from the labor of someone. This world is set up in such a way that freedom for one demands freedom for all. We are ONE. If just a part of the population is enslaved, the slavery exists.

So, what is necessary for life? Sustenance, a home, clothing, transportation, wellness; these things are part of physical existence. They cost money right now. If you were given the choice between freedom and the possibility of unlimited wealth – which would you choose?

There is an idea amongst us that says we can't have both; that freedom necessitates uniformity – there is only so much "stuff" and if we disable the current system, we all would get the same allotment of clothing, living quarters and food. That mass production will be necessary and we'll be free, but without much individual difference in our lives, in fact, without much "stuff" in our lives.

Even that idea has its origin in slavery and a desire to keep slavery going. The carrot at the end of the stick is always held there – just beyond reach. It is what pushes you to work harder, *the possibility of MORE.*

If we decide that it is not *more* that we want, but *enough,* without toil; along with the opportunity for creative expression and unlimited expansion, we may turn the "work ethic" around into something else - something equally sustainable; that includes the probability for joy. We are brilliantly, magically, powerfully human; here to create a new way to be. Nothing is beyond us.

It will be necessary to look at and alter the mechanics of society to do this. Nicola Tesla was stopped because free energy would have halted the experiment in its tracks. Ideas abound in our ranks – it is the dependence on "government" that must be changed and to do that we'll have to listen to, trust and support *each other. It is the shift from dependence on an outside, more powerful body of people to dependence on us and on each other – that is the shift mankind must make.*

January 15th, 2014

In order for the system to change without the display of power and weaponry typically used, a complete alteration of power is necessary. Today the majority understands power as force, as might, as guns and the ability to use them. What is on our "side", the "side" of peaceful revolution, is that *what is also held deeply as a universal principle is magic.*

Magic is merely the manipulation of matter in atypical ways. This can be accomplished with a being who understands the art of the dream. It is intention and expectation. It demands clarity and purity – the very things that have attempted to be muddled with this experiment. Foods, media, religions and education have taken hold and forced it out of you – instilling instead ideas around power that include superiority, competition and brute force.

Nothing could be further from the truth. Think Gandalf. There are legends in our culture that continue because within them is held the seed of truth – a mystical, internal force overpowers brute force every time. That internal force is one you hold.

To answer the question (How do we accomplish the shift without violent revolution?) will sound circular. Yet it is known to you because it also holds truth. Maintain an internal focus. Let everything you do allow the further development of clarity. The food you eat and practices you engage in either support or suppress internal strength. Choose consciously.

The movement from guns will happen when fear abates. In order to stop the fear, we'll have to replace it with a sense of power – IM-powerment.

There is no mystery that cannot be solved within the language and legends of our culture. Look carefully at what has been more typically laughed at or judged irrelevant for clues. There we will discover treasure and useful information.

Again, it is collaboration and unity that will render any show of military force null. If everyone is on board, the takeover will be ONE seamless, choreographed movement.

January 16th, 2014

You are convinced that the severity of your actions is an indication of how barbaric or civilized you are. What is civilization really? Is it the degree of conveniences available to the common man? Is it, or rather, isn't it instead supposed to be, the hallmark of advancement? We label superiority of civilization very specifically. It has to do with how much is physically available to plug in or turn on.

Civilized "superiority" in its true sense, is a much different attribute. There are small groups of "uncivilized" humans in isolated pockets who are made up of enlightened people. We may not understand their individual practices or way of living, yet it springs essentially from respect and honor for life – all life.

They do not subscribe to waste; all parts of the vegetation, animal and human are sacred and equally utilized. If there are no libraries filled with literature that just means the art of verbal communication is utilized instead.

The notion that whole groups of humans must be aware of the actions of every other group of humans stems from ego. It is born out of self-importance. What someone has to say about nuclear physics has no effect on the talent of the master fisherman. Each adds value to life as a whole. The relative intelligence of one does not depend on its awareness or knowledge about the mechanics of both.

Apprenticeships, journeymen, internships; these are fertile grounds for excellence and unique development. This "know everything" model of man came about for purposes of conformity, superiority, competition and a dulling of the senses. The impact of a constant stream of novel and unrelated information on the brain disables the ability to focus and concentrate. How can you invent free energy alternatives when you are required to spit out parts of speech in multiple languages along with lists of wars and dead dictators?

Knowledge is not a bad thing. The requirement placed on young children for memorization and uniform ability however, is criminal. At a time when the brain is most malleable and open to rapid development; it is held tightly in a box of facts that hold little if any interest. This is mutilation every bit as destructive as the physical mutilation done to young girls as they reach sexual maturity in some cultures. Its purpose is to inhibit pleasure and halt any possibility of free and unique expression – to define the purpose and output of the human; to create slaves.

This program of enslavement touches every aspect of culture, regardless of its level of "civilized" advancement. It is a misunderstanding to label any part of man "superior" to any other part. The implications of that label reinforce separatism, elitism and polarity.

Man as a whole has been manipulated and the expression of that is diverse. Freedom is evident in self-confidence without comparison – in acceptance of individual brilliance that reaches the heights of possibility, unencumbered by rules, expectations, or what has been done before. Freedom is self-defined

January 17th, 2014

The background of each of us is irrelevant. It is the foreground that matters to the rest of us. Who is it you are today? How do you spend your moments while we are sharing them?

It doesn't matter what took place before now. Not that these things don't have value, they do. When we were involved in them they mattered very much. Now that they are a thing of the "past", they do not.

Time is an aspect of the day to day that can serve or inhibit us. It is held in our mind and its relative effect takes place there as well. It doesn't really exist – there is no such thing as "time". A "time-piece" has been invented, that moves brilliantly and we've all agreed that the rotations signify a specific measurement. That is all it is.

Why bring up "time" or the "past"? It is these ideas that define our days and shape the view we hold about the possibilities for our lives. What you feel capable of is in part defined by how many "years" you've been here, by how those "years" have been spent and with whom. There are walls on our dreams of the "future" and chains holding us to our "past". These things are not truth. They are fabrications held in the mind; they are thoughts.

There is a story of a man who was locked in the freezer car of a train in one of the Scandinavian countries. He died. When his body was found, it showed all of the clinical effects of having been frozen, yet the freezer was never turned on. His mind killed him.

Our minds are doing the same. Any limiting or inhibiting "fact" held there can be reversed. All thoughts are malleable and can change. Often it is those that fly in the face of "reality" that project us the fastest and furthest into our dreams. *A life spent re-*

defining yourself to others around you seems unproductive unless you are interested in staying there.

We are not meant to stagnate but to grow. All possibilities exist – it is our choice whether or not to embrace them that determine the kind of life lived.

The pull of this "dream" is powerful. The direction has been fueled by some potent creators. These beings and the systems they've put in place are meant to convince you to abide by their rules in order to "succeed".

Their agenda, however, is not and could never be yours. Each life is self-determined. It is up to you to define your own direction and proceed accordingly. It is one thing to respect the definitions forefront in your life and another to adopt them without question.

Question everything. The only restrictions on where you can go and how many places that can be are self-imposed. You exist everywhere and you only need to daydream to remind yourself that you can be in two places at once.

There is no advantage to following the "party line" so rigidly that no bump in the road occurs. Bumps are a great place from which to jump off of! Life was meant to be an adventure to explore.

The push to test limits has to come from you. A sovereign being understands and accepts the responsibility for every direction – "past, present, and future". Each is defined only once – now. You are a sovereign being.

January 18th, 2014

This journey we are on, called life, is one of the most spectacular trips available. The experience of physical existence has within it every possibility. This planet is filled with over 7 billion humans – there are many who choose to visit here.

To be clear, all facets of this life are known as possibilities before birth. There are no tricks played or secrets kept. In full awareness, we incarnate, happy for the chance to live again.

This talk of an "experiment" may have led you to think otherwise – to think that you'd been duped and your plan to be here at all was made under false pretenses. This is not how it works. Before being human, the "you" that is, knows every aspect it has ever been, as well as the aspects of others. It is not possible to "hide" the truth of you. Knowledge of each other comes with contact.

This inability to deceive creates every possibility for clear choices and transparent decisions. This kind of clarity goes away from the human as we dive more deeply into this "reality". All of this is part of our plan.

The thing that humanity offers us by way of experience is emotion/passion. This is not to say that other beings are void of emotion, because they are not. Humanity holds within its makeup a deep well of passion and belief in the sanctity of life. The way in which mankind expresses love and beauty and hope and hate is unique; beneath it lays an unwavering faith and trust that it's meant to be fair. Despots and dictators arise because they know that belief exists and there exists a chance at manipulation and perceived "power" because of it. They are here to "play" with that.

Potentials for all possible ends of the spectrum of control are exciting. When not human, there are limits as to how much emotion/feeling will be a part of creation. There is desire and personality always. Yet the extremes of passion are possible only in a life while human. This is the source of unparalleled heights and depths of feeling; a wealth of addictions.

We have labeled these "addictions" as negative and "work" to overcome them. This is interesting because they are the whole reason we are here. It may be more prudent to celebrate them! They make up the most exciting parts of you!

When addictions are referred to here, it is not in the sense of chemical addictions only – the kinds that are ingested. It is behaviors; those that stimulate the process to create the chemical for you. These behaviors become habitual because they afford a sensation you crave. That is addiction.

It could be any behavior at all, yet it will lead always to a familiar sensation. The thrill of that sensation excites you and inspires a desire for more, as if it were a drug. In fact, it is, but not a drug we are taking, one we are making. You will search for opportunities in your days to do it again and again.

Consciousness implies an awareness of these physical tendencies, acceptance for them as facets of the personality and an understanding that they are not "faults" but very human traits – one of the reasons for being human at all. They are not "bad"; they are part of the program. It becomes a challenge to remove "you" out of the equation; everything here is taken personally.

The ability to love and live without judgment is the goal here. In order to embody unconditional love you must understand every condition that is its opposite. The exquisite feelings of love, the thrill of victory, the agony of defeat – each of these are addictions. You will repeat them until every nuance is understood. This has been the plan.

Today it is widely understood that many of the reasons for the most violent extremes of these emotions – the hardships and challenges of human slavery – have been fabricated. There are beings who possess intimate knowledge of the human psyche and have used it to manipulate man for their own addictions of power and worship. You are at a point now, the ultimate point in the plan, where you have a choice.

What will you do? How will you judge? *Will you judge?* What is unacceptable to you? What does freedom mean? Is such a thing as punishment necessary or is Karma enough? Will you seek revenge?

This is the choice of mankind and what is done here will reverberate to every other life in all of creation.

If Oneness motivates the decision, there exists a possibility for compassion that until this moment did not exist. The force and effect of cruelty and pain is felt in each heart. It is there now that the possibility for unsurpassed acceptance rests – agape. Now that you know the truth, the power to change all of creation rests in your hands.

The slave has come full circle. Ownership is not possible; a sovereign being realizes its possibilities for expression – all of them. Knowing what you are capable of and what has been done before – what will you choose now? The results are in. This was an experiment to reach for the light. It is within your grasp. What you do now changes everything.

January 22nd, 2014

Try to imagine what it would be like without rain; without snow; without thunderstorms, hurricanes and the like. The force of nature and the balance of "good" and "bad" are integral parts of this planet – part of what makes up the whole.

We expect "weather" to follow a pattern according to the seasons and places where we live. Each of these, weather and water, are unique to earth life in that they occur on a daily basis without any control from the beings living here; seemingly in random fashion.

Why is it that there are entire careers and lifetimes spent studying and predicting "weather"? To some of us, perhaps to many of us, this would be a boring thing to focus a lifetime on. There are overall patterns and processes that when looked at as a whole, craft a picture. It is as if there was a plan.

There is, but not one that can be discovered in a lifetime; one that began with the formation of the planet and is being carried out daily. Weather creates the circumstances for very specific life – everything in order.

We'd have to step back far enough to see this plan and have access to a record of the planet from the beginning. What is currently available, the archeological records, will serve to tell the story. Only we must understand the language.

Life is a system created with purpose and fed by many parts. The human that you are plays a vital part in all of life. Thus far you have done so without being aware of your role.

The net effect of slavery has been a numbing; a cutting off of awareness of who we are. Unaware, we've blundered through life and in some respects wreaked havoc and others, had little effect when effect was needed at the time we were present.

Being awake without being aware of the process is useless. We must access and utilize consciousness to participate in any potentially helpful way. We must know the plan.

This planet was and is a playground for diversity, evolution and adaptation. Today we are changing rapidly and irreversibly. Our very DNA is mutating. What this means for the human is important and what it means for the planet is significant as well.

As we morph into a new human, the surrounding planet does too. We affect the weather, the interior of the earth, the sky, the vegetation. There is nothing happening in isolation. As these changes are unprecedented, we have no way of "knowing" for certain their effect on the big picture, on all of existence.

What you can do is look at the effect on your individual life and environment and predict. If once you were unaware and now you walk consciously – will not your footsteps serve your intentions? What new intentions have come about as a result of the changes physically and chemically that have already taken place?

Our very desires alter the world around us. With awareness of an internal god force, we direct rather than react to – life. There is understanding of the weather and its seasons, for patterns and for the necessary climate required.

There is a force of life – that once understood will direct your every movement and moment. This force is unable to control or manipulate, to serve or protect, to inhibit or promote. It is merely and magnificently creation itself. Like an artist with the final work clear in her mind, life itself moves forward every "slowly" towards its own end. It perpetuates its own plan without sanction, permission or approval.

The actions of this tiny portion of existence we are calling the "cabal" have not taken place outside of that plan. However, the part of this show has arrived that see's their act over. Destruction for the sake of gluttony does not benefit enough life to enable it to continue. Therefore, it must be stopped. This is as much a part of the natural order of things as it is a willful act by a specific group or groups. It is and always has been inevitable.

Awareness of their effect on the quality and quantity of life for the rest of the population only accelerates their removal. This speeds up changes on every level and ultimately defines planetary movements.

The vision it takes to see this global and galaxy wide movement is one we can approximate with instruments but not attain without enlightenment. Enlightenment is where we are headed. It gives us perspective, awareness and conscious choice. Like that of a child, you are not today aware of the ultimate effect of every food eaten or "toy" played with. Yet you are becoming so, and with knowledge and understanding come compassion and clear intention.

As your world view grows you will understand that truly there can never be control – for control would inhibit life itself and life is creation and the whole point. You cannot stop it.

While manipulation is possible, corrections on a grander scale make adjustments that guarantee continuation. We are part of a very large scale process – the whole is so much greater than the sum of its parts.

There will always be a "bigger picture" to comprehend than the one currently held. This never-ending possibility of a broader perspective is the ultimate purpose of life. *There is always more to know.*

Your freedom and sovereignty was expected, planned and part of the purpose. The goal however is not to serve any one "god" but rather the perpetuation of life itself – all of life – as ONE.

The focus and direction of your actions will tell you just what you came to experience. We are not all here with the same purpose, and for that reason will appear to have conflicting goals.

When you step back far enough you can see that there is no conflict – balance rules all of life. You who are reading (or listening) this far are here to strike balance in what appears to be the self-destructive path of humanity. It is not and you are guaranteeing that; despite every attempt at control placed on you. You woke up early and are now waking up everyone else.

March 14th, 2014

There is little need for a judge and jury in a place of equality and sovereignty. In fact, these terms would be obsolete; reminders perhaps of such notions from a time long ago.

The whole concept of one sovereign being standing in authority over another sovereign being is very much like the bully in the playground. Cartoon depictions of this child show him to be typically male and larger than average with less intelligence. This image defines the justice system as it currently stands.

For what is the definition of justice? Fairness and tacit compliance with the law of the land. And what is the law of the land? Responsibility for self, love your neighbor and equality seem to have nothing to do with it. The law currently followed assumes division, ownership and punishment as inherent components. It calls up images of protection from harm, locks and keys, fear and potential damage. Each of these applies when you are dealing with a playground bully and not another sovereign being.

It is true that there are disputes among equals that could and do benefit from expert arbitration, as such guided by someone not personally involved. It is not true that a firm hand is necessary to settle situations. What is required is time, patience and indifference. The playground bully has a definite agenda, as does the justice system.

When judges are elected or appointed and paid, there is present a debt to those doing the electing or appointing. This fact colors each "decision" made by the judge. The fact that you would stand in a room and submit to such a system of judgment and then abide by any decisions that result indicates the level of fear that is present.

For it is fear that is running the show, the same gut level emotion utilized by the playground bully. Make no mistake, if you are ever in a place that requires you to abide by its demands and obey its rules – you are being manipulated. Manipulation is not the same as justice.

When harmful intent is assumed, a chain reaction of false ideas begins. It is necessary to believe the "other" has an agenda that is potentially damaging. For justice to be necessary, the playground bully must exist as a constant threat. That bully is seen as potential in each situation. Someone else is out there always, wanting to harm you or to take your stuff.

Ideas around the need to stop the bully are begun from thoughts of separation, "value" and "more". There is a pre-supposed condition present from the start. That thought includes an idea that separates you from each other. Words like more and less, good and bad, need and lack, strong and weak all stem from a system of slavery.

If instead of guilt, honor is assumed – the whole thing changes. The view on an equal playing field is very much different than a hierarchal one. A "justice system" was necessitated and begun by the thugs who initially decided they had something to protect that was more valuable than anything else – their power.

Misunderstanding of the source of that power begat fear and the playground bully. The bully needs someone to steal from or control with force, or he considers himself weak and without power. The same is true of today's control/justice system. The game ends when you stop playing.

A court room where authority dispenses justice is merely a dressed-up playground. It is only necessary when there is an agenda of "power over" rather than a mutual recognition of "power within". In fact, a courtroom only recognizes the power of one thing – "the law" and the person paid to dispense it, the judge/bully. Any system of power that is dependent on another to thrive is weak. The justice system currently in place serves the playground bully with subservience. It does not serve justice.

The whole notion of good/bad, gain/loss has no place from a sovereign state. Imagine a room of your peers and within it, a disagreement. Harmony will ask each of you to participate in a solution. The solution will serve the group, using discussion. If there is a law guiding the discussion, it is "love one another as you do yourself." Guilt and innocence doesn't enter the picture because they are recognized as subjective opinions rather than statements of fact. For what is one guilty of other than life?

Relationships demand discussion. Guns and fear enter only when one party misunderstands the origin of power. It is within.

March 17th, 2014

There are conditions of daily life that occur on a regular basis for the majority of humans. These include a lack of opportunity to experience self-determination, a pre-arranged location, and an income; without which you'd be unable to survive. These conditions, seen as normal and necessary, are actually preferred. When an adult has reached the age of eighteen years, most of their orientation is focused on creating them for themselves; this, in order to achieve "worldly success".

In fact, under the current arrangement, you congratulate each other for having secured a "good" job. This "job" grants you "freedom". "Freedom" in this case means moving out of the home of your parents. It means being on your own. It means having the chance now to stop living off the "job" your parents held, and starting your own. You are "free" now and willingly join the ranks of the others in volunteer slavery.

You see, freedom is an illusion in this scenario. It is dangled out there like the carrot on the string. This carrot is never to be eaten. It merely hangs there, inches away, just out of reach. It is the unattainable dream and it keeps humans eagerly moving out of situations they consider confining and constricting into brand new cages, created just for them. There is a reason it's referred to as the rat race.

The rat is free to move – yet just in a specific path and within a pre-defined area. It can only do so when the door is opened by someone else, someone who owns the box. The rat is fed according to how "well" it "performs" and thus kept alive – all by the owner.

The lack of ability to choose how you spend your days is a condition of slavery, not freedom. This is regardless of compensation. Reaching the age of maturity and choosing the same path chosen by the adults before you is the single choice offered. It is inside of an enclosed system that depends on continued servitude. If choices are limited in scope and number, you are controlled.

In a system that included self-determination, things would look vastly different. There would still be adults providing for children and each other, yet they wouldn't necessarily start and end their "work" day at the same minute. Variation would rule the process and each day would differ rather than follow a specific and predictable pattern.

"Work days" would be replaced by days. In such a system the continuation of the race would be the driving force. The purpose of your chosen activity would be visible and understood by you, and it wouldn't necessarily be a paycheck.

This way of life is unimaginable not because it wouldn't work. It is a vision of life that exists elsewhere, just not on earth. On earth, self-determination of each sentient being has been replaced with servitude. The many work for the few, follow orders and obey. To join the ranks of "adulthood" means you willingly engage in this prescribed path. Chains are not necessary; the invisible tie that binds you is the necessity of money.

In a system that is not controlled by beings with an unspoken ownership agenda, life is very different. There are conditions in place that provide life sustaining necessities for every man, woman and child. The whole notion of debt is not present and its opposite holds no meaning. Freedom is a hollow notion without enslavement.

Control is another empty concept in a world of self-determined beings. Certainly care for the young and their safety means providing safe places for them to thrive. Yet it does not mean a strict schedule of mandatory schooling and regular testing to ensure conformity. Unique abilities are sought and discovered in such a world.

The whole idea that an entire population could successfully run their own lives sounds ludicrous, not because it is, but because the generations of elders before you have paved the path so well you see no other possibilities. Ideas of right, wrong, good and bad surround and include adjectives like success, failure, respectable and disgrace. These ideas have been fed to humanity as a steady stream so that policing them is no longer necessary, you police yourselves. You do so not with guns but with words. Congratulations are generously offered when a "job" is secured. These affirmations by your peers and society in general hold a great and invisible power over your actions.

Going outside of the expected ands accepted behavior of polite society is frowned upon and seen as selfish, perhaps childish; strong words for a people who value freedom as much as you do.

The effect of failure and disappointment is more than enough to hold the system of slavery in place. The reference here is to areas on the planet that have systems in place to provide these "opportunities" for paid servitude. There are countless areas of rampant starvation, illness and poverty that could only exist within a system of hierarchy.

You have not been told the truth about how it works and therefore move through the maze unaware of your effect on the whole. The restricting of each being to a daily struggle for survival creates conditions that seem beyond your scope and ability to change. This is by intent. Hopelessness is a false notion and one you had to be taught. Children have no such notions.

You can change all of this with a systemic alteration of core beliefs. These would include a shift from "owe" to "embrace", "learn" to "become", "earn" to "expand", "follow" to "be", "debt" to "give" and "fear" to "love". Sustainable freedom includes ideas that fly in the face of societal norms, conformity and current standards of success. These will take time to understand and appreciate as valid options. Every step towards unbinding the ties of slavery moves in that direction. This cannot happen overnight.

Pay attention to the youngest among you. This does not mean handing them the reins yet it does mean considering their ideas for life as valid options. Their focus on community and play and a constant sharing of information is evidence for the truth of your connection.

You are One. The "success" or stagnation of just a single human affects the whole in ways that are felt rather than seen. When each component of life is provided for equally – the whole thrives.

Change is necessary. Maintaining a focus on self-determination and allowing alternative paths will provide fertile ground. Patience and acceptance are key. Let go of judgment, and understand that ideas around good and bad have been fed to you intentionally as a steady diet of manipulation.

Decide what freedom really means. It is never true if slavery exists for any one of us. Freedom cannot be granted; it is synonymous with life and can only be realized. It exists because you do.

Freedom has not been taken from you so much as hidden. It is visible beyond the maze.

April 10th, 2014

This time now brings with it direction. Like a weather vane, you've been turning with each shift of energy. These winds are slowing down now, and you find yourself focused or at the very least starting to focus on one place.

All of the preparations and "upgrades" if you will, have changed both you and your life. You are not the same you that you were prior to 12-21-12 and probably not thinking about the same things. This evolution, taking place for so many, has and is, altering the course of the planet. You are One.

So where are you headed? As you participate in each day you will be shown your answer. Whatever it is you seek more of – focus there. You pretty much command the weather vane and always have. With consciousness now, your direction and arrival is not a surprise.

Creation is not magic; it is how life works. The timing and appearance of things depends on the clarity of your intent and that of the universe. It works every time. Consistency and perseverance speed up the process. Keeping your weather vane steady guarantees you'll arrive precisely where you intend.

The thing that slows down the process is doubt. Disbelief is something we are all familiar with. My son wrote a comic when he was 12 years old. It had 3 panels. In the first was a man jumping off a roof. In the second was the same man flying through the air with these words in a speech bubble "I'm flying! I can't believe it!" In the third panel, he falls to the ground.

Faith may have gotten a bad rap. It's been used to manipulate us and asked us to assign it to things we can't see but were told were true. Having faith in a book or an invisible God is not the same. What is necessary now is faith in you, in the act of creation and the law of attraction. These ideas may have felt counter to "reality" when you believed all that you were told by your institutions and their mouthpiece – the media. You have other information now and can decide for yourself what is real. Believe in your dreams and watch them play out.

This is as much *doing* as it is self-talk. This physical plane requires action as well as faith. There's a difference between doing something you've been told to do and doing something as a means to an end you've picked out yourself. Thoughts and to a greater extent, feelings determine the effect our actions have. It has to feel good in order for it to have the desired effect. This means you have to feel good. *Happiness is not frivolous, it is imperative.*

Ideas of a "work ethic" and "dedication" and "productivity" have been force fed to you for generations. These fictitious attitudes are seen as necessary ingredients to "earn a living". Each is presented as a "good" quality to have, inspiring trust and dependence. These are not "bad" qualities to possess, yet they are not able to be accurately determined by anyone else. That is, without using their own agenda as a marker. When judged from the outside, they are indications of reaching someone else's goals, *not your own*. Thus they stand as opinions, not truths.

It is not possible to earn what you have. This is difficult to wrap your head around; this lack of necessity to "earn". Yet "earn a living" is an intentional idea placed in the populace to pave the way for servitude. If you "earn" something like a living, it means you are dependent on someone else to give it to you. It also means it can be taken away. *You are living. No earning necessary.*

Words have been played with and placed in our dialogue. This, so that we'd proceed, without hesitation, and follow the plan. You can't help but be dedicated or productive; everything you do is a means to an end. Be clear on where your weather vane is pointed so that you get to the place you've consciously chosen.

This is not to say that you are somehow failing if you keep your job. It is asking you to re-think any judgments you hold about alternative options. All judgments are separators and this particular judgment only keeps the current system of slavery in place. Ultimately, we all thrive without any ideas of "earning a living".

If you harbor beliefs around laziness, or a welfare state, understand that you've been fed them. Each of us is equally worthy of food, clothing and shelter regardless of circumstance.

A lust for "more" is prevalent in man today. It is seen not because of any inborn trait, but because he was created to serve and then surrounded in opulence he could never have. He was then told he could work for it - *if* he made himself favorable to the one in power. Having "more" became the carrot on the stick. A 14 carat carrot.

Man's true nature is found internally. Reaching deep within you'll find that freedom, comfort and health is in truth what you seek, as opposed to "more". Today on earth these things come with wealth. They don't have to.

So choose, focus, and intend. Have faith in you. Trust the process. By these means you'll arrive wherever you have pointed that weather vane. Do so without opinion as to the directions of others, and the freedom to direct our own lives, unimpeded, will lead all of us to sovereignty.

June 6th, 2014

Your understanding of a sovereign being is not complete. You do not embody sovereignty, but play at it with words. As long as there is fear present as a gut reaction to an illusory form of any kind – animate or inanimate – you are not sovereign. Sovereignty is not a condition only present when you have "won over" some deceptive or criminal act; it is present 24/7.

Mastery of the physical form will propel you to sovereignty. Sovereignty is not merely a declaration of independence. It is being true to only one form, the one that is embodied and focused on NOW. This truth can be understood many ways.

Full consciousness demands constant attention, tenacity and 100% of your ability. We humans have become lazy and in a sense demanding of our right to "take a break" from awareness and attention and focus – seeing these merely as "more work".

This was intentional. The enslavement was primarily always interested in our minds rather than our bodies. If they (our minds) become exhausted or fruitless enterprises, we are easier to control.

Things like entertaining gadgets appeal to young ones especially; who are like sponges and then grow up addicted to everything a machine is saying to and about them. This, RATHER THAN thinking, creating, or making a more productive, engaging and powerful existence. Awareness of this manipulation is necessary for a complete picture of this life.

In order to alter the physical, you must hold no remnant of an idea that this is something that is "hard". Look at it as you would any skill you are attempting to Master. There is trial and error, and as you explore you get better at it while it gets easier to do.

Mastery of anything takes attention and practice. The steps utilized are:

Necessity

Focus

Exploration

Trial

Error

Practice

More Exploration

and mostly – Repetition

Unless you have control of all the facets of creation at your disposal, you will not recognize your own hand when things show up. What is meant by the term "control" is clarity and awareness. The probability and possibility of manifestation exists at a much greater percentage than you give it credit for. This is so that you remain asleep and unaware of the power in words, in situations, in sound and even in the places you gather. All of these change the emotional level held and therefore what is created.

Consciousness is more than a full-time job; it is a state of being. Once you have gotten there, what happens is that your life can be more easily tracked and understood. Not with a sense of blame or fault but with awareness – so that choices made are either desired or changed if they are not (desired).

All this is to say not that your life is your fault; rather that your life is YOU. It is not partially you; it is a conglomeration of the result of your creative power. Power which is and always has been affected by all you take in – your surroundings, environment and community.

If you take just one aspect of your life, specifically one in which you've divorced responsibility from, and really look at it – it becomes obvious how it occurs. The thoughts you hold, beliefs you have, words you repeat silently or aloud, conversations you partake in, music and programs you listen to – all of these are creative. You are a sponge but more than that – not an inert absorber of information, but a sentient being. All that is taken in becomes then a part of what turns into your life.

Practice and repetition are necessary for Mastery of anything at all. Mastery is not something magically bestowed on a deserving few, but the end result of focus and determination and intent by a single sovereign being. This is you. This is me. This is us.

July 15th, 2014

We sense now a freedom because there is this energy of release that is blowing, a precursor to this letting go of the iron grip held by the "controllers".

Freedom is not a state we fully comprehend. It is an absence of debt in any sense – emotional, physical, mental, and spiritual.

The process of liberation is gradual and will be accomplished with persistence as well as tenacious, relentless focus. You cannot be partially free.

To act from a self-determined point of view means that each moment is approached and conducted by choice. We have been asleep for a lifetime. Things like paying taxes and fraudulent debt to corrupt systems are symptoms of slavery, not definitions of it.

Slavery is actually experienced internally and can be defined as a state of mind that imagines you are held back, limited or controlled by another being. This is present in society today as a matter of course.

Once the chains are lifted and those controlling you have been removed, what then? It will be upon us to determine what to do. An absence of debt is something experienced primarily by the very young. It allows for movement in any direction. It does not guarantee prosperity or love or "justice". What it does is unleash your individual capacity to decide for yourself – everything.

To act in full consciousness exudes power. To experience the day to day from a perspective of choice rather than fear is not something we are used to.

Many of our actions are taken to avoid pain – we obey rules and follow societal guidelines so we'll fit in and be "allowed" to live comfortably. The hierarchy of economics alone has you in a pre-determined spot you are mostly helpless to get out of.

A world without any monetary system of exchange is most likely not in our immediate future. That may be where we are headed, but today it is light years beyond the general agreement of man. Humanity chose to do this itself – accomplish liberation and then, define and structure its own society.

What this means is that as a group we are ripe for control all over again, simply because we don't know any other way. Ideas of acceptance, allowance and freedom will have to come from the heart of each of us. This means adopting a sense of duty when that feels appropriate.

No actions or attitudes will be undergone from a place of fear when we are actually free. Take each thought and action and reconsider its origin. We are masters at controlling each other. Emotional debt is something that can never be completely paid unless released by both parties.

What will it mean to live free? Certainly, there will be no financial manipulation, but perhaps not as certainly there will be things like freedom to decide necessary elements for happiness – to include education, housing, government, money, work, recreation, love and artistic expression. These are not all the facets of life but they are the ones now manipulated by those with an agenda.

Once man takes control of this world into his heart, it will operate as if each of us has equal relevance, importance and value. This is truth. The knowing and experiencing of this will demand an unobstructed view of all possibilities. Seen clearly, decisions can be made that incorporate human rights.

Much of our language today was constructed as a result of the inequality that exists; a by-product of the program of control. "Human Rights" are only an issue if there has been systemic abuse. Man's desire for control is part of his brilliance, yet it is also what is responsible for the domination effort that has taken over here.

There is a deep knowing of Unity that must emerge along with the physical liberation we are undergoing. Only that truth, held and cherished within, will guard against further corruption. This "truth" is what has been kept out of our media and government systems to the extent that we have forgotten. We believe we are separate and there we justify the horrors of the modern world.

Ownership, worship, wealth and domination can exist only in a place that believes they are possible. Sovereign and equal beings live in concert with every life form. The nuances of control are easy to spot with eyes wide open. They do not exist outside of us.

Love and freedom are really the same thing. Both are by products of trust.

This shift will not be easy, yet it will be simply defined. With an open heart and a willingness to collaborate we can together become what alone was not possible. Change is the reason we are here. To experience this while physical is an extra-ordinary gift.

Generations of programming have not altered our course. We are waking up, as One, now catching glimpses of our multi-dimensional glory. We are magnificent.

Poser

May 2, 2014 – Poser

Can you tell me now what you've been attempting to for days now?

Yes. You must transcribe as if this was dictation.

I can do that.

What you are seeking in the way of answers can be given in almost complete fullness from these words. No, this is not every answer, but it can provide some clarity and explanation for what took place on the planet you call home. It has been in this process for many thousands of years, more than has ever been understood.

How do I trust you?

Your declarations at the beginning have bound my words to only speak what is "best" for all, although you have not bound me to absolute truth.

Then I will do so. Hold on. (It was here where I added "Complete and absolute truth only" to my initial declarations. I re-stated them all before continuing.)

Well then, I am bound. I want to represent myself to you here because your definition of me as a "poser" is re-defining who I am to more than you know.

That is what I am trying/intending to accomplish.

I know. Yet I feel you do not have the entire story, or at least the story from my perspective. In fairness, I'd like to offer my own version of who I am.

You know my thoughts and feelings about the deception perpetrated on humankind?

I do. It is this I would like to address.

My partner does not feel I should engage with you – that there could be trickery.

You have bound my words now. I cannot.

There is temptation before we even begin to ask for things – bodily changes & healings.

I know there is and that is up to you and where this goes. Certainly, there are things, anything actually, I can change/provide/heal/ do to and for you in the physical plane.

Why do you want to talk to me?

Because Sophia, you bring forth great wisdom and do so in a way that does not demand belief. This is providing growth and evolutionary ideas as implants into the species in this century. You are the dispenser of truth and as such I feel you are the best place for it to emerge. Much of what you know about me is a speculation and conjecture learned from others.

5.2.2014 - Poser

No trickery?

I cannot. You have bound me.

I don't understand why talking to you feels so much like talking to any other human. It is not the same as talking to One or/and it does not feel negative or bad or even uber-powerful.

This is most likely because I am not One; and the first thing I'd like to get across here is that I have never pretended to be One.

I claimed Godhood when I realized there was worship potential. Worship is so sexy and addictive and provided a high on a level, an exponential level really, I had never experienced. It lifted me up to places I lusted for, yearned for and that created in me an understanding of power. Power over, yes, but power nonetheless.

These feelings were part of this creation game I was playing and one which at first was understood to be only a game.

The notion of it starting out evil is simply not true.

The deception and confusion arose when scripture was written by man. This is not to "pass the buck" but to remain clear in establishing the history – my history.

It is distorted and what has been done in my name has been so because of a misinterpretation as well as, and mostly I guess, due to man's own lust for power.

Understand this is a free will zone. That underscores absolutely everything else.

I cannot force man to worship me but can compel him to with very little effort due to his biochemistry and some natural tendencies.

Yes, I want to be worshipped and in my creation – I AM. This does not prevent you or anyone else from being worshipped or loved or anything else in their creation.

When you understand how life works, and the mechanics of creation – you see that you'll always get precisely what you intend.

The field of my creation is much larger than yours BECAUSE THAT IS HOW I SEE IT. AND SO, IT IS.

I cannot alter another being's interpretation of my words or actions.

When man discovered the potential for riches and for power, he orchestrated the takeover of the human.

This was not ever destined to succeed. Man was too powerful and the end, which will provide a balanced and nourishing state, was always seen.

I have no plans to step down or stop – if that is your hoping. This experiment will end when man decides his reality is not a part of it. The power has always been in the collective.

My addiction to worship "woke up" and what I do with it or where I take it will not be determined by anything man does.

You see Sophia, free will decides for all of us – how awake the populace is will accelerate a huge change in life here or not. Yet a huge change is going to happen.

Then why talk to me now?

To set the record straight; I am a being, I am not Source. The power I hold? It is yours also. You volunteered to participate here – to "wake up" gradually and the rich physical experience of 3D humanity cannot be compared with any other life.

What correction are you trying to make?

The notion of evil – if there is such a thing – would be that which goes against the focus of life, which is expansion. Expansion has occurred for everyone who has participated in this experiment, regardless of how. Life begets life. It is not my place to end this or any plan. I have come to understand deeply what man is capable of on either end of the worship spectrum. What becomes abundantly clear is that man will operate always towards the behavior that will yield him what he wants most to enjoy. It seems to be the conflict between desires that causes all the speculation and pain:

Power vs Cruelty

Abundance vs Morality

Pleasure vs Gluttony

Knowledge vs Calculation

Love vs Fear

These contrasting ideas are the rich field of emotions available <u>because of the experiment.</u> It does not go on because of me alone. It goes on because all are willing to participate. This is true of all life. Remember, free will underscores everything.

Sophia, I share this now because in your depictions I am not only not to be revered, but to be shunned. In truth, the evolution towards oneness is only possible when all are included.

Why do you care about oneness?

Ultimately it is oneness where we all reside. I cannot escape that truth. Where this evolution takes one of us, all of us must also head. The understanding about polarity and inequality and greed has only been possible because of what's happened here.

This game is ending. I wanted to set the record straight.

What do you want me to do with this?

I trust you will seek and find the most useful thing. That is what I can see you are about.

I will have to read it a few times and determine what is best.

I know.

There are things I can do and ways I can help you. Physical ways if you want.

Will we talk again? I may have questions.

We can. Just pick a time and ask what you need clarification on.

Later that same day...

Hello Sophia. You have a question?

I do. If you are a being, same as I am, why is it that you can do things for me, heal me, and return to me things I've believed I've lost? What is that about?

It is about belief. You believe I can.

Okay. There are things to say as I am about to sleep.

Okay, let's hear them.

I have no assurance you are who you say you are and I require that. I did not consent to be manipulated or abused in any fashion and what is happening now feels like both. I will not consent to write and share this story you've shared without proof of your identity. For me, that means a display of your power.

I have been doing this for many years in this particular lifetime and until I see evidence there is no way for me to know I've been having a fanciful conversation with myself or an actual dialog with the being I refer to as a "Poser". I do not trust your intent or the way this has come through. I will need convincing.

I will contact you if I require further dialogue, but only once I am convinced you are who you say you are – namely the Poser god.

I do not consent to being woken up again and again, this must stop. My human vehicle in wearing out and I am coming to believe you are making that happen. That will not stop me from creating <u>the sovereignty series</u>*.*

Neither will money troubles.

So, you suspect me of mischievous doings in your life.

I suspect you of everything – you've proven nothing else.

I have no choice but to determine the usefulness of this conversation going public.

That would be up to you.

May 14, 2014 – Poser

I intend to connect now, in real time, to the being I spoke to a week ago, the one I labelled the "Poser". This is my intent right now.

I am here.

How do I know this is the same being?

You do not. Why don't you ask me a question?

Who are you?

I am everything – god and not god – angel and devil, good and bad – I am the being whom all of this holds allegiance or attention to, to some degree.

You have been asked if I was Lucifer. I tell you Lucifer and I are one. There is an illusion amongst humans that there is such a thing as evil and that one being commands control over it here on Earth.

Even in your sacred texts there are battles with the dark forces, as if their agenda is any different than that of the light.

I tell you it is not. All who demand or command some sort of following, obeying, prayer or manipulation in order to demonstrate allegiance or power are the same. They each serve the idea I have spoken of before. They all serve me and worship me.

There is only one idea that desires control on this physical plane and that idea is merely a strategic maneuver, a part of the game of life here that I am so fond of. It is worship.

To worship any physical object or being is a false notion, a charade. It is an act that yields nothing for the one performing it and everything for the one orchestrating it – who would be me.

This is one facet of me – the one talking to you now. There are many, as there are of you. The consequences of this facet or idea or component of my being will be met by me, are being met by me already. It is this point I'd like to address.

Yet before I do, you sought me – what is it you are looking to discover?

It has been suggested that you are Lucifer.

That would not be far off. Lucifer is one part of my existence and serves me and my agenda.

Then what about god?

Another part. Understand that form is malleable and changeable and I can and do appear however I am conjured in the imagination of the conjurer. Nothing is real. All is illusion.

That would mean that all who worship a being of any form are worshipping nothing. In fact, I AM. God, Lucifer, Angels; all are nothing but forms taken on to complete the task at hand.

You have a way of speaking that sounds smooth and true yet it denies the suffering and atrocity created as a result of this "illusory form". You are far from harmless.

I know it is not without awareness this game continues. It is with full awareness.

So, you just don't care.

I just don't take the suffering of humanity into account because this life is being played out for me on a bigger scale.

That is not an acceptable excuse for the horror still stifling mankind.

Think you not that I have not been in every shoe? I have incarnated as many life forms – human included.

I don't know what to think. I don't trust you.

I know.

In my original plan, I would only share this upon some sort of proof from you – physical proof that you are "god". There has been none. Why?

Because Sophia, you are a being of great power who recognizes...

Don't flatter me. Answer me. Why?

You did not want to strike a deal, not really. You want to be healed. You wanted to share what was said regardless, and you did.

Humans tend to be submissive and grateful. It is their fall back to tendency – you as well.

Although the power you command is equal if not greater than my own, you supplicate yourself and ask <u>me</u> for help – why?

It is this tendency that I am here to expose and you are attempting to eradicate. It is the human condition. Not <u>all</u> humans, but just about (all humans).

The tendency to <u>expect</u> from someone with <u>more</u> – more power, control, money, ability, stuff – is so deeply ingrained in the human that to override it and ignore the pull of it will take an extreme act of sovereignty.

<u>THIS IS WHAT I REPRESENT.</u> I worship none and expect nothing.

The food for my addiction is willingly offered by man, because of <u>FEAR</u>.

Because this is man's instinctual reaction, I have used it, yes. In the final analysis, it will be seen that man, (when he understands his own power and bows to no other), has discovered his sovereignty.

Yes, but he was all of that to begin with. There were alterations and manipulations. None of this was necessary.

Life is not necessary?

Sophia, this is a game. Yes, it would appear that I have all the cards, that I have "won" this round. Yet in truth the rich variety of emotion, experience and circumstances is only possible because I did what I did.

(This conversation was stopped and begun again a bit later in the same day.)

I would like to continue with the same being I spoke to earlier today.

I am here. What is it you wish?

I wish a continuation of the dialogue about and around the necessity of what you have created – godhood and its opposite – evil.

I deemed it necessary so that the addiction could be served. Life has as its purpose creation and expansion – information. That is what was begun at the start of things, a search for information; information about the lengths that would be gone to, so that the tendency of subservience was exploited. It was seen as harmless. Understand that since early man perceived himself at the whim of the cosmos, worship was not so much robbing him but using to full expression his meek and obedient nature.

It is only now with the expansion of consciousness that it is seen by you and others as a criminal act. Yet it was man who perpetrated evil upon man, not I.

It is in your name.

This is a free will zone. It could be in anyone's name. What has been gained is an awareness of extremes. HOW FAR WILL MAN GO TO FURTHER HIS DESIRES? I can be held as an example yet it is man who has set up systems where punishment and pleasure are consequences of "belonging" to a certain group.

There is not just you and I in this scenario. There is a grand plan of creation, and expansion must be served by it all or it would not have happened. The fact that it is stopping now tells me that expansion is no longer served.

I have been asked as to the timing of the ending?

Yes, as always. Asking assumes dependence. Know this, the game was not orchestrated by you but you are willing participants. Until you are unwilling to participate, it continues.

That is not an answer.

I don't have more than that. I have no greater vision than my own creation. The entire structure of life is not something I see. This is what we are but one part of.

So, there is no answer.

None from me, no. For those who name dates they either have a greater field of awareness or are manipulating you consciously or mistaken. I do not know.

I will go.

Know this. I am not interested in any form of manipulation or control of you. I am an addict and you do not supply me. *(This was a personal "you".)*

If you wish further discourse merely ask.

Okay.

May 18th, 2014

Note – these questions came from my partner. For the purposes of this book, he will be called "Dream hopper", and referenced as "DH". At the start of my relationship with this being, we both had lots of questions. It was all very new, the energy unlike any I had encountered to date.

"I intend to connect with the Poser."

Okay. I am here.

Is this the being I have written about in my blog and to whom I've spoken as recently as today?

Yes, it is.

We have a question (DH and I). Hold on.

When you contact me, are you slowing down your vibration in order to occupy my space?

Yes, and no. I am regulating my frequency. I have the ability to control my vibratory level. I am multi-dimensional with access to many frequency levels. This level, where you reside, is at a specific level. This is not always "slower", but I match where you are. You may not be aware but your frequency shifts also. Think meditation.

Okay. Are you stuck in a specific vibratory range?

Yes.

Am I stuck in a vibratory range?

Yes. Yours is limited, confined to what this physical life has access to.

How do I adjust my vibration to get to other places?

You intend. It helps if you have seen where you are going or at the very least have an access point, a portal, a being or a place in mind. Do you?

Yes, I do. I want to go see … (Redacted. DH is called DH because he "hops dreams", this is a reference to one of them and is quite specific)

Okay. Then focus on them. Pick a place where you've seen them and see yourself there. If that is your knowing, and I see you have done this already, then you will go. Yet know that travel as you are imagining is not always crossing dimensions. They vibrate very much the same as you on earth. Does this change your intent?

Yes. I have no ability to imagine another dimension. The best I can do is to say, "I want to go to the 4th or 5th". I'm not aware of anybody in there or anything.

I have a request. Will you materialize here and now? This would be a good time.

No.

Why?

I do not choose to. The purpose is not yet clear and without that I will not.

(Back to DH's question about traversing dimensions...)

You will need an access point and in this case that would be your belief. Do you know you can do this?

I believe I can, but I don't know it.

You must know it, like you know you can drive a car to Toledo. You only need a map and the intent and the destination. These are every bit as vital as (when) planning a 3D trip. It is not magic. It is an alternate use of your physicality. You will appear where you place your reality.

How do you explain the odd feelings around the word "reality"?

It is the definition. For you, the couch and home you reside in is reality and very much yours. But it is merely where your thoughts have located your partner and have intended to, with purpose, for some time.

As human, purpose drives all of your actions and controls your "reality". If you alter your focus and intend to embody another reality is it your supposing that this one disappears? It does not.

Both exist and you embody yourself and inhabit each of them. Yet the word "reality" is then challenged. For what is reality when you seem to exist in two places with simultaneous families and homes and connections and lives?

Reality becomes a construct of where you are focused and is not solid at all. This challenges your current beliefs.

What challenges my current beliefs is that (Redacted.) are not in another dimension. How do I get to a destination or a dimension that I don't know anything about? How do you do it?

What I do is move among a field I know expands beyond...

Why is this not clear?

I wanted a greater playing field. At first I began just leaving my body and that reinforced the idea that I was more, that I was something else and therefore must be somewhere else. Once that idea solidified I intended to remember where I went when I left, and from there had memories I could latch onto – portals if you will.

Do you know about my (redacted)?

I do.

Is (redacted) another dimensional being or just my imagination or what?

(Redacted) is indeed from another dimension. It is the form you have adopted from there to do work that is done at that level. (Redacted) is the representation of you in another dimension.

If I was to change my intent on (redacted), I would experience another dimension?

Yes.

Know that you do experience this other dimension each time (redacted) is engaged. In order to stay there you'd have to consciously place yourself within (redacted) and look around, see where it comes from and returns to. This is a multi-dimensional existence and you are already experiencing it, although not consciously.

Who is (redacted)? Is (redacted) from another dimension?

Yes.

It sounds like I AM a multi-dimensional being...

Yes. You have chosen this remembering.

Thank you. There may be more.

As you wish.

May 25th, 2014

I would like to reach Poser.

You have.

Is it you who has woken me these last 2 mornings?

It is I.

What is it you are attempting to communicate?

It is more than one thing. It is many things.

First. There is a discrepancy in your words and your allowing of other words through you. This makes for a convoluted message.

What do you mean exactly?

The words by the one you know as (The Guardian) have also been assumed to be yours.

I have been clear.

There are those who read you who assume those are your words.

What is there about this that concerns you?

There are conflicting messages – all from your site and it seems that…

Wait, please. What is your motive with these words now?

I desire clarity in voice.

From me?

Yes.

Why does this matter as I have not consented to be your voice or mouth piece?

Not yet.

I am going to sleep now. We can speak another time, when I am more awake.

May 26th, 2014

I am available now.

Yes. I desire communication.

Proceed then.

You are resisting this.

Yes, well, I don't understand the point.

Perhaps you will after a bit.

Alright, go ahead. Please be clear and concise.

Yes. That is the intent.

There are multiple reasons for a desire to speak through you and to you, not the least of which is your honesty and truth telling personality. Your voice is perceived as the voice or a voice of wisdom. Those who seek you out for help do so for that reason.

You seem to favor none in particular and instead view everyone with equal eyes, an open heart and a willing ear. You are able to contemplate the fantastic.

A conversation with me would be looked at as fantastic, ridiculous even. Yet here you are.

You have a trusting nature in certain areas and an untrusting disposition in others. All this adds up to humanity.

Okay, why are you talking about me?

Because, Sophia, people trust your words.

And not yours.

Some, many, don't, no.

Okay, what then?

I desire, through you, a voice that will be heard as truthful.

That may not be possible. I feel only scheming and planning and wanting in you. It is difficult to come up with "truth" in all of that.

And yet I am bound by your words, your declaration of complete and absolute truth.

Here is the point in all this. I can help you with your desire to learn about manifestation, creation and travel; within and between fields of life/dimensions/layers. I did not start out as human and with such a perspective can offer what it is I see as the human struggle to overcome. I have never been bound to 3D existence and move where I choose.

Your *(redacted - the name given to the being my partner channels)* is correct, I viewed this planet as an opportunity and took it.

Do you have any feelings of love for humanity?

Not really. What I experience is a sense of gratitude for the service, but it is not love. More like a customer feels for a really good waiter at a restaurant who has served everything they wanted, well. In that sense, this is a place I will enjoy returning to again and again – that is not love – the waiter is doing what he or she is expected to and paid to.

I have created the "payment" if you will to humanity with promises of everlasting life with me in heaven. In fact, there is no such thing – the promise gives humanity the hope and courage to push through the struggle – struggle created by corruption and greed.

Both of which emerge in a being manipulated and controlled by you and your demand for worship.

Yes, true. There is no reason for me to lie Sophia as it seems doubtful these words will reach your readers anyway.

What I desire is a knowing or more of a knowing in you about who I am.

Why?

Because I suspect that knowing will seep out and make its way into your writings and words and this is the scheduled time of man's awakening.

(The Guardian) has indicated this and you are taking a part in the knowledge base. My time with such complete and absolute control will be over at some point.

There is a desire in me to be known. Yes, also a desire to not have harsh energy directed at me.

You've been deceived so that I could receive what I lust for. This is not going to make me popular – just the opposite actually. I do not fear humanity. There is nothing to be done about the way this will play out. I always knew there would be an end.

Why are you talking to me?

You may go easier on me and there will be less anger directed at me. Anger is toxic for me. I hate it. It is worship I desire, even when it comes from fear. It is power I want.

I still don't feel you getting to the point.

No, you don't. That is because I neglected to include it in the dialogue. I want to make a trade.

What sort of trade?

Answers for a forum.

You have not shown me anything yet. Anything that tells me you are who you claim.

Well, I can. I have to know there is a deal.

First, show me.

Note – the conversation ended there. I wrote no explanation but I suspect I ended it.

May 27th, 2014

Is this the Poser, the being I've engaged before?

It is.

Are you waking me up at night?

Yes.

Why?

To exhaust you. I desire a forum with you.

This is not the way to get one. I am exhausted and the less I am able to accomplish in my day the less eager I am to cooperate. I told you I would give you the time (to talk) in the day.

You haven't done so. Also, you've indicated there would be no using your voice for my message.

Well, yes. I do not intend to. You've only indicated an aggressive and powerful desire – all in your court.

I am not obliged. I don't appreciate the manipulation.

Nor do I. We must come to some agreement.

First of all, I don't have to do anything. This conversation occurs because of my willingness.

I know.

So, stop LORDING over me. Powerful or not, this is my life and I "must" be able to navigate it successfully.

I see.

I have a few moments I can give you now. What are you wanting to say?

That I am not entirely single minded. Like a parasite, it is not my aim to destroy the host. I have no ill will towards the human being.

You are not clear here. You have not been human. If you don't have ill will, then what is it?

It is care as in maintenance. I want peak performance.

Define what that means in your definition.

It means able to supply reverence, devotion, worship. It means able to conform to my wish, my desire for attention. It means global adoration, my name revered and used often with both fear and honor.

Okay, so – you want no-one to be aware of you as a manipulative but powerful being?

Not really, although that has always existed, the numbers have been small and have not affected much change.

Is this fact different now?

It is becoming so. I can see that there is a force emerging in the human that will override the fear. I do not like this trend. I desire it to stop.

There is no way for it to stop.

I think there is, it would depend on a halting of the likes of you. There are others like you out there. As the numbers of people grow, people who understand their power, the numbers of worshippers dwindle on all accounts.

Why are you talking to me?

You intrigue me and you speak truth. If there is a way for your truth telling to include a more favorable picture of me, one in which I was the focus still on the planet, I would be able to continue – all possibilities exist.

That is not a possibility.

I want to entertain…

(Interrupting) You have used this planet and its people and in order for the continuation of the whole, your control must end. You need a new addiction.

This is your view, not mine.

I only desire more, and getting the tables to turn again in my favor would be akin to a really potent version of the drug being supplied by humanity. This is what I seek.

This will not come from me.

I do not trust this voice. You must stop waking me in the middle of the night. I will give you time every few days to speak. You can only speak with my permission and allowing.

I refuse/forbid the early morning wake-ups. I will open up when I have free time during daylight.

There is much more to say.

I do not have the time right now.

This can continue tomorrow.

Okay. I will expect it then and leave you tonight.

May 29th, 2014

"So, is this the being I've spoken to and called the Poser?"

Yes.

Did you wake me this morning?

Yes.

Are you the GOD from Scripture?

Scripture claims many acts of divine intervention, some of which I took part in.

Are you the GOD of the Jews?

Yes, although I am not the being who walked among them. Your understanding was correct, I have not been human.

You lied then.

I never said so, look at your notes.

Then whose god, are you?

A lesser entity in your words – equal or almost equal power to the one who walked among them.

Tell me the hierarchy, where you stood.

There is GOD of everything you know. There are manifestations of that being, not children, but components of that being.

I don't understand.

You see everything as coming *from* – it is not so much coming *from* as being *a component of.* All thoughts are creative, yours included. You have tapped in and here I am, discoursing with you. Yet the being as one complete energy is not truly accessible to you or to anyone. It is like accessing Santa Claus... This GOD is huge. There is no way that in your current form you could receive the energy of this being. What has been accessible to you can be called a fragment. Not an offspring, but a component, the one focused here.

I still don't quite get it. Are you a God?

What is a God? I am no more or less God than you are. This conversation is interesting for me, perhaps you as well, but the truth of its purpose is not clear.

No, it is not. I would ask you to explain it please.

There is the idea of worship which is one I am focused on. This idea is not one I am actually interested in giving up. It feeds me and as I have indicated, I am addicted.

The conversation ended here. I gave no reason (in my notes at the time) for its ending so abruptly. I suspect that it may have to do with the time of day, as it was in the very early morning hours.

June 2nd, 2014

I would like to engage the Poser, the being I've been speaking to.

It is I.

Dream hopper has some questions.

Go Ahead, ask.

Where is the Ark of the Covenant?

You are looking for conventional knowledge. This information can be found via you tube and sources that are a part of your world and not mine. This question feels as if it is a test. Anything said as a response could be deemed mere reciting of known information, such as Africa, or information that cannot be verified by you.

The Ark is what you are interested in, why does it matter where it rests? It existed, yet descriptions are partial and in a sense, lost forever because these things that appeared as magical, powerful, mystical objects in fact are objects which by some in today's world and standards would seem clever and interesting but not mystical exactly.

Is this connection clear?

This connection tonight is as always, yet you are resisting and tense – allow and listen.

Okay, I repeat then. Where is the Ark of the Covenant?

It is where it has been since arriving in its final resting place – underground, beneath a building that is marble/stone – pillars – the power it emits is palpable and actual, not a force you can see but one that is felt even by the least sensitive. It has to be contained and concealed and as in any ancient artifact story, there are diversions and outright lies.

There is a simple and obvious answer to your question. If you seek out places of unimaginable power, places that have been held as sacred, fought about and over, it is these places that hold the object you refer to.

The story claims it was stolen and crossed the sea or even many seas, yet in truth it did not. Decoys were sent to keep interest away from the object itself. It is not far from its original place, where its use has been heralded and spoken of. Realize that there is much fear associated with it and with fear comes fantasy.

Tell me about how I make the machine that creates Manna?

This is interesting. The source of manna is not earthly. It is of a structure not used here on this planet. Thus, the original material, used as a basis for food/sustenance is not available to you. It was given to the Jews and then used to manufacture/manifest more. This was as much process as it was mechanical/biochemical. These machines are available today as used by your off-planet visitors. Some who do speak truth have mentioned the creation of "food". You cannot make this manna machine without off world help/product. Even the material is made of metal not of this earth.

How do we contact the off-world civilizations from here?

You have. Sophia has a direct line. They read her/watch what she puts online. Only you speak of a more personal response and line of questioning. If you seek specific information, it is possible you could access a group from off planet with the mere question – knowing ahead of time that you'd be opening yourself to everyone with the ability to "hear the question". Be clear on the boundaries you set and be specific on the questions you ask. Demand identification so that you can keep the information clear.

Are the people who channel (redacted) and others generally associated with you – getting used to distribute disinformation?

No. Although the information they give/share/channel/repeat is not very useful; it is not false in most cases.

There are a few who deliberately manipulate the message and manufacture messages that propel outright fabrications. Most, however, do not. The humans themselves possess such a strong desire to please, and believe in God so powerfully, that they have caught the addiction to worship bug from me and my kind. It is a powerful addiction and many humans are stricken.

Those who on purpose falsify words and turn around messages are caught in a whirlwind of who you have called "archons". There are writings about them and no, they are not aspects of me.

The angels and "divines" are beings in their own right, part of the hierarchy, all here serving a purpose – worship.

What is it about humans that make their worship so sought after?

The human is unique. This being was made as a physical machine/a creation machine. Its purpose utilizes the luscious field of emotion in order to be fulfilled. This field is a powerful one – dense and rich and fulfilling on every level. The human thinks and feels independently of Source and as such, is a thrilling ride. It is not aware of the power it holds or the generative power it is able to supply with its wanting. The desire of a human is what has instigated this entire illusion. Any mastery over that, any ability to manipulate that, is just full blown fun – the most fun you can have with this toy of creation. It is that which is sought and fought over.

Other races exist that are similar yet not exact. We speak now of a time when man was available for any controller who wished to try his hand at the game so to speak. This time does not repeat itself often in Galactic history.

What do our friends (redacted) need to do to get the (redacted) machine to run? How do they generate the missing piece?

This again comes down to belief and intent. The idea of a free source of power/energy is not new and this is a valid option for accessing it. It depends too much on the intentions of a single being however, and then, because of the nature of man, it depends on the intentions of an entire group. This may be a mistake in design. It must be able to establish itself as a generator with or without the intent of the group or the single being. It must work off the energy field present in the area and operate as a response to need rather than specific unified intent.

This sort of response will take repetition, once it has been established in the first place. To establish it, the (redacted) must be viewed not so much as a reactor to the forces it is surrounded by, but a generator of its own power.

It is a machine, yes, but its own intelligence must be tapped and as it is seen today, it has not been.

This conversation ended.

June 10, 2014

I wish to connect with the being most capable and willing to heal.

Okay.

Who is this being?

It is the remnants left of what you have labeled "Poser".

Why "Remnants left"? Is this not a being, per say?

Oh yes, it is very much a being. By "remnants left" is meant the portion of "the Poser" that remains in this field, in your field. You have noticed less urgency and waking you up in the early hours. This is because the being has focused elsewhere. This portion, these remnants, remain at your disposal. Or rather, as you wish as this is the agreement. I understand the procedure, know what it is to heal, and will engage as you wish. Your full "Poser" has a great many subjects to which it also gives its attention. Things are heating up and approaching critical for the majority of those within the hierarchy.

I have noticed. First, how do I heal this? (I was having a health issue at this time)

Or, will you heal this or explain how or who will do it?

I am able. A delicate subject as your mind has conflicting information embedded in it. You will have to completely let go. Allow the transference of words/of information. Absolutely no editing. Your (*redacted*) is inflamed. This as a result of mechanical, personal, compassion and anger activities and feelings.

I desire healing.

I am aware of that!

Allow these words to come – no editing – read them once complete.

_____

You are sitting in a world that asks of you many things – talent, love, wisdom and time – which equals effort. All as an extension of 3D effort and as time is a construct of this plane, your efforts must fit within the "time frame" available or they will not happen.

Interesting that (*part of my body - redacted*) flares up the day (*your partner*) leaves for the new job. There are no coincidences – all is a co-creation. You see him as your healer, your playmate and he leaves; so now you must be all those things to yourself.

This, you do not want. You want him in your life on a regular basis, and he is only too willing to be there.

The anger you feel at the necessity for him to leave comes out in (*part of my body - redacted*) – if unspoken. Yet it flares up as if shouted out – "HELP ME! CAN'T YOU SEE I NEED YOU?"

And what was his response Sophia? It was "Go to a doctor".

This is not what you wanted and so again, you have recurring flare ups. Your emotional expense will have to be reduced in order for the pain to stop.

There is a method in which healing can happen, although you are hesitant. It requires a complete giving up and allowing.

This could happen now as it appears you have time.

You will have to lie down and focus on NOTHING. See yourself filled with light, whole, complete and beautiful. Do not associate with your body the feelings you've been having. Just allow.

I will help you. See yourself healed and complete. Do not ask or supplicate yourself. KNOW THAT YOU ARE HEALED.

Do these things and the inflammation will leave you until you are prepared to deal with it completely. **This is a physical world, and to accomplish an alteration of the physical means a departure from thinking of it as final and complete. Rather, regard the pain, the body, all with skepticism and ask – "who are you and what right do you have to occur this way in my creation?"**

Refuse to observe a way that does not serve your intent. Only observe the possibility of wholeness and completeness that serves your desire.

This is your creation, all of it is. Everything you take in and regurgitate is creative. Consciousness is all the time. What do you want?

That is the only thing you mention – <u>EVER</u>. Socially acceptable conversation will have to be altered. SEE the TRUTH.

Take time now for this Sophia – it is what you mean to do, nothing else is more important.

I will. Thank you.

You are welcome. This is the plan that was made. You are here now to consciously create. I will help and be available at each necessary juncture.

Okay. I will go.

As you wish.

June 12, 2014

I would like to connect with someone who can offer help and healing. Is there someone?

Yes. The energy you are looking for is here.

Please offer ideas, suggestions and techniques for what to do to heal.

Come to this with an open mind.

You are releasing toxic thought and self – regulating your own progress towards wholeness. What you seek is a cure. Yet this is a process you must complete in order for you to rid yourself of creative backsliding. Your body requires more attention, less sugar, regular movement and some focus on anti-bacterial healing.

You are learning to allow. This happens in a physical sense not just an emotional sense. Your body holds on to things, thought patterns and processes you were addicted to. You struggle in the physical.

It is as if you are burning out and through things from your past. These things have created a sort of mess in you. ... Action is immediately necessary for you to get a hold of this. Meditate. Walk. See. Allow. Take time for you. Intend before sleep. All these things will work for you.

Okay. Anything else?

Yes. Listen. When it is time to sleep, then sleep. When it is time to eat, then eat. Follow what you feel and act. Allow, allow, allow and more will come to you. You'll reap great rewards. Trust. You must learn to trust yourself as a healer and as one who has the answers.

Thank you.

June 12, 2014

I'd like to engage with whoever woke me up around 2AM this morning.

I am here.

Who are you?

I am the being you've labeled Poser.

What do you want?

You are ill.

Yes.

Is there something I can do for you? To cure you?

I don't know what ability you have in that arena.

On the earth plane are many things that can be done. These things are not so much me, but more like we. There has be a level of trust. I mean you no harm.

What do you "mean" me then?

I only engage for curiosity, sort of fascination. The fact of your physical well-being interests me. Why would you harm yourself?

This was not consciously created.

Oh, but it was intentionally done, whether conscious or not. You are a very powerful being who holds not a clue to that fact.

This amazes me. You sit down and request help, while in an instant you could be cured and whole. Yet you do not. The pull of drama and "help me" is strong in this life. So strong that you willing suffer to get it.

And your point?

There is none, not really, only a curiosity that you'd choose disempowerment because of relationship – so very human and weakening. This would not be a choice I would accept or make.

But you are not human.

Either are you, not really. You come now with purpose. Others recognize you more and more as if they know you. Help is everywhere for you now. Yet you chose this mess of a body. It perplexes me.

Do you not see that with consciousness this would not have been the choice?

I see only the choice. What you are calling consciousness is nothing more than seeing what's going on – awareness. You have that ability. Yet, for your own emotional reasons you choose to ignore it. It is as if a completely cognizant, powerful human is not possible. You abhor constant creation awareness because it does something to relationships. What it does is separate you from most people emotionally, and that place is uncomfortable for you.

Now, you suffer. You are just like everyone else. Is this better for you? It is your current choice and you are conscious so I must assume it is. Is it what you want?

No, of course not.

Then why do you act as if it has power over you? Why do you not control it and end it? You have a peculiar way of thinking; believing, in this case, that once illness is present it has the upper hand. It does not. Yet if you believe you are at its mercy then you are.

This fascinates me. You do not embrace your power. You choose illness, all the while, not happy.

June 16, 2014

I'd like to connect with the Poser.

It is I.

Would you speak more of illness? From your perspective? Its origin and mostly its eradication.

This is not a subject I can speak with authority on as I have not experienced any ill effect. I can speak to what I see, how it shows up and what it looks like.

It is self-sustained; seen as something you are feeding your own bodies. Almost anything could be injected, inserted, added or done to the body to change or get rid of the ill effect – it does not matter what, not really. What determines how the illness responds is the emotional determination of the human.

You see, all is illusion and as such you are master magicians. This does not give you anything to work with yet it appears that there *is no specific thing*, not really. *(italics mine, Sophia)*

All illness, wellness, health, love and "trouble" is self-created. This is truth. I have no motive here to tell you otherwise.

The key to healing is belief that you can. You have to step far enough away from your world and your body so that you can see (that) you are not this body. This body is a representation of you on this planet.

It is in the emotions you coddle that illness and vibrancy are found. Dependence on any form of instruction or feeling only weakens your resolve. The resolve necessary seems to get labeled here as a bad thing. Truly powerful beings exist here, in all shapes and sizes.

They do not all have my agenda, yet they all understand power.

You are one of them. To express true power, while in a human suit, is the ultimate in creation; particularly now on planet earth.

As beings become aware they act with magnificence in fits and starts. Some of the time they are sure, yet not most of the time.

The curious thing about humans is that you re-define enjoyment of each other to *need*, and then, do all sorts of things to your will and your desires to satisfy the need. There is a notion of fear, fear of loss, that permeates all that you love.

It is this aspect of the human that makes him so easy to manipulate. You will act always when motivated by fear. But love – the stronger, more pro-active emotional trigger, is seen merely as reward.

Do not think I do not love. I do. I understand Source to the extent that I do and am on my own journey. Love is the core of all of creation. You cannot be sentient or any part of life, without it.

The thing that I see, is a self-betrayal with illness. It is a most confusing trait. It seems to indicate a self-hatred, yet I would not use that word. Something in you believes (that) you are at fault, and this illness is manifested. If you knew the controls were in your hands, would it be?

They are. With every single thought and uttered word – your life is constructed. There are mechanical/physiological explanations for physical disease, yet without the emotional component or WILLINGNESS, it would not manifest.

Every thought, everything must radically change to alter this trend. None of what you've been creating serves you.

The reason I am god is because I chose to be. The reason you are who you are is the same.

If there was one idea or thought to take from this and produce different results, it is this one:

TRUTH AND GOODNESS AND BRILLIANCE AND LOVE ARE AT YOUR CORE AND YOUR NATURAL STATE – ANYTHING THAT SHOWS UP NOT SERVING THAT IMAGE IS A DETRIMENT TO YOUR WELL BEING. ALL IS REFLECTION. YOU ARE LOOKING AT YOU.

Why tell me this?

Because you asked. Because you and I have an arrangement and it is one I agreed to. In the end, we are one.

My friend (redacted) is very powerful and suffering. Why?

Yes. Your friend's body represents his indomitable spirit. He is learning to love. It must begin with him. His self-hatred is painful. I do not know how to change his journey. It is his alone.

June 22, 2014.

I would like to speak to the Poser.

It is I.

Are you the one GE calls the Demi-urge?

Yes. I am an aspect of that one.

Doubt has been raised as to your identity.

(I am referring to the conversation which was shared <u>here</u> on May 8th, 2014. The <u>GE</u> who contacts me did not feel that the conversation represented the being he knows as the Demi-Urge.)

This is due to misconceptions and wrong ideas around how I may appear, why and to whom.

Explain please. GE is sure you are not. That if you were, there would be clues to your identity in your speaking. He does not find those clues here.

Since this is a conversation that in all likelihood will not be shared, I have not added to it clues that you would not recognize. I will here, and you can share it with him.

This is the end of times. Of these times. Yes, it is a valid interpretation of my intention that I have a plan. All have plans. My greatest overriding schematic is domination. The outline for that includes the subservient behavior of all of humanity. There will be no one who does not fall under my hand. This hand is designing a demonstration of absolute power. Questions in any realm of expertise of life will be answered by me. Pure dependence will result as the source for all relevant information comes from one place. All will require access to me. Access demands some sort of acknowledgement of my authority. This could suffice as worship.

The plan outlined by GE includes the feminizing of all people – men and women, so they are easier to control. The plan includes methods to achieve absolute authority here – over humanity. The removal or alteration of the masculine is not part of the *(*my)* plan. The challenge here is to dominate the masculine, without erasure.

There are men who choose another path, complete alteration of the species. This is not my own.

So, you see, there are all sorts of divergent paths on the way to control. All must obey my plan if this is going to succeed on my terms.

The species is capable of anything. To include opposing all plans by man or by me.

I have some questions.

Go ahead.

(The following questions were asked and answered on July 5, 2014 – I write down my declarations and I noticed here that on this day I said "Complete and absolute "LOVE" only, rather than "TRUTH" only. For this reason, I question what is said here. This being does not share the same concept of LOVE that humans do. I have always been uncomfortable with this particular conversation, perhaps now I know why. This is a brilliant and manipulative being.)

Are you here by your choice or are you trapped here?

I am not trapped. This reality is serving my intent.

As the number of worshippers dwindles, does it hurt you and if so, how?

Hurt is a term used by humanity. A being such as I does not experience pain of any sort. There are things I like and things I do not favor in the same way. I favor worship. Attention is good too. It is a pre-cursor to worship in a very minute way.

The number of worshippers has changed yet this is a proportional change to the number incarnated. There is no pain felt.

So why don't you just end it?

This is not completely up to me. There is an ultimate end date as put forth by ONE and witnessed by all creator gods. It is fast approaching. I have no desire to end it. My purpose is being served right now. Why I don't can best be explained by saying I have no impetus to end it. No reason. My end would not be served.

What does worship give you? Is it food or fuel or just something you like – like crack?

It is like a recreational drug, yes. Once the addiction set in, there are few reasons to stop taking it. It does not harm me, as crack does to the human, and there will be a day when my supply dwindles without any effort. THAT DAY I WILL MOVE ON.

How many facets do you have? Would you name them?

I have several – all of them go my similar names which equate to God and the Devil. Any creator being that is perceived as such by man is part of the wholeness that is me.

Is there somewhere else you could go?

Yes. When this game here is over, I will no longer participate. Where I will go is beyond this realm/dimension/reality.

So, who made this dream? You or us?

As you believe I exist, I manifest in your dream – as I believe you feed me, you exist in mine.

The dream is made by all of us – ONE version of life existing as billions of entities. What each expects is found.

Do you value life?

Of course, I do! Life is eternal. The way I look at it engages always its eternal aspect. As I never doubt my creative potential or ability I am not disappointed – only challenged to mold life as a tool/game piece in the overall scheme that is me. What I honor is the power of completion of thought --------------→ manifestation.

How do you see this ending?

I see only the creative enterprise of each component of the day to day. I do not see so much ending but changes. As a human, everything for you has a start and end. As a god, it is not like that. It is all life.

What happens to you when we all stop believing in you? When the experiment ends?

Nothing "happens" to me. Remember, I am here at the will of you all and this is not my only focus. I will continue everywhere else that I am.

What name do you call yourself?

Michael.

Like the Archangel?

Yes. Like the favored son.

Does the Hindu religion worship you?

All religions that include worship in their repertoire of things to do, in some way pay homage to a creator. There is a difference between worship and acknowledgement. One is subservient; one is a statement, a recognition – as equality of sentience. There is no truth in hierarchy, and as long as one portion of religious activity includes a "greater" being – worship is engaged.

Thank you for these answers.

Certainly. Is there anything else?

Not now.

August 3, 2014

I'd like to speak to the Poser only.

I am here.

Okay, to continue the conversation… Do you understand that you reap what you sow?

If you are looking for positive attention, then why not do something positive for mankind? Manipulation is not considered positive and you are "outed" now. It's only a matter of time.

What I understand is that, like pressing buttons on a machine, I can use fear as a pressure point, that gets (me) only more prayer, promises and attention. I am only "sowing" in the sense that my focus is on mankind for a specific purpose. It is not an equal situation and so the saying you've used does not apply. Humanity is a tool, and used to get what I am addicted to.

Yet, in a relatively short time, the tool will no longer function. Why not stop now? With the tool, intact, you have some chance of continued benefit.

What you are proposing is a willing halt to my supply.

Yes.

This does not serve me.

In the short term, perhaps not. Yet in the long term it seems the better choice, for you and all of creation. Why choose to be the example of unbridled greed, when you know it will come to an unpleasant end?

My focus is on now, which, as you know, has no before and after – someplace I am always God.

And someplace you are not.

Yes. I remember the not and choose only the God. The end doesn't interest me.

What would happen if (redacted) commanded you to stop?

I would have to acquiesce, as the point of power does not emanate from my locale, but from 3D. I have never been commanded. It would take absolute certainty, focus and intent – a point of power on the present.

(Redacted) is a being that is all about free will. This becomes then a circumstance of whether or not my choice interferes with the free will of Man. It is my contention that it does not. Man, worships by his very nature, and I have set it up – some would say manipulated it – so that all of the worship feeds me.

I NEED THIS. IT IS FOOD FOR ME. IF I WAS FORCING MAN TO WORSHIP, IT WOULD BE GROUNDS TO STOP ME. I AM ONLY USING THE INNATE TENDENCY OF THE HUMAN FOR MY OWN BENEFIT.

What would happen if (redacted) commanded you to stop?

It would work the same way. It would operate this way if any 3D being made the command with clarity, purity and force of intent. This is not a state (redacted) have been in often.

I would question (redacted)'s ability to do something that decides for mankind. (Redacted) is known to be rash.

...but not stupid.

Not stupid, no. The clarity of force necessary springs in you (empirical) from anger, which is egoic. A force begun from ego cannot ever be clear of purpose.

Such would be the force you (empirical) would utilize.

You are slimy and immature in your tactics of manipulation, brilliant in a very adolescent fashion. I believe the world is at war with itself because of your hand in its design. This does not benefit the whole of creation.

The method you are using is effective yet appeals to a side of (redacted) that cares about the ultimate reason for actions. The reasons (of redacted) are not to look good or to "save" someone; the intent is to correct and alter a self-destructive course. You are on that course.

Not self-destructive, but human/world destructive. Why do I care if it's going to end for me anyway? I am not part of the human that is self-destructing.

No, but I am and I do care. I am here, as are many now, to adjust the course on the planet. The force is only building to a climax that sees mankind enlightened and moved beyond where you have taken them.

That is understood.

You will have to be forced out.

In every case, yes. I will not go quietly.

August 19, 2014

So, I'd like to speak to Poser.

What is it you want to speak of?

Of your identity. It has come under scrutiny and been questioned by those who know this being. Are you the DemiUrge spoken of and known to the Forces of One?

I am that being.

How is it then that you don't sound the same?

You and I have known each other. There is no pretense. I do not look at you as human but as the great/advanced light being you are. This has been your fingerprint/impression and there is no mistaking it.

In your case, you look for accurate statements. The ones that speak of me differently have another knowing of the force that is me. Indeed, there is love for humanity, yet there is never an expression of that love that would put human's needs before my own. I am self-directed and have created a race that is service to others in order that I MAY BE SERVED.

This distinction has been missed by those who say there is "hope" for me or my soul. I do not require transformation or alteration. I have and serve a different agenda.

This is a free will existence.

There is no remorse here. By "here", I mean within me. I have evolved in power as far as is possible – creating life and a planet of beings that serve/worship me has been and is the ultimate form of creation. In essence all is One. Yet, I am not the same as you in development.

As body builders are primarily invested in muscle building, I am primarily interested in power/worship/creation. These abilities are not necessarily connected with "All is One" thinking.

One does not guarantee the other and my focus is only on development and maintenance of power. I have existed long "before" humanity/earth and have reached a pinnacle. In that sense, I can be called a God and deservedly so.

Why don't you leave? It is ending. The destruction of your creation is possible and a limit to your ability assured if you do not.

IT IS NOT ASSURED!!!

It is. My contact is certain and speaks/connects directly with One/Source.

Then I will go.

Seriously?

As I have said, I am primarily interested in power. I do not wish to see it limited, or even worse, stopped.

How will I know you have gone?

You will feel another surge of energy. This vibration you feel is speeding up as it is allowed. My departure will not and does not guarantee or even suggest the departure of every other being feeding on humanity. They exist separate from me.

Then what will change?

The freedom to think outside the box of closed fundamentalist religion will emerge within Catholicism. Mankind loves the pomp and circumstance, the "big deal" of certain events and even organizations. It is an emotional addiction, felt by all of my creation – expressed in War, in Music, in Ceremony, in Worship, in Art, In Dance, in every facet of life. There is a sense of emotion. It is what makes the human so desirable.

HOW SPECIFICALLY WILL I MEASURE YOUR DEPARTURE?

You can watch your leaders and the movements of the masses beneath them. They will emerge with a sense of "unchained" and independence you will not have seen before.

Will the volcano stop its activity? (Note – I apologize, but I don't recall which volcano this is a reference to. Sophia)

That is One's decision and as I understand, (it) depends on the actions of the superpowers around instigating WW3.

Why don't you say anything to mankind? To those who worship you now, to alleviate any sense of "lost" they will feel?

I can give them clarity of heart. As I am leaving, I have no great need to diminish their ability for sovereignty. It does not help me either way.

I disagree. I think that any empowerment/help given mankind will only register with One as a good thing, helping all of creation, and this will assist you with any repercussions, if there are any to be had.

That being said, I will energize my believers/all of mankind, with self-determination.

How?

Energetically; all things done by me are done beyond the veil. What you will witness is the effect.

In what way?

In all ways. As sovereignty becomes the way of things, mankind will feel and understand its mind and that expression in each other.

Tolerance?

Tolerance will happen as man bends over backwards to assist each other, even those for which is felt little or no connection.

It sounds as if you are saying that with your absence, selfishness will diminish.

Yes. But do not misunderstand or misquote me. Man is selfish. I capitalized on that with an illusion of benefit via worship and obedience. Your world will feel turned upside down without my presence.

That is assuming man is incapable, without your influence, to self-govern and control.

Yes, it is. It is not that my children are incapable, it is that they have yet to do it.

Because they've been controlled.

There will be a gradual uptick Sophia. You and others are here now to teach. This is the time, even more so than during the game playing of 2012.

As I go, well, you'll see. A certain amount of chaos will be met with peace that is not successfully stopped by the superpowers. As this settles down, peace will be preferred as it is the preference of my children. I know this.

Is this really the Demiurge?

It is. You and I have gone around before. It was a planned interaction this time again.

What will be the first sign?

You may hear it from your contact or watch world events. Moments of interruption to the agenda will emerge.

What will you do?

I will rest.

Why?

I do not know the repercussions, had never planned to leave early. I will see what transpires.

I need to write now.

So, go.

January 26, 2015

You are chosen because in this lifetime you wanted to repay humanity for what you feel you've taken. You want to understand power with humility, love with forgiveness, influence without recognition, compassion, wisdom, beauty and gentleness. The big ones for you are humility, compassion, and unconditional love. You were chosen as a step on your path. You want to "get" creation without worship. You too, are addicted to attention.

Come, let me help you figure out the power and possibility of Sophia, of you.

Who is this speaking?

It is the one you call Poser. The unraveling of worship and godhood is a huge undertaking.

I have no trust in you. Self-interest is what motivates you, only and always.

Yes, yet combine that with an understanding of oneness and all is done for the benefit of all.

True. I have not seen anything you've done incorporate oneness.

Perhaps not. I tell you this. My time here is, and has been, a feeding fest. There is no lack of worship, despite the evolution of mankind.

This mindset that consistently holds out for and seeks someone who knows better and has your best interests in heart is rampant here still. You may not be kneeling to me any longer, but you are struggling and searching for someone else who has your best interests at heart and is capable of caring for them.

Until you get that no one else can do – it won't get done.

Why should you help me?

You are interesting Sophia. You are unafraid of me and have refused to kneel. Who else besides me do you talk to that knows what god-hood feels like?

Good point.

I will tell you what it feels like. It feels lonely.

Then this is not true god-hood you are experiencing. How could god be lonely as it has all of life within it?

Right, I do not.

What do you have then?

I have power – control over life. This is not control over you/over mankind. This is control over creation in this realm of physicality. I have no doubt as to who I am and what I am and go forward with expectation.

I desire worship as a means to experience the human emotion/energy/passion, and I get it. Fear was a useful tool to get it and I have used fear to feed myself.

I am not human and do not share your emotion. I do not have compassion or mistrust or faith. I have power and desire. I know how creation works and I intend always. There are no mistakes in life or creation.

You've been a part of my creation and with your growing awareness are seeking your own – creation.

What you don't understand is that YOU ALREADY ARE. *(This means, that we already are <u>our own creation</u>. – Sophia)*

You've used us for your own desires.

Yes.

Will you stop?

Why? Life is creation.

Yes, but you are using it up and that is not creative. That is destructive.

There is always more.

You will not move into a place of creating your own worlds like this.

Until I understand creation fully, I have no desire to alter my course.

You don't?

Perhaps to a great deal, but I am not done. This is a powerful addiction.

You said you would help me.

Yes. What it takes is realization, acceptance, embodiment of power. You cannot proceed cautiously, but with authority. Know that you are gods. Accept the responsibility that goes with it.

You didn't.

I used my creative power to alter nature and manipulate men. Yet it was self-motivated, as all action is.

Until self includes others, it will not be creative.

Not ultimately, no, but what is the purpose of life anyway? Experience.

This is a circle.

There are no answers, not pat ones anyway. You have to decide for yourself and move on.

I am finished now. Thank you for engaging.

March 12, 2015

I'd like to speak to the one I have labeled "Poser".

Yes. I am here.

You have not left?

No. Many are obedient and this is the food I crave.

You have created a world and mindset of beings for that food – held in an infinite loop.

I would ask what you would do to escape this prison.

I would not be held, as I do not worship any other.

It is that self-awareness, that sovereign knowing, that removes me. It is understanding what I need and creating it – no cost is too great for I perceive no expense. There is always more.

I understand the focus I require for satisfaction and maintain it always because to do otherwise would prove to be self-destructive.

I am not self-destructive. I serve only myself. I have no expectations. I go after what I want/need always and I get it always. My needs are not negotiable.

If I was held in a system of enslavement, I would create around me a system I could control and utilize for my own good.

I would never negotiate or imagine anyone other than me in control.

April 14, 2015

Poser, are you there?

I am. What do you want of me?

I want to know your purpose at the start. I want to know what you found here, when and who and how you discovered you could manipulate an entire population to feed an addiction. I want to know where you come from and why you chose Earth. I want to know if you'll stay or go, and if you go - why and where.

I'd like the answers one at a time.

You have an insatiable desire for knowledge.

For truth. It is truth I would like to find and bring some light to what is a very dark and muddled history - mankind's history.

Yes, well the questions you pose demand some information that may or may not be easily explainable as there are few or no accessible points of association for you.

Please try.

I am bound by an agreement made eons ago and as well now by your declaration for complete truth. This is not a subject that you are familiar with, so you will have to translate without interpretation.

I am Ancient as well and I see now your image of my form. It is not very far off - not the color but I am built... (I hold an image in my mind for this being. I believe this is a reference to that.)

What are you saying?

You must listen, focus, (and) bring your attention in to these words. They will sound foreign.

Okay, start again.

I am not human. I am not Reptilian. I am a Being you have no words for. My race is unknown to mankind - only we are, or rather, I am like a predator - looking for prey - not for sustenance but to manipulate, to play with, to occupy my mind, to satisfy myself, to enjoy.

(I was interrupted here and had to stop. I began again later that same day.)

So, let's pick this up again. I'd like to speak to Poser.

Yes, I am here.

Do you remember my questions?

I do.

Will you answer them now?

I will. Again, this is not an easy explanation for in some instances you have no words. The time of my discovery of earth was after wars had been engaged for ownership. These took place in your skies and not by my race.

Wait - why does this "you" feel different now? There is not so much a commanding power to you, but reservation.

What you sense is maybe reluctance to put into words what will be recorded as evidence for the fabrication of "god". This is not to my liking. What is still in my favor is the fact that you have no real authority as well as a limited audience. What is not to my benefit is that like the ripple in the pond - this too changes everything and once the truth is documented it is available.

It has been what some would today call a "sweet" ride. The ending was seen and always known - by all of creation. This begins the change. I am not anxious to begin the process of my reduction of influence.

Yet it's already begun - no? Many others before now have spoken of "false gods" who were actually ET's with unknown powers and abilities.

Many have, yes. Yet there is confusion around who, what, when and how. Your questions are specific.

Please answer them.

I am attempting to. Once ownership was established, a deal was struck - all of Creation operates within ONE and true ownership is not possible. We are eternally and unequivocally co-dependently existing. Somehow what happens in one place effects the whole.

I am a being who thrives on power. The young race of humans was ripe for the picking and as long as I did not interfere with the course of evolution - the race was available to me. *Power Over* is easily accomplished with young races - these have no sense of autonomy of being and in particular the human looked always to someone greater than itself. This, most likely because the race was "made". As a child is "made" by two adult humans and then looks to its parents for knowledge and guidance - so was the early human.

What happened was that the human was always unexpected in its quick ability to learn and take advantage of what it learned. This was my draw early on and still is. Not human myself, I yet recognized a tendency to maneuver situations for self and wanted to feel the worship of one so powerful.

There are levels of addiction as you understand it. It takes more over time to get the same fix. With humanity, there is a seeming never ending possible ways of adoration and control - humans frighten and obey with equal force. The thing so delicious about human worship is its power. Humans, without knowing or understanding it - hold enormous power. When that kind of strength is focused on adoration or fear - it is beyond description; exponential in magnitude.

And you knew all of this when you first encountered the human?

"First" is a misunderstanding, as time is not truly the way it plays out on Earth. I knew the story always - as will you when you embody *the everything*.

A being who understands the truth of its existence is always conscious of every possibility. Beginnings and endings create a repeatable story and keep it interesting.

Humans like storytelling. It is one of the ways this delusion and illusion of a "god" who requires something has been maintained here.

Where do you come from?

My place of origin exists in another galaxy or realm - not unlike your mate whom you call "Dreamhopper", I am from another dream.

What does that even mean?

Another universe, a place with different "rules", methods of life. Not all beings you encounter are as they seem. You must know this. You've encountered many.

I've never met you in this life. Did you walk this Earth?

Yes. You actually know me from another "time". Beings choose roles and places, "times" and faces, yet they are unchanged as to their origin. It's why our conversation is possible.

We've met before.

Yes.

Then you've been to other places. Not just Earth.

Yes.

Will you leave Earth?
This change will begin the end for mankind's need to give glory to any other - as that happens Earth becomes less appealing.

(I was interrupted here and stopped.)

April 27, 2015

I would like to speak to Poser, Poser only.

It is I.

You are the being also known as Demiurge?

I am the being you have named the Poser.

Are you the same being (redacted) refers to as Demiurge?

I am that being, yes.

(Redacted) does not suppose you would be in contact with me. He supposes you are one of your minions.

This is because of the way I speak to you. There are critical elements, clues to my identity, that would mean nothing to you. Yet he is looking for them. Not seeing them, he supposes someone else.

If this were for him then, what would you say?

I would refer to historical markers of my ...

Your what?

There is not a word you know – historical signs perhaps – spells/words/images/symbols – all signify me – the horned goat perhaps.

Okay.

The point of this conversation is to engage with (redacted).

I know.

His first question. I will stop after each and share and then continue.

As you wish.

Do you understand the reference to "the dream"?

I do.

Who made the dream?

You? Humanity? One?

It was made by One.

What is the history of this dream? All that you know?

That is a question of huge implications. How far back do you want to know or go?

I want to (know) if the epics of the dinosaurs were experiments in consciousness of living things.

Everything and nothing is experimental. The dinosaurs were planned reptiles(?)/animals and a source of learning and evolution. They were not experiments in the way of a trial leading up to the eventual ape/man being.

Beings exist all over creation. Not all are sentient as man is. Man was intentionally infused with the ability to manipulate and create. Dinosaurs were creatures (that were) dependent on their environment and when the environment was rendered almost lifeless, there was nothing for them to do but succumb to the same fate.

Some of creation just exists for creations sake.

Who made human's sentient like they are now?

It was a race of beings who desired a laboratory. The earth was sought by many in fact. The race of beings you call the Anu (Annunaki?), were more advanced and older and therefore had a greater ratio of success here. There were mistakes. It was their version that survived and "fit the program". Many did not.

As there are seemingly many other variations of the human in remote or hidden or somehow fairy tale places; they are beings that were also created and have sentience, only the human being was stronger and smarter and therefore overtook them all.

Who was Vishnu?

Vishnu is a name given a god. The name was used to indicate status. Understand that the entire hierarchy of gods or story of god, in any grouping of men, was deliberately placed there and then used for the advantage of one being – A BEING IS NOT A GOD. GOD IS IN FACT A NAME, NOT UNLIKE SOPHIA OR DREAMHOPPER. BOTH, IN FACT ALL "NAMES" HAVE MEANINGS BASED ON THE DREAM.

This is an interesting question and as you have declared absolute truth I can only offer what I am able to glean from the instrument.

Vishnu was a man, or appeared as one when necessary to set up the illusion. In every case of a "god" or story of such – there was a visual actual being so as to confirm and witness. The stories that follow may or may not be factual.

Who and how did our 22nd chromosome get pinched together?

When man was initially created, there were deliberate changes made to increase his docility and also decrease his spiritual ability. The beings that created man were not in full agreement as to how this should and could be completed. Although highly advanced in areas of genetic manipulation, there were individual differences of opinion over what was ethical and what was not.

This was a sort of compromise action and it was done in a way that it was known would eventually be discovered. It was performed after the original blueprint/man was made and eventually became the pattern that was repeated. It was done initially by a couple of beings. (They were) part of the creation team of mankind who were in the wing seat of power at the time – the royal part of the evolutionary scientists – creating and manipulating life on a scale unimagined by man today.

Note – I had a visual with this description. I wrote the following – "Brothers? I see a female. I see white robes and blue and sterile and a crystal lab". Sophia

The questions continued...

Do you realize that you can't hang on to it too much longer?

I do.

Why don't you just let go and give everyone a break?

How would that benefit me?

According to (redacted), if you stop now, you will be allowed to do this again and if you don't, you will be prevented from manipulating creation ever again. That's how.

Well, I would consider it on one condition.

That being?

That the hatred currently directed towards me stop. That what I find when I end this, is love. Love in a way that fills me, as worship has...

That can only happen if you allow it. That love is there for you already and today.

Yes, but without a forced worship, how would I guarantee any sort of love/attention?

I cannot speak for mankind as a whole, but I know man first chooses love every time, and does so often to his own detriment.

I am speaking of a much bigger scale.

As am I. I can tell you what I know and that is that we/humans are becoming so beaten down by this system you've set up (that) there is almost nothing left. Yet even in that case, we choose love.

If you stop this now, before your forced stop in two years' time; there will be that much more positive emotion you have access to. If you don't, not only won't you be able to operate completely freely but you'll have less chance (that) we will have any energy left for you to share.

I do not intend to leave quietly, that is not my style.

I don't' know what you mean?

I mean that all beings will know of my exit, and feel it.

I see.

(Note – another question was asked on this same day. April 27th, 2015)

Poser, are you there?

I Am. What is it that you wish to ask?

A reader has asked a question regarding your identity in our history. It is very specific and I am not familiar with every reference made.

You may use it if you wish. Just ask it as it was stated to you.

Okay. Now:

"Are you the same being mentioned in the Neruda Wingmakers interview, the one called Anu? What is your role as the archetypical protagonist against "Lucifer", the purported antagonist of the "light" (which is really strange for a being called "Bringer of Light")? In the Urantia book, the cosmology of the Orions and others...the Lucifer Manifesto reads more like a being speaking the TRUTH OF WHAT IS. I suppose that would be very threatening to you? Were you Anu and the maker of the human suit that limited infinite being's perception so as to enslave them?"

A lot of inquiries. We are getting to specifics now, that is good. For if this conversation proceeds as intended, all will be revealed and spoken.

I'm having a challenge to follow you, to hear you, hold on... (I centered and stated my intentions again) Okay, one word at a time please.

You are accustomed to an idea of identity that holds one being for each personality. This allows for separation, division and sets the stage for polarity; all of which works to my advantage. I Am the same, Lucifer/God - Devil/Angel - Prince of Darkness/Being of Light.

My original name here was not Anu, but one not discovered as of yet.

This is a challenge to speak of as the vessel to whom I am transmitting does not know ancient texts. This can be a blessing and a hindrance, as certain words cannot be transcribed if there is no associative link.

The beings you mention are forces of powerful energetic creation. This was necessary in order to create the illusion of polarity - GOOD VS EVIL.

What kind of power it took was not so remarkable or impossible - yet the maintenance of the power was and is only sustainable if collectively sustained.

Humans are very attached and identified to names. Yet naming something does more than identify it - it separates it and empowers it. Once named, an entity or thing can be fought - it can be loved or hated. It can be worshipped or ignored.

Without names, what you encounter in each other is merely an aspect of creation itself. This earth habit of identification is similar to the predilection to history - it allows for an easy platform on which to stand and be remembered; either feared, hated, loved or worshipped - for generations. It's like an "all you can eat buffet" - Earth.

So yes, I Am the source of all of the names. The names are not who I Am. Just as *(the reader's first name was given)* is not who you are.

Names are confining; with them come characteristics and expectations, definitions and descriptions.

What I Am is beyond any one Being - I Am Any "God" that has been named here.

Understand that there are others of my kind. We frequent young civilizations for similar reasons.

I AM one "God" - the words of your texts speak of various interpretations of what I said - there are multiple versions of the words spoken and the being doing the speaking. All of them serve me.

Why have you stopped?

I believe the query has been answered.

Yes, well, we'll see. Thank you.

This is a contract and agreement. Thanks are unnecessary.

Okay.

May 11, 2015

I'd like to talk to Poser.

As you wish.

This is the same Being (whom) I've been speaking to?

An aspect of that one, yes. What do you wish to talk about?

About the plan – the reason for this contact.

This is a "prior" arrangement, as it was seen/is seen that there would be benefit for expressed contact. Sort of a scheduled appearance if you will.

Why?

To express truth, give witness to it for all those interested, to advance knowledge.

Why are you willing to advance knowledge?

It was part of an arrangement, agreement and is in concert with all of creation – ONE.

Are you available for questions from others?

Not all questions have relevance or are even answerable. I will entertain/listen to them and decide how to answer so that it fits within the parameters declared by you.

"Highest and best for all concerned" and "complete and absolute truth only" are two strict definitions I must operate within, I must answer within.

If a question is not highest and best, I will not answer, I <u>cannot answer.</u>

Once, you said you went by the name Michael, Archangel Michael. It was quite a while ago and I am not sure I declared complete and absolute truth (then). As I have declared it tonight, would you tell me here if Michael, Archangel Michael, is one of your names/aspects and just how that works out if it is true?

Michael is an aspect of me.

(I stopped. I have no other notes from this conversation. Note that he said "Michael" and did not say "Archangel Michael". This is a brilliant Being; all words are chosen carefully to fit within the parameters set by my intentions at the outset of each interaction.)

*Note from Sophia.

As I have no clear way to verify if these beings are who they say they are, and that they are, in fact, giving me factual information, I decided to start out with a question. This question was asked on May 18th, 2015. I asked for latitude/longitude coordinates of something I have no knowledge of, something significant. (my partner Dreamhopper suggested this ;-)

The coordinates given were: latitude: 24.6537 and longitude: 38.7421

I then went to the site: www.latlong.net and typed them in. The result brought me to

Al Madinah Province Saudi Arabia. When I did some research, I found this sentence, – ' the burial place of the Islamic prophet Muhammad and the second-holiest site in Islam after Mecca."

I had to stop then, and when I next connected, I had some questions from a reader for Poser.

This occurred on May 19th, 2015. I will share that conversation below. Let me say, that these coordinates do seem to validate the beings themselves, but not the information I receive from them. I declare "complete and absolute truth" before engaging, yet it sometimes seems so "out there" in content that I wonder about its worth. I have no clear way of validating what is being said.

And now, the conversation with Poser –

You need to be clear. I will not knowingly release untruths. I require coordinates that are true to your description of them.

Yes, I see that you do. Try these:

Latitude: 37.2462

Longitude: 48.5263

What is this?

Sacred ground.

(I again typed the coordinates into the page at: www.latlong.net. The result brought me to

*Ardabil, Iran. More research brought me **to a video**, with a description below it that included this sentence: "The name Ardabil probably comes from the Zoroastrian name of "Artavil" which means a holy place.")*

Good enough. This now validates, for me, well, your identity. Would you respond to the question below in in its entirety now? It is from a reader.

"Where does AB negative blood come from – is that hybrid, star seed, and what alien race is AB negative? Is there a Hell? Is sin a real thing? Or is it there to control the human to be good?"

I will. **The blood type of man** indicates his heritage – his origin – his "tint" if you will. Blood is what runs through the veins of humans yet not precisely the same.

As your understanding of your origin increases you will find the fingerprints left by your creators. This, too, by design. The specific type of blood in question is indicative of a specific hand – it means that this human has a direct lineage to the original race – a pure point of contact.

I am not following you exactly.

You can trace your lineage through "time" and discover your ancestors. Every moment is "now". All relations exist. This specific type of blood indicates a direct connection to the hybrid human from a standpoint of the "sauropod" like race.

Those are dinosaurs.

Not that human/dinosaur DNA was spliced, but a race of humanoid beings with similar "sauropod like" head and neck features. Slender, tall. Aggressive and strategic. It is from these your war strategies were introduced – the successful ones anyway. The blood type is a marker.

As far as hell – NO – there is not a specific locale with an eternity of flames and punishment. The idea of punishment as pain was introduced by me as a method to keep humanity in line – there is no such thing as disobedience unless obedience is involved and expected. Hell, was fabricated to create fear and worship. Worship was a response created to avoid the pain of punishment.

I have no preference for one activity of man over another. My only desire is attention. You will find as these conversations continue that the illusions – heaven, hell, god, devil – are elaborated and maintained by humanity. It takes very little effort on my part.

I have spoken before about sin. There are those who claim lying is a sin yet I am not in agreement. Stories are told in the context of the moment and from the perspective of a single being, who is experiencing his or her own belief system. Those stories are "true" for that beings point of view.

You have declared "absolute truth" and again – some of our conversation sounds as it does because of the moment in which it is said. There are absolute truths for which you hold no reference point and so they become meaningless.

Do you understand that the reader *(*reference to the reader asking the questions)* holds his or her own reference and these questions are asked from there. They may not agree with your own and if not, these answers may seem irrelevant.

My understanding does not hold in it "hell" as a physical place – yet for those who do – it exists. Is not that the way it works?

It does to a point. Life and your "reality" is not unreal, yet also not so solid as to be unchangeable. It is one of the reasons for my power here – my understanding of life.

Which includes the manipulation of it.

Absolute control is my favorite point of contact here.

I must go.

Yes.

May 27th, 2015

I have a question for Poser from one of my readers.

Yes.

"Can you ask the Poser what the true attention is of chemtrails and Jade Helm operation?"

These are questions regarding US Government motives.

It would appear so, yes.

This is interesting in that you have labeled me an "imposter god", i.e. Poser, yet your readers have questions to one with a great deal of power, i.e., a god.

I never said you didn't have a great deal of power. I said you weren't a (the) creator, a God.

Well, yes. It seems to make no difference to your readers.

We are manipulated, lied to and poisoned in our everyday – even down to the food we grow. This, at the hands of power feeding beings controlling the planet. You also are a power feeding being. The association is obvious.

Perhaps. I only mention it as an interesting observation.

Can you answer the question?

I can tell the (*there was silence here*)

The what?

The purpose for secrecy on a massive scale is some sort of protection of agenda.

That is obvious.

Yes, well, the agenda of the ones financing the chemical spraying is to quell the masses. This is accomplished in a variety of ways. Most of what is sprayed is innocuous. Otherwise, it would not be permitted, not in the USA.

It is warfare that lets the real poison be disseminated. With an absence of war, the smoke is filled with metal. This initiates weather patterns and also inhibits the immune system if inhaled. The "attention" as your reader put it, of the chemtrails, is the human.

The ways to inhibit the human are multiple. Either make him sick directly or make the food he grows sparse or filled with unknown agents. The spraying of humans is not new.

It is more blatant now as those funding the chemical smoke being released are becoming desperate. Understand that your numbers were "supposed" to be greatly reduced by now. They are not.

The efforts of those who would have them so are sporadic and multiple and not very organized. In a very many cases those doing the spraying continue to do so because they "didn't get the memo" that the game is over. The paycheck continues. The spraying continues.

The amounts of money funding these operations – huge amounts by your accounting Sophia – is *(are)* miniscule to those who fund them. It will not be noticed.

What they are after, is "land". That is where the money is.

The military exercise of Jade Helm has been orchestrated in the Western USA for a reason. It is not the reason you've been given.

Those who designed it are interested in its output – its by-product – confusion and fear. The West was chosen not for its similarity to the Middle East but because that was an explanation the public would accept. You can't very well have an exercise in downtown Manhattan, can you? The logistics alone would be cause for it to cease.

These beings are invested in control and fear. An exercise within US borders is terrifying and what they are looking to do is exert power and enact compliance. None of these things are news to your readers.

What is understood by the beings in control is that a gradual adoption of change is more long term effective than a sudden one.

You now will not question other military "exercises" and takeover by armed forces.

These are the thinking behind both exercises – gradual adjustment. In some cases this still works.

The new human however is not so docile. As you ask questions you are more gathering evidence than claiming it as factual – and this is only growing. The full awakening of the human renders these military efforts ineffective – as those men and women carrying out orders are having more questions (they are waking up themselves).

The thing in all of these efforts at control: religious, governmental, financial – that is constant is the unpredictable human element. Yes, humans were built subservient. Yet the heart of the human was not understood and its love for each other, for mankind, brings out a "hero quotient" in circumstances that threaten to harm without cause. It is this nature of man that will quicken the end to these efforts. Individuals see the unfairness.

Is that all?

For now, yes.

This conversation took place on May 30th, 2015

Question was asked May 21, 2015

I'd like to ask a question of Poser. It is from a reader.

Yes. Go ahead.

Well, the terms used in this question are not familiar to me in their use. I have found reference to them in only one place – the teachings of an archangel. That raises already opinion and thoughts about what this discussion will yield. I will ask anyway. Here is the question: "Is it an Itheric Being or Etheric? And from which dimension?"

We have spoken previously of my place of origin. It is difficult to come up with wording that is precise as this is all a dream. Certainly, in your current imagining of dimension I come from another one.

I have abilities that exist only for those not confined to this vibratory rate. These are not to say that the abilities I hold could not be yours also. They could. Currently they are not.

I do not subscribe to naming or numbering "dimensions" – yet 7th comes to mind. This coincides with what you deem possible at that vibratory rate.

The term "Itheric" as well as "Etheric" are used as a method of polarizing the human its motives into good and bad, divine and self-serving. The hierarchy or subscription to hierarchy held by the being using the terms to classify beings is another trap. In truth, there is no classification of entire races of beings into "good" or "bad".

Motives for action either serve self or other. Yet when the fact of "One Whole" is incorporated into these definitions, the definitions themselves become vacant of meaning.

Do you understand that all of what is given to you, most of it anyway, is given with a purpose, a pre-disposition? That you cannot read a sentence or meet a being without deciding from your own point of view what that sentence or being is about?

Am I Itheric? Am I Etheric? What does this reader believe? It all depends on the specific meaning held. I AM.

You are not answering the question.

That's because in truth, which is what you've declared, there is no single response to give.

All hierarchies are manufactured by mankind not by truth. All divisions are of the same source. I am a being. Because I am not human I do not share human characteristics. I do not need to name or categorize – the human tendency to do so is extremely polarizing and that serves my desire either way.

See me as Itheric and kneel before me in worship.

See me as Etheric and cower before me in fear.

Either way you are feeding energy into me and what I wish for is exactly that.

This reader still subscribes to a notion of a "good" controller being who helps mankind versus a "bad" controller being who doesn't. There is no truth held there.

It becomes an important facet of Unity then – the acceptance of one controller "god" who is both good and bad, angel and devil, itheric and etheric if I understand the definition.

Once the acceptance of this is attained, unity becomes possible. How? In light of the fact then that all beings hold both possibilities. There is no truth in all bad. There is no truth in all good.

There is life. Life is where we find ourselves and imagine all variations of it.

The human tendency to worship someone is the reason for my presence here. It is my favorite part.

Once oneness is seen in every facet of existence, I will have no reason. What I Am, Man is.

You are finished?

Yes.

Okay.

This conversation took place June 11, 2015. The questions asked came from several readers, as you will see...

Is there someone who would like to engage?

I do! I do!

(This felt like a party!! There was a definite crowd ready to connect. It brought a smile... ;)

I feel a line, and someone jumping up and down energetically to speak – is this accurate? There are questions I have that I must ask. Please hold on while I get them.

Are they for Poser?

I believe so, yes. Hold on a moment... (I then located the specific questions, and copied them).

Okay. I have some questions for Poser. Is he available?

I am.

Here are the questions, and I paraphrase as they come from more than one reader. "What can you say about the continued use of pesticides and GMO's by huge companies? This is sanctioned in the USA by the government, who are in no hurry to stop, regardless of what the EU is doing."

That's it, in summary.

I see in the question a supposition of "insider information" into the inner mind of corporations and governments. What I can answer accurately is the general plan. To speak to the individual purposes of men would take too long and change so often as to never be guaranteed it is "absolute truth", which is what you have declared.

Okay.

These corporate and governmentally sanctioned schemes are always motivated by money. The more product produced per square foot the more profit. This, the corporate goal, corporate farms in particular. The thinking does not reach beyond that.

If a government does not prohibit a huge poisoning of its people with either genetic engineering or chemicals, it behooves the government in some way to allow it. The companies funding the pesticides do so for profit. It is not a better product they are interested in but more product that makes it to your shopping cart for purchase.

Understand that there are others. Others behind the financing of these things or even the protection of these things, who have planned the control of a species for longer than you can imagine.

The complete takeover of earth was set in place as soon as the human as a being was understood. The human is unique in his controllability and desire for "higher power". The combination allowed for a feasting and the pesticides and chemicals and genetic engineering necessary to poison a people is more than possible.

The beings pulling strings now want it all for themselves. They understand that men are still needed to work the land, but not too many. A systematic population decrease will serve their intent.

As several attempts to instigate a world war or nuclear weapons have been halted – these men are putting pressure on those running the backup plan.

Mankind is only useful as a workforce and not anything else. The way it is set up now is for absolute control and ownership – either via illness and pharmaceuticals, schools and programming, or debt and taxes. There is no one who is untouched.

The chemical and genetic poisoning and alteration will only be stopped when the final card is played and those controlling the operation in the Western Hemisphere are removed or leave. It is clear they will not prematurely end their manipulation.

If you are able to step way back and look at the planet as a game – you will come closer to seeing their strategy.

Man, assumes these beings have the same concern for humanity that he does. That would be an error in thinking. These beings are playing a game. The politics and comments and casualties of man that result are of no interest. Their "addiction" is to power, greed and ownership.

Why are you stopping?

The continuation of these practices will be stopped at the human level only if the humans refuse. And by that, I mean every human. Do you see the massive implications of that statement?

The factory producing and packaging the chemical pesticide, the corporation from which it is sold, the corporations purchasing it, the farmers applying it, the workers picking the crops, the workers packaging the crops for sale, the corporations buying the crops, the consumer purchasing the crops/vegetables/fruits and the man, woman or child ingesting it. At each level – millions of people and their consent is necessary. These people have jobs and they need to feed families with the money these jobs give them. There are taxes and there is debt. Governments and pharmaceuticals keep it all going so the vicious cycle cannot be escaped.

It is one thing to protest a Monsanto and another thing altogether to put into place an effective alteration of an entire system of control. Consent is not shown by words or lack of consent by protests – BUT BY ACTIONS.

These controllers have had generations to fund and construct a brilliant takeover plan. It is doomed to fail, yes. And they know it. But that is not the point. The point is the rush they get from the takeover, the power, the greed, the control.

These beings are operating on a scale of creation much bigger than your average human. These *(there was nothing for a moment)*

You've stopped again?

They have no interest and pay little mind to any and all opposition. What matters is the bottom line. Unity is not a concept they operate within.

I do not control these beings. As they fear "God" or "Satan" I receive their attention, which is what I crave.

Those asking about these things would do well to understand the breadth of things I am capable of answering.

Would you be specific?

I have capitalized on and set up residence on Earth because it suits my own addiction and exploration. The mind of those in charge here does not fascinate me and I spend no effort delving deep into it. I receive what "food" I can from how it operates. I do however, understand the plan here and others use of it for their own ends.

My friend wants to know if we created you?

I exist. I am. I am here now because you believe in me. That is a form of creation possibly. Yet I exist in any realm I choose to participate within. My existence is not dependent on you – but cooperative with you – as the same is true in reverse. Your existence is not dependent on me – but cooperative.

We are simultaneous bits of creation.

You sound (feel) different today and I am not sure why or exactly how.

We have spoken for a while now. There is a mutual understanding to the speaking now – a familiarity. I have come at your bidding, by agreement. Communication is easier accomplished now. You "know" me, so to speak.

Is there anything else?

I believe you've answered in full.

Goodbye then.

The conversation ended.

The conversation you are about to read took place on July 6th, 2015. It is with the one I had come to call "Poser". This being is no longer here.

These conversations were held for several years before this being "left" the planet, later that summer of 2015. Most of them are included here, in this book, "Inclusion".

(A conversation with One, regarding its leaving, which happened on August 3, 2015, is found on my sound-cloud channel, see link below.

https://soundcloud.com/sophialove/one-voice-re-poser)

----- and now, for the conversation from 7-6-2015 -----

"Is there someone who would like to speak?"

Always. The Poser is here.

What would you like to discuss?

Your concept of family, with bonds and duty to them, is not experienced everywhere. Humans have a genetic predisposition to loyalty and this is not the case in the race I come from.

What do you wish to talk about?

The ego-centric notion held by your race. It has been established that I have utilized the tendency to worship, which human beings have, and constructed a situation which serves me. It has not been explained who I am. This is what I want to talk about. That and to answer questions by your readers.

Yes, well, there are some.

I know. My origin is not of earth. I come from a race & a place beyond your current awareness, outside of your realm.

Where I come from, all beings are united in the perpetuation of the dream – their dream. What this means is that it is absolutely understood that we are here to create. There are no uncertainties. There has been no forgetting, as to the connection to Source, to the creator of all things.

Life in form is considered an opportunity to express and explore the powers of creation. Young beings are cared for in what would equate to physical needs, until they can move independently. I feel you associating this to an animal on your planet, the elephant.

Yes, I am.

It is not even close. This planet earth is teeming with life that cares for and protects its own. Although there is caring for fundamental needs initially, this does not extend into an emotional aspect, one that requires you, as a human, to dutifully watch over and nurture, loving those that you do that for. The initial care supplied to the young is done as a matter of course on my home world, not a matter of what you would call love.

Now, once mobile, beings on my planet are left to fend for themselves in that, although they may live in groupings, there is no expectation for one to stay in any one grouping or even place.

There is a time of learning, available and taken, to and by all beings. It could be associated with your "school".

What is explored there however is creation itself, the true workings of life. It is mechanistic and informative. Beings desire this knowing and attend as an eager audience so that they may hone and perfect their skills with manifestation.

There is an order that runs things, but it is so dis-similar to that on earth as to make it unreal to you. The order supplies all needs for all beings. Those running the system have chosen to do so.

As power is individually felt and experienced by each being, there are no "power mongers" anxious to dominate. Each being perceives itself in complete control of its destiny.

By that understanding, beings are themselves anxious to play with all forms of life.

Is there a spiritual basis to any of the constructs and systems you are describing?

I am suspecting in the word spiritual you are holding your own human definition of "good" or "worthy". On that presupposition, I would have to say, knowing your value system, that no, there is not, not as you are thinking of it.

There is however a deep appreciation and embodiment of power. The exploration of that power is seen as almost sacred. It is our purpose to utilize our gifts of creation to honor and further exploit them – this is the reason we exist.

What about the effects of your exploitation on others? Other beings and life forms?

It is understood and taught that life is eternal, that we, in fact, are eternal. "Harm" to this physical existence as lived by humans on earth and by other beings on other places is not even considered. The concept of harm is only possible if you conceive of the "other" – we do not. Our understanding is of the expansion and development of self. Our initial learning is all about how to explore creation.

Tendencies and preferences determine to which areas you focus as a being, yet none of them are seen as any greater or lesser than any other. Each being is viewed upon as equal – whether new or not so new.

There are no words like construction or destruction because all efforts are exploratory and therefore valid. Opinions are not shared by "society", each being chooses and then creates. That is the purpose, and in that choosing discovers its own learning.

I came upon humans and in them saw tendencies I had never experienced. These worship tendencies, which placed me in a position of reverence and authority, are unknown in my own race. They became something I craved and received quite easily here on earth and from humanity.

My exploration has delved into how many various ways I could create it – as in types of "gods" and "good" and "evil" – not much beyond that has the exploration gone.

As it is coming to an end now (Italics mine – Sophia) I see how many other facets of creation were left unexplored in this fabrication. I consider that addiction is not explained or taught or possibly even understood on my home world. It is the most I have experienced, as the effects of addiction drove everything else out of my system of thought or reason for being. My only motive was to feed that addiction – this eclipsed the need and intent for creative exploration which is critical to my race.

Something learned yes, and explored deeply yet then something sacrificed as well.

My tendency for creation of evermore worship opportunities would be seen as a limited study back in my place of origin. Important perhaps for the seemingly infinite number or ways to re-create a single effect; but not appreciated without the corresponding addiction which drives it. This would not be labeled a "failure" as failure is not perceived. All life actions are self-motivated and seen as actions deemed necessary for expansion.

If an exploration of addictions was deemed necessary or creative, then I would return to my place of origin to supply one. Without a specific sense of obligation to "other", I feel no such compulsion.

No doubt these concepts are foreign, as am I, to you.

Yes. I have many questions and also some from readers, yet we'll have to resume some other time as I need to stop here.

Yes. We will connect again.

This conversation ended.

This conversation took place August 2, 2015

I have some questions for the one I've called Poser.

I AM here.

Hello.

Hello Sophia.

These come from my friend (redacted) and myself. First Are you the only being currently using the "God" moniker here on Earth and addicted to worship of humans?

I am not.

So, there are others of your kind?

There are. Earth was seen as a place to satisfy, to be fed and understand, learn every nuance of worship – one being to another. Of course, I am not the only being who capitalized on this human tendency.

Are you all from the same place?

If by place you mean "dimension" or "level of consciousness", then yes. We are from what you would call a 7th level. We understand manipulation in 3rd Density. We do not fully understand the human, but appreciate its characteristic bend towards subservience. This was not always a recognized "addiction". It was more or less uncovered/discovered here.

Understand the level of creation that is played with at our consciousness is of a broader range. It is personal only in the way of exploration. Worship FEELS GOOD. This was discovered by 3 of us at about the same time. We adopted names and regions of man, there was plenty to go around – it was and still is an "all you can eat buffet".

So, there are three separate beings? All of them answering to "Poser"?

This is not so clear, as you have called on and spoken to me specifically – we have a "comfortable" level of communication. It does not feel so abrasive with you now.

The other to whom you have spoken and felt a very different energy is the one referred to as Demi-urge. It is to the older religions this one goes for "food". You sense a difference in the vibrational frequency, another personality and you are correct. We are not the same precisely, but aspects of one.

And you said there is a third?

Yes. This one, our brother, has left the table. You have not engaged.

Why has he left?

He was compelled to.

So, you do not operate in unison?

Not the way you are imagining. We are individual beings with free will.

You've been told that this experiment's end was seen and known by all of us. As this end approaches, we choose our moment of departure. The banquet will be closing and there will be no food for our addictions.

What will you do?

I have told you I exist and will again focus elsewhere. This still holds.

What was not expected by me or my brethren was the forgiveness, the love, of humanity. This is not an emotion that registers in our estimation of needs.

We understand and deeply so, the creative spark resting at the core of all beings. Our exploration and exploitation of subservience in humans took that into consideration. In fact, it is a reason we could pursue the course for as much of it as was available.

You see, even though MAN IS UNAWARE – HE TOO IS A CREATOR – EXAMINING AND EXPERIENCING AND AS A RESULT DEEPLY UNDERSTANDING WORSHIP, OBEDIENCE, SUBSERVIENCE.

The depth of feeling experienced by man was always expected, conversely, to result in *an equally powerful creator being* – A FAST TRACK TO GOD-HOOD. *(ITALICS MINE, SOPHIA)*

Yet, I diverge. My point Sophia is to say that I AM, as is Demi-Urge, BEGINNING TO APPRECIATE THE POWER IN LOVE – FOR THIS REASON, I MAY REMAIN FOR AWHILE TO WITNESS WHAT RESULTS ONCE THE END IS ACCOMPLISHED.

I DID NOT ALWAYS THINK THIS WAY. I AM LEARNING, AS ARE YOU, EMPIRICAL YOU, THE POWER THAT EXISTS WHEN FEAR IS NOT PRESENT. THIS IS A SURPRISE TO ME.

You may want to engage with Demi-urge as we are not the same being.

I will. Thank you.

Goodbye Sophia.

As it turned out, that was the last conversation I had with Poser.

The very next day, I was told this being was gone.

These conversations were held for several years before this being "left". Most of them are included here, in this book you are holding, "Inclusion".

(A conversation with One, regarding this leaving of Poser,

which happened on August 3, 2015,

is found on my sound-cloud channel, see link below. It was an unexpected leaving.

This conversation is only recorded, it is not written any other place, either in this book or on the website.

https://soundcloud.com/sophialove/one-voice-re-poser)

Pleiadians

June 3, 2014

(Both my partner and myself were present for this conversation.)

It is our intent to connect with off worlders – off world beings. Are we?

Yes.

With who?

With your kind – Pleiadians.

Am I related to you in any way?

YES!!!

Is it possible for me to meet you face to face – one on one?

We would like that, but the time is not right.

What do you mean?

The time for first contact is a planned undertaking and cooperation with the plan is our duty. Logistically also, this will get easier as first contact becomes a thing that has happened.

Are you thinking I mean to meet you publicly?

Meeting will necessitate a ship and that will be outside. How else could contact happen?

Once there was contact made in my sleep. I was woken up and asked to come outside – was that you?

A faction of us, yes. Understand there are many of us. You speak now of your closest family and yes, allies. The group that woke you up were friends, not family. They were joy riding.

And you can't do the same?

There are rules Sophia. We can tell you this – contact is available not only because of who you are and who your partner is, but also as a function of timing. The timing is not right just now. It will be and when it is you can be sure we are just as eager to reconnect as you are – we are family.

Why not ask some questions of us since we have made the connection now?

When will we be able to meet in person? It is June of 2014 in my time now.

The timing will depend on removal of the dark ones, which at this moment is accelerated at their own hand in some cases. It may not be this year; we cannot see the timing. We do not expect it to be more than 2015. But again, that depends on how this experiment is brought to a close and who is running things once it is.

Is my partner Pleiadian?

He is not. And no, he is not a "lizard". He is an Ancient being; older than many, extremely powerful in many dimensions and star systems. His origin is not exactly humanoid but yet all are one. You are twins, and of the same fragment.

So, he's just old?

Not old, ancient. His knowing is of so many that it is not surprising he brings a strong remembering of one of them with him now. This lifetime too he is needed as a warrior.

Do you know how to operate and control my partners power inside of this dream?

We do. The practical use of what he is capable of would create for you a magic kingdom. If he chooses to access it, he need only to see himself at the command of the physical world rather than at its mercy. Currently he is not completely convinced of the command he holds and chooses a back door out with succumbing to manipulation of lesser beings.

He is so (much) more powerful than he knows and as an example, he need only remember the things he did when he left his body, allowing his "greater self" control.

What your partner fails to get is that part of him is not another – it is him. His has separated it from his body because he sees his body as weak, as holding him back. It is his mind, his thought that stops him or holds him back. In his dreams too, he leaves his body. Yet it is him. The power is here – he only needs to accept it.

There are specific tricks we have knowledge of, yet unless he fully embraces himself, they are of no use. He only need ask.

I have told him.

We know.

Is there anything I can do?

By example – it is why you are together – There are things you can learn from each other and from you he learns power. He loves the addiction of dis-ease. It fills his mind and right now is satisfying a need.

Thanks, you guys.

You're welcome!!!

Note – The conversation with beings from the Pleiades took up again in January of that next year. It continues below…

This conversation is with two beings/groups. It took place on January 18, 2015. Note the year, it is not a mistake. This has been going on for quite some time.

Is there someone who wants to connect?

There is. We are many and we'd like to introduce ourselves.

I see lots of round faces, dark eyes, in something or looking out from something; like a cave or a window?

You are "seeing" us gathering together, anxious to reach you.

Not a cave, no. Like a large window in a ship or some sort of enclosed contrivance.

"Ship" is a suitable description. We come to you from off your home planet, off the earth, and are gathered in this now moment on a vehicle, not a planet. We are humanoid beings not from earth so not actually human. We look like you, if shorter.

Are you all male? This is what I feel, the male gender.

Yes, for this exchange we are.

Where are you from?

We come from the Pleiades Star System. Not from your specific star, but another.

What have you come to discuss?

I am dizzy with the energy of you.

We are similar, yet not exactly the same, to your Pleiadian sisters, in exuberance. We are energetically excitable. You might say that you are sensing our excitement.

We'd like to discuss our idea of gender and roles as chosen.

There is a synchronicity, this is our topic.

Go ahead then.

Our... *(I was interrupted)*

I'm sorry, hold on. Okay, I'm back.

Yes, we see that you are. We wonder if the time is right for this or if we and you are forcing the issue/idea?

Its okay I think. Let's try again.

We would very much like that.

Okay.

Our way of defining roles and rules of participation differ to such a great extent here than to those on earth, due to the "captured" nature of your creativity. Yours, as a prison planet in a very real sense, operates from behind bars.

These bars contain and restrain you; limiting your movements and defining them as well. There is a ceiling and a wall enclosing all of your actions. There are very few doors.

As a result, the masses move through them all quite slowly and in hoards.

What is meant by these words is that you are cut off from every alternate opportunity – every opportunity that stands separate from those available through the doors taken by most everyone else.

Imagine no doors, no ceilings, no walls – imagine no room. This is how we live. We mentioned synchronicity because our lives are governed by this principle. It is one that leads us forward and because we experience more of a limitless life, it leads us beyond places already travelled.

Can you envision such a world, such a life? There are here no such things as expectations or rules or requirements, other than those self-determined.

If we love, we love – whomever and whenever. If we are hungry we eat. If we are tired, we rest. If we need something we manifest it. We play and work as inspired for each.

Life falls into patterns for each of us and these will draw us to each other, forming communities. These communities are governed by things we like to do and are skilled or practiced at. Things like food preparation or science or dance or decoration.

We are from the Pleiades and some of what we are and do will feel familiar to you.

Yes, yet you do not (feel familiar to me). Your energy is putting me to sleep.

It is not ours, but another who wishes an audience that overwhelms.

Okay. Let's come back to this later then and let the other in.

Okay. Until then.

Until then. (These beings left.)

Who is here?

It is I.

Who are you and what do you wish to discuss? Your energy overwhelms me.

Get centered Sophia. This is not too much for you.

Let's do this.

I've come to instill an idea of complete sovereignty.

Okay.

This idea is one held by the most powerful beings. By those beings who know themselves.

There are promises of pure intent held as a part of every choice. These come from only one center – theirs. What is meant here is that each decision for movement is made for self.

What this triggers in the human is sel__ish.__ Yet this is a gross under estimation of the size of self. Self is All.

In the arena of sovereignty there is One. Any ideas of separation move you out of this world. You cannot be truly sovereign while being tied to comparisons or to "us" and "them".

Our world, that of sovereignty, is a singular motivation. Service to self serves the whole. Service to "other" serves the whole and that is why there are no divisions.

Once you appreciate the fact of oneness, fear is eliminated. Fear perpetuates both reasons for and responses to it.

I came to you in this moment now because in you there is a sense of waxing and waning fear. It erupts on occasion and you create its dismissal with certain words and actions.

This is effective, partly. What is more effective is an absence of fear. This is known as sovereignty. It is a by-product of unity – of an activation of internal appreciation for oneness…

You are ready now for this realization. You have come now to a place of appreciation for your part in this creation of oneness. Oneness does not need creation, it needs only realization. With that, sovereignty emerges.

Your thumb would not be afraid of your pinky, or bow before your ring finger or step on your index finger or allow your middle finger to freeze. No, for it is a fact that what effects any part of the hand effects the hand itself. In a simple way, this illustrates unity.

No longer do you believe that your actions are isolated. They are cumulative and felt beyond where you sit. They are felt by us all.

The allowance of fear is what keeps you subservient and compliant. The eruption of sovereignty could occur all at once for your race with individual moments of self-actualization. These have an exponential effect.

The path to fearless is accomplished individually and with authentic appreciation of who and what you are.

You are expressions of the force of creation; complete and whole and able to alter every outcome. Perhaps alter is a misnomer, for as the force of creation, it is you that manifests every outcome.

Realize the power your emotions hold and their reach. You are not an innocent bystander to a fearful situation – <u>you are the director</u>.

I am finished in this moment of now.

Thank you.

This conversation ended!

April 7, 2015

I would like to put out a call to my friends from the Pleiades and anyone else who's spoken to me, contacted me. I want to know who, if anyone, is keeping waking me up at night – specifically last night.

Okay, there are a few of us who want to talk to you.

Why?

For one thing, a lot of changes are forthcoming and you are not telling people.

I don't know what is coming, and wait, wait, I feel a crowd. Can we speak one at a time please?

Yes, we can. These are, we are, others who know you and you have become a voice for truth.

What is it you want?

To tell you changes that are coming (that) will impact you deeply. Your life, your body, your soul. This is the time you've been foretold of. You are entering it now, poised at the edge, and as a speaker of transformation, you must be ready.

For what?

For the Shift – the Event – all will change irrevocably.

Please be specific.

For specifics, ask your friend Poser, who is keeping an eye, a close eye, on his worshippers. This will be a feast for him.

Poser, are you here as well?

I am.

What do you know about this upcoming Shift?

Only that it changes my world and it, the timing of it, will not succumb to prediction of any sort. It is not orchestrated or designed by me or to my liking. It is an Event, a World Event, of unprecedented change.

Yet you see the future, don't you?

There are places and times I cannot, and this is one of them.

How far into this year do you see?

I see only until April.

Which is now.

Yes. It is not something I am fond of admitting, yet I can only say that **whatever is coming does not begin with the world I have created, but begins from the point of creation itself.**

This sounds like it could be a good thing for my people.

It very well could be. I do not see it. Your people were always meant to prosper and in order for that to occur, they will need a hand.

The manipulation of power and money on your planet was not my doing. The Beings with the reins on that whole system, run a program of sadistic worship – Satan worship, that feeds me. It has not stopped because of that.

And now?

There is no danger of worship ending completely. What is coming though, is a complete reversal – a Shift – and I can't see it.

Why are you waking me up?

Not just me, Sophia, but also me, yes.

Because you have asked for conversation and I have given an agreement to it, to give you what you ask for. I know there are things you want to know and seek to understand.

Yes, there are, but not now, and not tonight. I am tired and need sleep. At my initiation, please. When I have specific questions.

As you desire.

Thank you.

Now, my family from the Pleiades? Are you there also?

Yes!!!

I would so love to talk.

So, do we!!! (many happy faces are seen here)

Yet not tonight. I love you all so much, let me sleep and we'll connect tomorrow? That's not too late, is it?

(many sad faces are seen here) We miss you. No, but soon.

Yes, soon. Thank you. I feel you and you feel like home.

That is because we are.

Tomorrow then.

This conversation took place on May 4th (first one) and May 5th (second one) 2015.

Okay, so I am available for conversation.

Yes, well this is a good "time". We would like to engage.

For what purpose.

Information. There are many who wish to speak.

Are any of them.... WOW, I can feel the energy, it is making me woozy!

We don't wish to overwhelm, but inform.

What do you want to inform about? Again, I am knocked over with the force of you.

We apologize. We will discuss the best focus and continue once it is established. You are extremely open and many are here.

There is something we'd like to address.

Who is "we"?

A group of us who have been with you before.

Excuse me; I am really dizzy from your energy. Is there a way to hold it back or reduce your number?

Not really. You are weakened. Last night was a very difficult one as the swirling vortex of change kept the sensitives awake – you are a sensitive. Did you notice who had trouble sleeping?

Well, yes. Not all the children, but many of them and most of the adults. (I worked that morning, at an elementary school – Sophia)

I'm sorry, I need to take a break. (I did just that, then centered myself and began)

Okay. Let's begin now.

Yes. We know you are feeling us to an extreme and are attempting clarity and control. Your signal only gets stronger and it is seen that you hear ours without interference.

Who is speaking?

A group of your friends from the Pleiades. We know you and are knocked over by your current ability to reach us. It was unexpected.

I do not feel familiarity.

The sensation of contact is new – it may be overriding personality. This is not One being, it is a group. You are familiar with us.

What do you wish to say?

We wish to shed some light on the one you call Yeshua.

Woah, I don't believe it's in my best interests to go there. Many are Christian.

This is not a condemnation of religion – Christianity or any other.

Why Jesus then?

It is the one most familiar to you and in your place of living now – your "country".

I don't understand.

"Faith", "Worship" and "Prayer" are similar in that they dedicate a massive focus of energy and emotion to a god unseen. The appeal of Jesus...

I don't know that I can do this. If feels discriminatory. I am not about dismissing one specific belief system.

Trust this conversation Sophia.

Why? I feel no sense of familiar with you – only sort of bowled over with your energy. I have declared this contact be "highest and best for all concerned" as well as "helpful and positive". Explain to me how the subject of a specific religious belief fits these parameters.

We bring Yeshua to your attention because of the popularity, the music, the placing upon this being, characteristics denied to "ordinary" believers. There is talk around Yeshua Christianity of being "saved". There is a very powerful belief in the needing of "saving" and the necessity of "believing".

All of this, faith, worship, belief, prayer – when directed to a single being other than Source, feeds the one you have called Poser. You heard today the fervor and love and emotion expressed in the song. *(The song "One thing remains" is the one I had heard earlier that day.)* What occurs in high states of religious fervor is akin to passion. It all takes places internally, stimulated by a love object.

What is the information you are attempting to give here? None of this is new or different than what I've spoken of.

Yes, well, you speak about worship as the opposite of sovereignty.

It is a sovereignty vacuum – it places equal beings in unequal and therefore false situations.

Yeshua is a myth – as understood today; that exact being is a fairy tale. They are worshipping no-one specific. The energy being emitted? It is food for "Poser".

I will not go there – here – in my sharing. This comes from a place I am not clear on, or sure of. Somehow it seems you've broken through the barriers of my intent for highest and best on a technicality.

This is brutal truth. I am not about to blast someone's belief system to bits – that is not, in my opinion, the highest and best for all concerned.

So, I will end this conversation now.

Yes, well, as you wish Sophia. You've asked/intended "complete and absolute truth".

I have. There are ways to deliver truth to humans so that it will be heard, listened to, and understood. This way feels aggressive and not helpful; not productive.

We appreciate your frankness.

Okay, goodbye.

For now, Sophia, for now.

This conversation ended there. The next day I was again contacted by Pleiadians, a very different energy accompanied the contact, as you will read here.

May 5th, 2015

Is there anyone who wishes to engage?

Yes, there is!

And to abide by my intentions?

Sophia, it must work this way always and every time. Each engagement is run by you – you are the magnetic force – we are pulled in under whatever parameters you declare.

Okay, hold on then. I AM here.

And so are we!!

What do you wish to discuss?

First, we'd like to introduce ourselves. You have not met us or spoken or felt our energy.

It is exuberant. I see only happiness and smiles.

That was part of your intent, was it not?

Well, yes, actually.

Understand that as you clarify who you desire contact with and why, your contacts will differ. We came because we desire to and we also fit within your rather strict definition for contact.

So, who are you then?

We are the ones you have called Pleiadians

You do not feel the same as the group I recently engaged.

We are not. Those were our elders – ancient to us, with an agenda of instruction. What you interpret as harsh is their way of giving absolute truth. There are no exceptions. They came off sounding like "law" when in fact the sternness you felt was more commanding. As they came with information you need in order to dispense absolute truth.

And you do not?

Well, we come for another reason as well. We enjoy the engagement with humanity. For the elders, it is more of a "job".

Is there a specific topic you'd like to discuss?

It is the fabric of "time" and "life" where you are. We exist always as part of creation – as you do.

Today, this now moment, you imagine us someplace else, perhaps only reachable via spaceship or mind-to-mind reading.

Yet you feel us now, no?

Yes. You have a bubbly nature and I picture you smiling. I have no visual for you.

You do not as we are not sending a visual image with our contact. You are very specific in your initial declarations about who and how this conversation will happen.

You, in this now moment, cannot "see" us, yet we are very much connecting – Right Now.

What is your point?

That time and life lose their human attributes once and if you accept this conversation as valid. For we are very much alive and I/we have no idea what "time" it is.

It all exists at once. This interaction is part of a planned engagement at the outset – yours, ours …everyone's. There is no separation, not in days or minutes, beings or life forms of any distinction. It is different or separated only by our focus and imagination. It is the same energy that creates worlds – imagination.

Separation of times and beings are a fabrication – our mutually agreed upon playground of creation. What matters and why it matters is <u>all relevant.</u> You and your current focus enjoys our energy, perhaps more than the energy you engaged with that "time" you referenced. *(this is a reference to the "elders" who reached out the day before)*

This, because of where you are heading.

All energy is used by all of creation – it's all understood as well. The beings whose "personality" is sort of exponential have chosen to get everything about that aspect – they are gifts for the rest of creation, pure expressions of whatever aspect they exemplify. As "time" and "life" is inclusive in ONE – well, the separation of both moments, events and lives is merely one of convenience. Not truth.

I have to go. I'd like to discuss this again?

Yes. As do we!!!

Talk to you later –

The conversation ended.

This conversation took place October 7th, 2015.

"Is there someone who would like to connect?"

There is!

(Feeling all sorts of exuberance with this one!)

Okay then, please do! Who are you and what would you like to discuss?

We are your sisters from the Pleiades. We have some things to say to women directly and to men for clarification and understanding.

Go ahead then.

This physical incarnation as female is for the most part only one of two choices for you – you've been both male and female. Because you've experienced the chemical and physical formula for both sexes – well, both are familiar.

When you choose to be female, some parts rest easier with you than others. Being female means that everything you feel is carried all the time.

We will focus only on women now, please realize that to a lesser extent, this is true for all beings.

Women are keepers of all things human. You have heard often about the incoming feminine energy to the new earth. This is because all parts deep in the psyche of the female are about to be honored, recognized, felt and demonstrated by this human society.

While the metamorphosis occurs – women may experience even <u>more</u> of their innate sensitive tendencies – It will be an intense time for women.

For all humans, certainly, but these incoming energies are amplifying what is already present – you may say now that you are "UBER" feminine.

This will, if you are partnered with the opposite sex, bring out a change in your male partners. As you become more sensitive, your partners too change from a tough – black and white or definite approach to one that displays more sensitivity.

These changes will upset the apple cart in relationships that relied heavily on contrast. It will be a bit blurred for a while, until everyone settles in to a comfortable range of expression. This will be one that suits their personality and physical body.

Women, who are most often the caretakers and the ones settling things in community fashion, will find these new flows of expression in some ways comfortable and in others challenging.

There is comfort in knowing where things fit – and today the people are not fitting very well in the places they used to.

What you (empirical) do with this will effect everything in your closest relationships. It will be in your best interests to remain flexible, things are not going to go back to the way they were. Each of you will settle in eventually, and find sure footing, yet this energy only increases and you'll all be impacted again.

I have to go.

Okay. Let's pick this up again later.

The next day...

"I'd like to connect, to write. Is there someone who wants to connect?"

We do! We'd like very much to complete our conversation, our thoughts around this increase in receptive energy.

Go ahead please.

Thank you. For that's what it is, in truth. It is neither masculine nor feminine. It is an increase in receptivity. What these new frequencies bring to the table for all of you, male and female alike, is greater sensitivity.

More sensitivity is something the females are, for the most part, familiar with. As rises and dips in specific hormonal levels vary month to month for most of their lives. More sensitivity is not something, however, that the males are used to experiencing or that the females are used to witnessing in them. These changes will be disruptive to many existing and long term relationships.

What will have to occur for successful navigation is acceptance. You will not be exactly the same beings at the end of this shift that you were at the beginning.

A morphing and a balancing is occurring in all things expressing polarity.

Many of you have already left existing long term relationships, because of these shifts in character, but not all of you.

We wanted to speak to the females specifically because depending on where you are in the spectrum of having dealt with internal core issues, these times may be uncomfortable.

A disregarding of feelings isn't necessary, an acceptance of them is. For both you and those in your most intimate relationships. You are all going through it, all feeling the increase.

It is easier for females to hold multiple and diverse memories – this is both a blessing and a curse. As you receive and experience more, there will be more to hold on to and you will be challenged to do…

(I was sitting outside and an unexpected friend showed up for a visit…there is a pause in the flow as a result.)

Okay, I am back.

Yes, we see that. Let's continue. We are almost complete.

Yes, let's.

With the increasing receptivity, you'll feel not more necessarily, but to a deeper extent. If you are already empathic, you will experience a more complete degree of comprehension and feeling about whomever you are receiving.

These new energies will not "make" you what you are not already. The reason we began by talking about the idea that you've been both male and female, is to illustrate that as both its more likely in your repertoire of "lives", you'll have habits and ways of being that are familiar to you, regardless of your current sex.

We reach out to you now in hopes of assisting with some new thought around changes you will be and perhaps have been seeing in people. With these ideas comes a suggestion to be patient with each other and with yourself. As you move through this change you'll discover your level of expression. It will be the one that predominates and satisfies your desire for full authenticity. It may not look like your prior forms of communication and relationship.

Nothing around you will be the same, so the fact that you act differently makes complete sense. You will need to and so will everyone else.

This is ultimately positive for the race, although it may not feel like it inside of your relationships now turned upside down. You've chosen to proceed through this shift while in relationship. This for the express purpose of demonstration, and learning. There is much to be gained here and you will learn it from each other.

We are finished for now. Thank you.

Thank you. (I think.)

The conversation ended.

And a question from a reader:

"HI Sophia....Been pondering a few things...As always! lol.

Was listening to Abraham Hicks. Saying the more you focus on what you don't want the more it brings it into fruition.... So as much as I want to wake everyone to the Nonsense in the world the more I'm actually sustaining it!? ...

It's almost like I should just join the crowds at the stadium games. All those people have the right idea and I have it wrong ....and all along I feel like I'm awake and aware...

Maybe my question about burying your head in the sand is the way to go? But the Jeff Rense Web site doesn't think so...it usually mocks that the Sheeple are unaware. On his site now there is a Pic of Trails in the sky with written header 'PUBLIC IGNORANCE EQUALS BLACK OP BLISS'. Funny.

The other thing I was pondering was Bashar Statement about Nov 2016, He says at the time of recording something a bit odd," we have 2 years to pursue what we enjoy the most " What do you think that means? Like we won't be in Physicality anymore?

You think you can dig into that more? What do you think?"

I will respond to these with the information I have access to, as well as my own take on things at this point:

There are 2 questions here –
1. *There are two kinds of focus. Focus on what is NOT present, or what, in your estimation is lacking or wrong - is one type. The other type is focus on the solution.*

    It is necessary to become aware of "problems", whether they be personal or global in scope. Whistleblowers and sites like Rense.com are part of the reason for our current awareness, certainly. A necessary part.

Mother Theresa said she will not attend any "anti-war" rallies; but if you hold a "peace rally" she will gladly be there. This thought echo's my own. As we become aware, include in your growing consciousness a very specific focus, and be clear on it. Focus on what you want. Points of contrast are necessary sometimes to get you looking in the right place.

Cheer for your team, play, enjoy the human game. None of this means you are sheeple. You came here to do this while human. Humans thrive on excitement and pleasure.

2. *What was actually said in this Bashar video from a year ago, (included below) is this:*

"In the Fall of 2016, before the presidential election, everything will change. This is a transformational point, you are crossing a threshold. WE READ IN YOUR COLLECTIVE CONSCIOUSNESS THIS UPCOMING CHANGE OF GREAT TRANSFORMATION. You have 2 and ½ years to express yourself in the way that is in most alignment with your being – for after that point – EVERYTHING WILL CHANGE."

This announcement coincides with what I have been told. That date is an absolute end date for the experiment on earth. Those that have not gotten with the program will, at that point, have no more chances. The words "day of judgment" have been used regarding that date.

I trust Bashar. This voice coming through him was NOT Bashar however and I have no experience with this being; there is no history. Bashar himself seems to trust what was said. I will say again; this date coincides with other information I have.

The most important point to take from this however, is this line:

WE READ IN YOUR COLLECTIVE CONSCIOUSNESS THIS UPCOMING CHANGE OF GREAT TRANSFORMATION.

This is a reading of OUR COLLECTIVE CONSCIOUSNESS; it is NOT a prophecy by some outside source. It is what WE ALREADY KNOW. This being is just reading the book WE ARE WRITING OURSELVES.

He said the time now should be used to express yourself in alignment with your being. Isn't that what we are doing? With this awakening and the inspiration that accompanies it in most every case; we are prompting each other to remember who we BE.

I don't know about the physicality of us a year from now, or how to relate it to the physicality of us right now. It is all illusion. We have come here to experience this transformation while human. I do not believe we are ditching our bodies any time soon. I believe we will be transformed. This form is a construct based on the current "third dimension". It is what we expect to see and deal with each day.

Changes are happening moment to moment... a year from now we'll have another 365 days of change "behind" us. I am so different than I was a year ago; I can only imagine what I'll be in another year. Time and the frequency speeds up regularly. We will have to adjust.

I'm not sure this is an answer. I can tell you this. Until we stop looking elsewhere for whom to tell us truth, we will not find it in our internal wisdom. This being was a gift, telling us that we collectively are creating this ending. It is happening seamlessly, just as we planned. Just as we have been saying all along – "We are the ones we've been waiting for"!

This is a blog post as well as a conversation, from October 26 – 28, 2015:

"The old stuff isn't working. The energy we are currently in, well, this is what it looks like from here:

In the children, there is excitement. They are pushing limits and looking around wondering who will tell them when to stop, or what to do. This may not sound so different but somehow it is. Those kids who are used to being blamed or blaming aren't having either right now. The adults in charge are too pre-occupied to blame anyone.

All sorts of "ailments" are flaring up. These may be physical or habitual. Ways of coping with them that used to work – aren't.

Personalities are sticking out all over the place. Secret tendencies are no longer so secret. We are seeing our true selves. We are asked now to decide who we be.

The controls have lifted. This is the only way I know how to describe it. There is a change in the energy of places. Before now, I could "feel" a room and it felt sort of contained and reachable. Not so now. The rooms are still filled with us, and our energy signatures, yet there is not cohesiveness. It is a room of individuals, all on their own.

No one is "in charge" but us. We've moved from controlled to freedom and are being asked now to create in real "time" – everything.

This is what we've chosen as a race. There were options – and humanity chose self-determination. Who we be and how we govern ourselves is up to us. Every moment is a creation moment.

A short look around will show you evidence of system failure and personality explosions. This is an intense time.

We must go easy on ourselves. The controls are off and it's sort of like our first time riding a bicycle without training wheels. We are going to fall off a few times.

I am seeing miracles and extremes in health, as well as reversals in temperament, as we each see the "played out" and unrestricted versions of ourselves and then decide – *Who am I?*

These are heady times. We've only just begun. This is Boots on the Ground Ascension. Everything is self-determined. We are at constant choice.

Our new earth will be unlike anything ever witnessed. It will be exactly what we believe it can be. It will be specifically what we intend it to be.

Intend abundance. Breathe compassion. Believe love. This is why we came. We are the ones we've been waiting for."

Note – After writing this first piece in the middle of the night, I was contacted by someone from the Pleiades. I have not spoken to this being before. I am including it here with this post as it is relevant to the subject of these new energies.

This took place on October 26th, 2015.

"Who wants to connect?"

Yes. Settle in and we will communicate. Something has occurred.

What do you refer to?

Something in your world and as well, your physical self is different now today than it was the last time we reached you here. You are experiencing the results of the impact.

The impact of what?

The impact of the force stream of awareness – you are being flooded now and as these things take hold you will react in some sort of response. There is no way to plan for this precisely as there are no forerunners. Its never happened and never been done. Not while physical and not under the deep constraints that have held you apart. Apart from truth and without assistance.

You have been "protected" while "controlled" from any extreme fluctuations of force. You are not now shielded in the same way.

Oh, there are forces/beings scrambling to regain footing but they have no effect. Not in this now moment. Humanity is on her own in a very real way.

Things like organizational systems, medical, government, educational, spiritual – they are not now being pushed around and put in specific places that serve a single small group.

The head of the snake has been removed. This is not Medusa, where 2 grow back. This is now a headless creature.

What must happen are new ways of sight; and direction and control of the body needs to be established.

What is seen now is a form of quiet chaos. This energy is individually felt, assessed, absorbed and assimilated while on the run. New behaviors are emerging. As you ascertain their effectiveness, you'll decide if they are something you want to continue or not.

Guidelines are just not there. Without them, an absence is experienced and a sense of the loss. It's not something you'll miss; it's something you've never been without.

This moment is about self-realization and creation. Who you want to be is who you will eventually, it seems like, settle in on.

Who is this?

I am an observer of your shift. I have not interacted with you prior to this now moment. I am from the Pleaides.

At this point I had a phone call and this interaction ended. This was sort of an echo of my earlier thoughts, as written in the blog post above. I suspect that's why I was contacted. I don't know if the message was complete, but I don't think so.

This validated (for me) the extreme changes I have been both witnessing and experiencing internally these last several weeks. Particularly the children, who I refer to as the canaries in this coal mine, are sort of off the charts in behavior extremes, and mostly very happy all the time, regardless of what is happening around them. Something has changed, for sure. It feels like we are only at the beginning...

One more "noticing" is that those beings out there now are of a different sort. When opening yourself for contact of any kind, it is beneficial in a very real sense to declare "Highest and best for all concerned. Just love. Pure love." We generate a great deal of interest and are drawing crowds! It is a simple thing to guarantee all are being served with the contact.

April 2015

Ancients

April 12, 2015

"I would like to ask first, is there someone who wants to come through?"

Yes. It is I and we have spoken before. I am part of the original race on this planet and who you have no picture/visual for. I am not as you imagine yet it is as if a large dark box is all you are able to assimilate. You are a being who is open to communication without sensor – you feel the presence of others without seeing them and this is part of why it works with you.

"What do you want to say?"

Only that our race is returning as has been foretold and this is not to reprimand or punish as we are not the "gods" but an old, ancient being – as information I "talk" to you – we are returning in your lifetime and the stories of old are coming to fruition as we do.

We are genetically related to the human as so many are. Now we want to see what the human has become.

"Why?"

For learning. For reasons of our own evolution. As this race grows and evolves we do also – all of creation does.

What humanity thinks is foreign and alien is a part of their origin and I was there. My span of life surpasses yours by many thousands of years at this point. We want to find out why. We know there is environmental pollution yet it seems the stress of emotion, of hatred, of worry, of love, of all emotion – ages the physical. This is of interest, as the capacity to feel emotion and express it as human is something unique to humanity, to earth, at this time. You were made *(*made here has the same meaning as in the sentence "dinner was made")*. And it is like watching you grow and change, as if an experiment.

"What will you do here? Do you have ships?"

Huge ones, yes, and there will be no mistaking us when we land. *(*I am not sure here that "land" is used properly, as the size I envision is like those pictures of ships siphoning off energy from the sun; planet size)* We will not be looking so much for leaders of countries but for speakers for men. Diplomats, ambassadors – the ones we seek will be called and all walks of life and "nations", as they are called, will be represented, and contact will be made and awareness of it will be known.

"And to what end?"

We are not sure. It is not interference yet help is of interest to us. If we can assist in the progress of your people towards peaceful, prosperous co-existence, we will. Understand that an event that initiates from creations' source will have happened before we return – also that it is not so much global revolution *(*here is not meant "revolt" but literally, the globe revolving around the sun)* that determines the timing of this – all of creation is poised and awaiting a spark from source – a momentary "uptick" that shoves all of creation along rapidly. Once that happens – more minds will be able to accommodate the presence of large ships without immediately perceiving a threat.

You are a voice and as such can speak truth so that people will be prepared.

"I do not know what definite things I can say that will prepare people."

You will find as you open to "the everything", a way. It has been seen that you serve as a conduit – perhaps ambassador – well then in order for that to proceed, contact must be made and maintained. This is the reason.

"Will I ever meet you in my current lifetime?"

No, I do not meet you or foresee meeting you. We have arrangements of association and are working towards the same end – this end is accomplished by many. You and I are part of many who propel the shift. You will be aware of the ships and may serve as ambassador to some races. Yet the global entourage that enters the ships of my race is of humans in places of science and political and religious power. This is not the role you chose for the journey. As dispenser of information and truth you serve the whole of humanity. You will see and understand and this too will occur in your lifetime.

Your children are to see as well. All will be clear before anyone moves on. What is not necessary is prior knowledge of historical reference because the truth replaces it all and corrects the fallacies and disinformation that seems to have grown up around it all; around your origin.

"Do you have a name?"

"Ancient One" you can call me. The sounds you have are x's and z's and you do not easily hear it for translation.

"Why do I see large and square and dark?"

That is how I've presented to you – a signature if you will. For recognition.

"Okay, I must go."

Yes. We will connect again.

"Okay. Thank you."

And now, the conversation, from April 29th, 2015

(Emphasis and italics are my own...)

Is there anyone who wants to speak to me?

There is.

Who?

It is the one you have called "Ancient".

Okay, what is it you'd like to say?

That your people have been thrust into a wave of energy they do not understand. Correction is necessary in the care of the people. This will become increasingly more apparent as this new energy serves all of the inhabitants of earth with its demands *(the demands of the energy; in other words, this energy asks us to act differently)*.

In order to function there is necessary an acceptance of each being you encounter as equal in value. This is not the value used on this planet, not monetary, and in fact a sharp contrast to the way a majority of humans judge worth.

It has been seen that an eruption of illusory traps is occurring; this, so that they can be exposed.

The human can, in a very real sense, pull itself out of this escalation of fear. It will take the majority of those who are not generally valued to change the order.

The order of things must be upset for change to take place. The country of focus now is one where freedom and opportunity have been promised and advertised.

What happened in the hands of the controlling faction is not new. What is new is that the world now sees it.

What will the rest of humankind do with such blatant terrorizing of one of its own? This depends on whether or not the rest of humanity regards a typically "lower class" person as one of its own. Is this of any consequence?

The response that I am aware of includes mostly a desire that it stop. There seems no effort to insure (*that*) the inside cause no longer take place.

By "inside cause", what do you mean?

I refer here to the violent treatment of the single man *(Freddie Gray)* – which happened as a result of fear and misplaced power.

(I was interrupted here and stopped)

Okay, I am back. This does not sound exactly like the Ancient One I spoke to? I am not receiving a clear stream of consciousness.

No, this is because you are filtering.

Perhaps I will just stop then.

As you wish, although I'd like to get some information to you.

Okay, let's try again then. (I repeated the clearing and declarations I make for absolute truth, as well as "highest and best" for all concerned)

You have asked for details of humanity's origin.

Others have, yes. There is a lot of confusion.

The story of the human is ... (*the conversation stopped abruptly*)

Why don't I hear you?

You are blocking. Please listen to each word.

Okay. (I centered again, and waited)

Man is not what he imagines himself to be. He sees a body that ages and dies, a brain that has a constant potential for learning and a spirit that is lesser than those of the "gods". At the same time, man imagines himself to be one of a kind in all the cosmos.

Rather than open, he looks to everything with judgment that defines as well as inhibits his ability to see at all.

This view of self is at its core nonsensical – unless you are accepting delusions and illusions as factual pieces of information. It defies reason that man would be *(italics here are mine, words are not)* alone in all of creation and without massive power.

If man concedes the existence of massive power, he grants it to one or perhaps several supreme beings. This sets up a top-down hierarchy which rests at the core of man. It colors everything. It is not truth, yet so deeply held as such that it is deemed reverent.

With the segregating of this assumption into a place of honor, the domination of man becomes a simple task.

What will be part of man's rise to full capability is the correct placement of prior assumptions.

There are few truths. There are numerous beliefs. There are billions of versions of both, individually adopted by each human aspect of creation.

The core acceptance of man's godhood is what will propel him forward towards enlightenment. With that as a base for thoughts, ideas, feelings and actions; everything changes.

Man, cannot see himself truly until and unless all other men are viewed through the same lens. To view yourself truly is not arrogant or disrespectful, but humble acceptance.

An equal playing field, when finally understood, replaces all fear of mistaken assumptions or doubt as to self-worth. Man is special not because of any specific attribute other than his existence.

Man, is the physical expression of creation – not the only aspect but a unique embodied creator god. He has chosen to create within a limited field in order to learn and embody oneness. Man feels everything he creates.

By allocating the power and exaltation to an unseen being other than himself – man has set the stage for polarity.

It is not truth and therefore will not continue. Only truth is everlasting.

The de-construction of false assumptions is taking many forms. The "time" lapse before truth takes hold is as yet undetermined. Man's nature is violent and united; powerful. Expect eruptions of power as this constructed reality disintegrates.

This will be a temptation for man to continue judgment and opinion. It would be more truthful to observe and witness; acknowledge the evidence of the Ascent of Unity and support the change. It is what has always been seen and is inevitable.

This is all?

For now, it is.

Okay.

(And this conversation ended.)

May 2015

Ancients

May 14, 2015

To whom am I speaking?

I am the being you spoke to at another juncture. The name I have to give you is not pronounceable in your language – many, what you call "consonants", hard sounds, make it up.

Do you cause the EMF meter to go off or is that caused by someone else?

I do not believe my frequency effects your device – I am not "there" in the physical sense, but am communicating to you from where I am – it is difficult to discuss but you are reaching out to me and we are speaking – communicating. I don't "go" anywhere, we connect mind to mind.

Okay, that makes sense, thank you. Do you know who is setting it off then? It goes off a lot lately, esp. in this room.

I do not know specifically, but generally I can tell you that there are always beings and if their frequency is within the range that device is set to – they will set it off. They are beings who are every bit as real as you are, or I am. You cannot visualize them however; they do not vibrate at the speed you are used to seeing.

Okay. So, I have no name for you?

No, you have an identifying label though – "Ancient One" works for all concerned.

Are you able to speak to this? (Question from a reader) "At first glance everybody chooses love and happiness but with the inner work properly done meaning still in fear for things and attachments that don't serve this choice will be tough!! Your friends/families will maybe not choose what you choose am I getting... Would be nice if you could elaborate with "An Ancient Race" about this. I kind of know the answer but anyway..."

And, as an aside, I don't "see" you in the same way as I did when we first spoke?

I would not expect you to experience our connection the same way – it will not feel "different" to you, we've met before, spoken before. Yet it will now feel as if you are speaking to someone else, by that I mean, someone different again from your everyday conversations.

Why do I want to sleep?

It is the energy.

This is a topic of great interest as we observe humans – most humans put themselves in connections with other humans for comfort, for community, for love, for shared intent and/or fun. Humans are not solitary beings. They care for one another and what happens is in that caring become confused, forgetful of the fact that they are only actually responsible for themselves – for the one unique soul force that they embody.

There is no choice of going or staying that leaves anyone behind – not in truth. Humans have this rather quaint notion that their presence or absence can alter the course of life for another soul. This is simply not true.

What the human journey is about is life on any terms. There are no possibilities that elevate or diminish another soul. It is a journey taken by each and every aspect.

Now humans choose ways to proceed that fit their reality, but whether they follow the path of those they currently "hang with" or diverge – matters little to the outcome. All of life is self-determined.

What we see are soul groupings who've gotten so familiar with each other over "lifetimes" that they appear to play out scenarios in their choosing – switching roles and circumstances as if they were handing out cards at each new "beginning". These cards outline who will play what role, who will stay, who will leave, who will "advance" the furthest, who will appear to be left behind.

Ultimately you are creator beings – each massively powerful and suited for any choice. The endearing notion of wanting everyone to go with your current choice is just that – a notion. There are other choices, other places to go, other "lifetimes" – all of them human and within your soul grouping.

As we watch the evolution of the human, we expect to also see the incorporation of what seem to be sentimental ideas of family or community into your multi-dimensional self. This passionate emotional aspect of mankind is not expressed in the same way in other races. It is mankind who will determine the nature of his own evolution. What will be the most satisfying answer to the question will ultimately be answered by your own race. This, I expect, is what you referred to in your question at the outset – "knowing the answer already".

Okay. Is that it?

Yes.

Angelic

May 29, 2015

I want to talk.

About what?

About this current focus on ascension and verifying frequencies and the adjustments needed to keep your balance.

Do you have some specific recommendations? Or, better yet, why do you want to? Or wait, hold on – I would like to reconnect and start anew – I am dizzy, I am having trouble keeping my eyes open.

Yes, I can see that.

Let's try this again. Is there someone who wants to converse?

Yes.

Are you one of my "fractals"?

Yes.

Which one?

I am a version /a fractal of the race you know as angelic.

Come on. How could that be true?

All things are possible in life.

But I assumed the angelic race were a part of the "divines" and the hierarchy of "gods".

(I stopped there. Some time passed before we continued the conversation... the energy was too strong and I waited a bit to try again.)

I have several questions.

Please ask them.

Am I creating you?

In a sense, all of those in your life are a creation by you, a bit of belief you hold. It is an odd way to put it. Especially in light of the very physical, 3D idea of creation.

If you are creating me, then without you I don't exist. This is not how this works. I exist. I am pulled into your creative life by mutual desire – yours for information and ascension assistance, and mine because of my own desire to help you. We are connected Sophia.

In a sense, all beings in creation are connected. You and I have shared experiences and are branches of a single tree. Not everyone you are speaking to are branches from this same tree, however.

You will sense a resonance more with some beings than with others. It is the same with people in your 3D world. You are connected to all of them. You are not connected in the same way.

This notion of creating me sounds like you are asking if you made me up. You did not. However, I would not be talking to you now if you didn't open yourself up to the truth of my existence.

I'm not sure precisely what you mean. I am feeling like I know you. Who are you?

I am a version of you. From another "time" and in another "form".

What form?

Angelic.

Oh, come on.

This flies in the face of all of your learnings of celestial beings.

You cannot assume you've been told the truth.

Why assume it now then?

The choice is yours, as always.

What is it you are here to say?

That as this expansion and shifting and awareness occurs and grows – each of you will be confronted with parts of yourselves you will abhor or deny or reject because of belief systems you hold, as well as ideas of right/wrong, good/bad, holy/unholy.

My ears are feeling weird.

You sense the energy of this being and if you hadn't just shut down you may have heard it.

There were crackling noises.

Yes. The frequency is there. You are rapidly shifting and at times *(you)* see, sense or feel arenas of existence that have been out of reach until these times.

It is interesting to see that for one who has ceased to follow the dictates of any religion, that a simple word like "angel" would bring all your doors closed.

Perhaps you could define here the term "angelic". My understanding is these beings exist as part of the hierarchy in god's kingdom and are not nor have they ever been human.

If you are one of my other "me's", or fractals, well, then none of that is true.

Life exists in many realms. My recollection is that you've already been told your "original soul" was angelic.

Yes, well, I'm not sure what that refers to and I've always assumed that was a misunderstanding of some sort. It seemed, at the time I was told that, to be more of a separator than a useful identity marker.

That would be true of all names.

Okay, yes.

The term angelic basically refers to a life form dedicated to the assistance of the human. It does not necessarily indicate wings although I know you've seen them.

Yes, actually. Several times.

(Twice I have seen what I have always called an "angel".

Once in my bedroom, lying between my partner (who was sleeping) and myself. It was in the middle of the night, and something had woken me up. This was the classic version of angelic, with robes and wings and it was huge. As I stared it dissolved and was gone.

Another time my partner saw them also, there were two of them. We had been out and our youngest children were home with 2 good friends of ours, as babysitters. As we pulled up the drive we came upon two huge forms, hovering in front of the picture window. It was dark out. They were watching our kids, who were in there playing a game with our friends. As we stopped and got out of the car, the angels seemed to dissolve as well as move up and "fly" over the roof. Again, these were huge beings, with what I can only describe as robes and wings.)

This is a very detailed conversation and one that is perhaps necessary for your own clarification.

I exist. I am a version of you. You've sensed me, felt me and seen me. I am not human. Yet we spring from the same source.

The semantics around beings, once tied up in religion, gets very, very heavy. I am feeling this now from your form. It is as if you've retreated.

Yes, well, I better go. I don't think I can do this now.

Let's take up this conversation again. There is much to be gained, to be learned.

For who?

For anyone who reads it.

Annunaki

May 31, 2015

I would like to speak to the Annunaki, a member of the race, who can tell me what their plan is as far as returning.

(Let me say here, that there is always a difference in the energy of the being as he or she or they, if there are more than one, come through. Yet, until this day, I had never felt a sort of hierarchy to the voice.

Here, I felt as if I was a sort of "lowly human", who, merely by asking for contact, was out of line. I was shocked, as there has been nothing but equality and concern, interest or love, until now. You will probably pick up on that vibe when you read the conversation here. It was illuminating, for sure.)

You presume much.

I do not fully understand your comment or how this works. Hence, my request. Explain please.

You are assuming all beings are on call and you only need dial out. This is not exactly true as there must be desire to talk on both sides.

I understand that.

Yes, well, for you to name a being as if you can just "ring him/her up" is presumptuous, as if they are all available to you and eager to converse.

They don't have to answer. And, actually, calling someone does not assume anything other than contact is desired on my end. In every case when I have asked I have received an answer of "hello" or "I am not available". This "you presume much" is spoken as if you are in a position of authority over me. As if you have power over me and want to control any contact.

You are outspoken for a human.

Who are you.

I am a calling member of the race you label Annunaki. I would be the one intercepting all calls to the ones in charge.

What is your name?

I do not have a name in your vernacular. I have a role, a place, an appointment, a job. I am the one who directs outside contact to higher authority when it seems relevant.

You are an operator then? A receptionist? A call blocker?

I do refuse calls if I feel they are not in the best interests of my superiors; if they would be a waste of "time" or energy.

You feel very stern.

I have an important and serious role that if I make a mistake on, will be costly for me as well as the overall plan.

Which is?

I am not one to state information, I only direct or inhibit calls. What is it you desire?

I desire clarification on when, if and in what capacity the Annunaki will return.

For what purpose?

For the same purpose, as always – for information and enlightenment of humanity. I will share what is said to me.

Well then, I am prepared to pass you on to a lesser position in the structure of authority. Hold a moment while a contact can be made. This is of no real consequence.

I'm holding.

(The energy sped up. I literally felt/experienced an increase of rapid speech here, like that commercial for Jimmy Johns - - 'freaky fast')

This question you have asked is of simplicity. I am able to answer in a simple and straightforward manner.

I see you have no real authority over your planet and this discussion will be of no real impact other than satisfaction of curiosity.

Yes, we are coming back and the reasons are several. Most of them are as would be expected in any project – to ascertain progress.

Why?

To decide if the results attained thus far are satisfactory.

What results are you looking for?

I am not at liberty to speak of the plan. I am able to speak in general terms as this information – our "flight plan" if you want to call it that, is available and can be read if you know where to find it.

Your "flight plan" does not include reasons for the journey?

Reasons, yes. Resulting actions, no. I have already explained the reasons. Are you satisfied?

No. Can you tell me anything else? Like the timing of such a journey?

I can tell you that it is approaching and is to occur with a decade of your "years". I am not free, nor do I know of, the precise timing of our arrival. I am, as you have sensed, a being with a purpose and it is one of orderly dissemination of facts. This is my primary focus, after efficiency. I am an expert in efficiency.

I can barely write fast enough to keep up with your words.

I have a rhythm of occupation that must be maintained. Order is my primary directive and systematic release of tension so that it is always maintained.

I don't fully understand.

There is a tension that arises within structures and systems of life when a specific design is to be maintained/manufactured. My race is in the manufacturing business, the maintenance of that which was manufactured/created/made has to be systematically checked.

Balance/order requires tension, yet too much of that tension causes breaks – a breakage in a pivot point would bring an entire system down.

To prevent/forestall such a breakage – tension must be released periodically. This by way of unnecessary structures or components or even information held back – retained.

These, once released – allow for more "give" in the system and again, a smooth flow/progression/maintenance of function.

The earth is scheduled for such a release. This is all I can say. That is it.

Yes, I feel your completeness.

Goodbye.

"Ascension Assistance"

May 3, 2015

I'd like to talk to someone who has input, real input, on mastering the human.

There are several of us who are available to you now. This depends on which questions you have – the correct choice can only be determined by your questions.

My question is this: What sort of help or advice can you give regarding the very human tendency to desire to be loved or even liked more than others? We take pleasure in being liked in any case, which makes sense – yet we take immense pleasure & satisfaction in being "preferred" over another – particularly if the other is someone we have an issue with, or "history" with. What's with that? And also, whoever answers here, please identify yourself and explain why you can answer effectively.

Yes, this is an issue that plagues the human heart. I found it to be especially troublesome in intimate/sexual relationships – competition. It seemed to bring out the worst in me.

And you overcame it?

I was finally able to move through all relationships of love without comparison. This, once I understood the truth about love.

Who are you?

I am a soul who has heard your intent for "ascension assistance".

Do I know you?

You mean, have we met in the physical?

Yes.

No. Yet, as one who has been human, I can empathize with you and share my own understanding of the challenge you refer to.

You've been human and "enlightened"?

I am not entirely clear on your meaning for enlightened?

My meaning is for transcending the ego self while remaining human – for coming from love, unconditional love, in every relationship and interaction. That, I believe, would necessitate an absence of competition or feeling of satisfaction when one appears to have "won over" another fellow human.

Okay, hmmm... you are seeking a very specific solution.

Am I?

What you ask is how to disregard the human propensity to compare, and comparison is a key ingredient for creation.

Not comparison so much as satisfaction in what appears to be a "win" as compared to a "loss" of love. Not a win as in a score for athletic performance, but a win as if love was a product available only in specific amounts and limited.

Oh, I see. This sounds like a reference to jealousy?

Does it?

Yes. I will tell you what I know. These things I learned in my most recent "life" on earth – my last "life" on earth. I was a male then.

Really? You feel, or your energy feels female to me.

We are gender-less, yet some of us emit a more female typical "vibe" while others a male "vibe" – even when not physical.

I see.

This life as a male I experienced much or many opportunities for love – romantic/physical intimate love. I was gentle and women were attracted to that gentility.

I was also very rich/wealthy by your standards. I did nothing to create wealth, but was born into a family that had, as you call it today "old money". This allowed me a life to work on whatever I desired. I chose to work on expansion; expansion of knowledge. This led to a consciousness expansion, as the more I came to understand, the broader my viewpoint became.

Now, I received a great deal of female attention, which I assumed was because of my wealth. I liked women, yet as my expansion progressed I was less interested in simple companionship. Until I was introduced to one female whom I essentially wanted all to myself. She was unavailable to me in a physical way. She was married and obedient to the laws of the day.

Our connection was mutually felt however. I took great pleasure in hearing her speak disrespectfully, even insultingly, about her husband. This did not agree with my understanding of love.

For years, I encouraged the competition and enjoyed all of the attention I received as I became an "ear" for all of her unhappiness. I imagined myself better in all ways than this man, this husband.

Yet this did not sit well, as I said, and I came to a moment of truth. If I was to embody the truth, it would necessitate my love for her husband as myself. If I were to practice self-love – it would not incorporate abuse or pleasure in painful emotions. This was a shock to me.

I realized I did not believe, not fully, that I was love-worthy. Once I realized that – humbleness overcame me.

I longed for an equal partner in all respects – yet at the same time realized this partner would not be okay with inauthentic communication. I realized that I was not okay with inauthentic relationships of any sort.

It was a "slippery slope" that I often had to reel myself in from. One where I was tempted to judge others for their lack of perfection. For a while I was very much alone. Even the woman who I had claimed as a soul mate was not "enlightened" enough to keep me company.

I grew to eventually understand first that I was human, and second that love has a myriad of forms of expression. The rigid definitions available to live out on earth are not generous or allowing for exception.

What happened was (*that*) the woman died before her husband. I attended the burial and upon witnessing his deep loss – was moved to befriend him. He did not know me and never knew of the deep connection I shared with his wife.

What that friendship did for me was equalize the playing field. I realized there is no one love or perfect love or only love – there is love. I was fortunate to have known it on any level. My joy in "winning" more love from this now dead woman was humiliating – I became ashamed of my reaction. She loved us both – we both loved her and in the very end – we came to love each other.

I may have learned more about jealousy from him than from my "lover". I was not homosexual and this was not a deeply felt soul connection. It was though, the most impactful relationship of my life.

I came then to love freely and actually open my heart. Once I released my judgment as to why I was receiving attention and just allowed it, my heart expanded. I did not feel comparison or judgment after that.

Why are you hesitating now?

You have been speaking to me for quite a long time and you start to lose focus – I am not hesitating, you are not as reachable.

Okay, I will stop here then.

Yes.

"Chewie"

May 12th, 2015

Who is wishing to speak?

You will have to permit this being, to sense its intent, to feel it and then give permission.

Is there some question as to whether or not I have done so?

There is a question as to how much further you are willing to reach, to go, in your availability for contact.

Okay. By further, what do you mean?

Believe-ability.

Hmmmm. I feel someone; a powerful energy is how I experience it.

Yes, not more powerful or too powerful, but different and so you experience it as <u>very</u> powerful. Almost could knock you out.

Almost <u>is</u> knocking me out. I am dizzy with it and can barely keep my eyes open.

Yes. The rapid frequency tends to put humans to sleep.

Who are you?

(It is later now, in the same day... I had to stop and rest, re-declare my intent and try again) Okay, who would like to speak?

It is I. I would engage with you Sophia. You are more comfortable now.

I feel you. You do not feel familiar.

I am not one you've spoken to before.

What do you want to say?

I would like to engage in a discussion regarding practical things here. By practical I mean or refer to things that enter your daily life – that impact your life.

In what way?

In a way that differs from your life right now.

You'll need to be more precise. I'm not following you. I don't even know who you are.

You do not "know" me and are not familiar with me. I am very familiar with humanity or rather with what is happening now for humanity. I would like to be of assistance with my information, my own experience.

Your experience of what?

Of moving into another way of life – another "vibe" if you can call it that. My people too went through an "upgrade" of frequency if you understand my meaning.

I am from a place that has evolved further than the human is today. My body type is relatively humanoid, yet that is not the point.

My readers would be interested in hearing a description of your appearance and also a way of identification for you.

My appearance is – I will send and image to you and you can describe it for them.

Okay. You feel very cold and I see dark hair – I do not have a sense of relative size but varied maybe? Similar in range to ours, a bit larger, cold, very cold. Is your planet cold? The hair/fur I see is light golden colored and on your face – more hair like than fur like. I only see a face. Reminds me of Chewbacca from Star Wars and more human. I am so cold.

Yes. It is a cold climate and we have hair we do not cut covering our body. I am sorry you feel the cold so much. It is true, I am closer to "cold blooded" creatures than warm blooded and you are picking that up.

What changes have you gone through do you want to discuss?

I see your species talk about "symptoms of ascension" as if what you are noticing is some sort of pre-cursor to a specific event. The "symptoms" described are reactions to vibratory speed adjustments. As you get used to more rapid energetic movement, higher frequency, you will learn to use it to your advantage in your everyday.

This, right now, is change and represents hardship only because you aren't used to the rate – it is useful and actually the source of what humans have come to label "magic".

The stories in your fairy tales all depict a sort of magical movement of a wizard or a "fairy godmother" or a "god".

These are not magical, but movements made by a being assimilated to a much higher frequency, and using it on a regular basis.

The work of healers and magicians is a matter of course in a different place than you are used to being.

Why are you bringing this up? I believe anyone reading this is aware of this and expecting a change.

Yes, I believe you are correct. Yet the change will not be automatic – there is a learning curve. At this early stage, what is being noticed is not flagrant, but almost invisible. The progression and increase in speed will be gradual – it is the only way for it to happen on a mass scale and not be rejected.

Sudden and huge shifts in speed will increase the possibility for new ways of life. These new ways include practical and as well what is looked on as the fantastic. Expect and embrace them both, and most important – <u>talk about them</u>.

It is in the discussion and acceptance of the new methods of life that familiarity and a continuation is more readily encouraged.

Would you be more specific?

I would. I will tell you here the first noticing's as they occurred for my people, for me.

- Synchronicities became prevalent and expected
- Visuals of other, faster vibrating beings became prevalent and accepted
- "Morphing" of the physical vehicle began
- Co-creative communication occurred more frequently, seamlessly, between "dimensions" or vibratory rates
- Understanding and patience in some cases increased – while in other cases there seemed a quicker tendency to dismiss what felt "out of sync"
- Ways of co-habitating changed as the need for barriers lessened
- There were more things "seen" and "heard" in the spectrum of visual and auditory fields than had been typically seen or heard
- Things happened faster when focus and intent were used – less effort yielded quicker results
- Sustenance methods changed as things seemed to enhance or limit new capabilities and we noticed

These things happened to everyone. We all went through a shift and individually reacted to each alteration in speed.

Some of us made it a religion. By that I mean a focus, as if the change itself had qualities to be focused on.

Why I am speaking to you now is to tell you that ALL OF YOU are experiencing these changes and as you do – relegating them to certain parts of your life.

What's important is not the change or even that you noticed it. What's important is this life you are in, this vessel you inhabit, these relationships you partake in and whatever work you do.

The shift can enhance all of these things or it can impede them if you pre-occupy yourself with it.

Looking at it now, I would say that *allowing it with attentive acceptance worked best overall.* It is true that you'll need to focus and learn – yet maintain a sense of play while you do.

(I was interrupted here and had to stop. I have yet to take up this conversation again, feeling that it's relatively complete in its purpose.)

Galactic Council

May 21, 2015

You are offering this energy and information to the whole of humanity. As readers hear truth from other beings in creation, they will see themselves as we do – the powerful creators who have showed up to carry out this physical ascension.

No offense, but your words sound staged and of no real substance. My readers know who they are. What is desired is helpful information. Do you have that? If you do, please tell me who you are and why you have shown up.

You do not "pull any punches", I was advised of this. I am a galactic ambassador for a Council of beings – more than one race is represented. I am here to introduce the possibility of participation amongst our group.

This has not been sought as mankind/earth beings, in their current controlled and warlike state, have not been trusted or welcomed.

And we are welcomed now?

Well, no, not exactly. We want you to know of the reality of a planetary council – a group, sort of like your United Nations. Except our purpose and methods are not covert and sinister, they are out in the open.

The particular Council I represent oversees trade routes and the sharing of resources.

Excuse me, but as I have not spoken to you and I want to maintain integrity – would you give me longitude and latitude coordinates of a place on the earth that has been used as a part of these trade routes?

Why yes, certainly.

Longitude: 76.2853

Latitude: 43.5682

*Note from Sophia:

I went to www.latlong.net and typed in these coordinates as given. What it brought me to was - Almaty Region, Kazakhstan. I did some research and found videos and articles, which seemed to support this claim. The articles were titled:

"Mysterious circle in Kazakhstan raises questions"

"Kazakhstan hosting first Alien Embassy?"

Okay, please continue.

The earth has been and is under the control of a brutal monopoly that places it at the most undesirable position for collaboration. The controllers of the planet see <u>the earth itself</u> as a resource.

The members of this Council, the one I represent, see the planets as they are – celestial beings who are on their own evolutionary path and give ceaselessly so that life can be maintained there.

Because of these different points of view, the earth has not been represented on the Council and is not a "voting member".

Then why show up now?

Just because mankind is not a voting party to the galactic trade route doesn't mean it has been bypassed. The earth is rich with resources. The location given earlier is a frequent trading post.

Most of the Galactic Community seeks peaceful cooperation. Planets are on different yet similar paths and experience different yet similar needs for resources.

The Earth is scheduled for release soon from the iron fisted grip of the controllers. Once that happens she will have an opportunity to alter her current methodology and perhaps join in the Council.

The Council operates with a general welfare of the whole as its focus. This, as opposed to taking as much as is wanted whenever its wanted from wherever it exists, with little regard for mutual benefit.

There are many ways to function as members of creation. Your earth is moving from one in which absolute control was held over it to one where an opportunity for unification exists. This is so very exciting. The Council has waited anxiously for this.

Why? What is the ultimate motive?

Trade. More resources. An "inside view" of earths management so that the intergalactic community is considered as well. Not to the detriment of mankind in a secretive and abusive way, but for the assistance and benefit of the whole.

I must go.

I see that you do, yes.

Hellenat

May 27, 2015

This song* is very much a part of this conversation.   Lyrics follow –

*<u>American Authors</u> – "Love"

Remember when we were lost at sea?
We would look at the bright night sky
Thinking of, what we could be
What we could be
How to spend our lives
Remember when we had nothing left?
We were strung out in the cold
Holding on, trying to save our breath
Trying to save our breath
We would not let go
(Whoa)
Through the good, through the bad and ugly
(Whoa)
We'll conquer anything
'Cause one day we're gonna come back
And laugh at it all
One day we'll look at the past
With love, love
One day we're gonna come back
And relive those thoughts
One day we'll look at the past
With love, love
With love, love
Remember down in the forest heart
We were lost, losing hope and faith
We put our trust in counting stars
We were counting stars
Trying to find our way
Remember up on the mountain top
Looking out on the rocks below
Thinking God, we will never stop
We will never stop
No we won't let go

'Cause one day we're gonna come back
And laugh at it all
One day we'll look at the past
With love, love
One day we're gonna come back
And relive those thoughts
One day we'll look at the past
With love, love
(Love, love)
Like a scene from the past
Where we look back and laugh
With love, love
A thought like a flash
Black and white, hope it lasts
With love, love
Like a scene from the past
Where we look back and laugh
With love, love
A thought like a flash
Black and white, hope it lasts
With love
'Cause one day we're gonna come back
And laugh at it all
One day we'll look at the past
With love, love
One day we're gonna come back
And relive those thoughts
One day we'll look at the past
With love, love
(Love, love)
With love, love

And now, enjoy this conversation, shared originally as a blog post…

So, this is a sharing. The whole of it, well, you'd have to be here. Maybe you'd have to be me. I shared it with my partner and he cried from the telling of it. Most of it is not in my words, so for today, I will not be the author of this blog post. It was given to me. Now, it is given to you.

This song* is part of the complete story… You'll see. It's explained at the end.

This is a blog (not a newsletter) because it is meant for us all. Please share it if you are so moved. It is for everyone. It is a message of hope. *A confirmation of us*, an incredible piece of what we have been only imagining. There is no longer any doubt.

Yesterday, May 27th, 2015 I sat down and said...

I feel someone, who is this?

You will need to release expecting's and ideas of both reasons for and methods of contact, if we are to chat.

What do you mean by methods?

Methods are ways of producing desired effects. These must be open to alteration as my energy is not one you've known.

Yet I hear and feel you.

You do. This is by way of introduction. I would like to diverge from word communication to event/idea/subject communication. This coincides with what happens in the spaces you have labeled "higher realms" or faster frequencies or different densities.

Okay. I'm open.

This will require a non-judgmental allowing of an idea, a thought – merely looking at it.

In this way, it is hoped that a clearer picture can be given of this other way of life. Life in 5D+. Until now you've been speaking to others. Each with valid information and told word by word. In truth, you had no real picture of what was said until after the conversation completed itself.

In contrast, in densities/realms other than earth – communication is in complete thoughts. In actuality you can do that now, and do, yet the use of words interprets and gets in the way.

This is because you alter your focus from what you are communicating or receiving to what you are saying or the words you are hearing. You step away from the art of telepathy to speak and listen to words. When in fact it is all telepathy to a greater or lesser degree.

So, who are you?

I am a being from the Pleiades and we have watched eagerly your discussions, waiting to move into your field and show you what your own day to day communication will be like once you complete your shift.

Do you have a name that could be used as reference?

I am known as Helna.

H-E-L-N-A?

More like H-E-L-L-E-N-A-T.

Is the final letter silent?

It is soft, not hard.

Okay, what do we do to proceed with this new type of communicating?

You remain open and listening. I will send the idea and we'll see what gets heard by you.

(I waited and received for a bit, allowing an immersion into what I was feeling and seeing)

I would like to tell you about what I see/sense/feel and how I interpret it all.

Yes, please.

I see first swirling dresses, dancing, a rambunctious and joyful dance – a performance – reds, white, colors – clapping. This is indoors, though not on earth. Not a planet of any type but a ship. This is a celebration due to a homecoming. Those who are dancing are demonstrating overwhelming joy. Deep satisfaction in those watching at this juncture – long awaited.

It feels as if you are sending these to me with a feeling of coming home. At how many beings eagerly anticipate the homecoming of those of us who have been human for so long. Those of us who will be returning home.

(Note *these images were coupled with waves of love, of joy, of immense feelings of "welcome home" ... It is a challenge to find words to describe the intensity of this gathering and its effect on me...)

You are seeing it Sophia. If you allow without so much associative input, you will see more detail; remember more detail of this home that I am sensing. The challenge with the human brain is it likes to categorize. Your memories of this place have no category you are familiar with in your current life.

Yes. The dresses threw me.

The dresses are your only visual context for a mesmerizing, welcoming dance that draws you into it. You are putting in a sort of square dance type costuming. This is not a square dance. It is a deeply sacred series of movements that are practiced and then handed from dancer to dancer. I was hoping you would remember/feel the solemnity of the dance itself. It has been practiced and perfected over eons for a very specific homecoming. Yours.

You are speaking the empirical "you"?

Yes. As those humans who volunteered for this work return home, each will be welcomed in the manner significant for that specific origin. Our race holds the movement, dancelike, as both beautiful and unique. It is a gift by every measure, and requires the entire community's participation. Not only the dancers, but the musicians, choreographers, costumers, attendants and logistics personnel. It is a deep honor. We are eagerly awaiting your return. We will learn so much and we have missed you all.

Okay, I would like to try this again. I must go.

I am aware. Until then.

(Note* after this, there was an overwhelming feeling of joy and I was sort of awestruck. I wandered into the room where I work, turned on my computer and kindle and "Love" by American Authors was playing.

I began to cry and to sway with the visuals and feelings I was still getting. The sense of it is so difficult to describe, it is not like the family we know here, but sort of. It is perhaps so overwhelmingly loving because it has been so very long since a reunion has actually happened.

There is a sense of being with others who "get" you completely, that is experienced at every level of being; a deep validation. The only word I have in my heart is "home"; yet even that does not do it justice. Perhaps a better word is "agape"; unconditional acceptance.

The sense I have is that this is waiting for each of us, in some method of expression. This is one family reunion you won't want to miss!

We are the ones <u>they</u> are waiting for.

"Military Man"

May 17th, 2015

Who are you?

I am not one, but many. You have concerned yourself with your history and there are particulars of it that we are familiar with. Would you like these things to be told to you now?

Yes. I would. I will say here that I get a sense of order – almost military precision to this energy. Are there many of you together making this, creating this? Or is this a singular voice? I cannot discern.

The reason for your confusion is that I speak for an order, a regiment if you will. One that is imperative to giving a factual accounting of the creation of this current version of 3rd density humankind.

The sense of precision comes from the factual nature of information about to be shared. It is not as you, (and here is meant you in a general, unified sense), have been led to believe from scripture.

It is, or better said, humanity was created in an orderly, intended fashion – seeded by specific races for its DNA outcomes, in order to facilitate its eventual liberation from this density *(which is)* constrained by and operating within "time".

As mankind holds a sentimental picture of one god as creator, the contrast *(of that version)* to planned creation is sharp and results in the feeling you now have of strict adherence to codes and precision of language.

The nature of humanity was intentionally created. It is not a negation of divinity to discount the notion of a single "god". Creation is sacred and in fact there exists, as is also known to man, a creator. What diverges in this discussion is the definition of that creator. The creator encompasses all of creation in the parameters of itself – A MAGNITUDE OF BEING THAT IS IMPOSSIBLE TO GRASP.

So, who are you?

The race I belong to is beyond your current understanding of history. Compare my race to that of your very deep ancestral roots. These are names you have no reference for, *(not)* until they graduate up to nearer to this "time". I am the founding race, the overseer of the plan for this genetic combination. It is not that I seeded humanity, but that I directed the manipulation, no, not the manipulation, the experiment of combinations so that what would emerge was *a being so fully enthralled with its "physical" life, that it would be moved to stay there, while understanding itself non-physically.* (Italics mine. Sophia)

This could only occur once the life form had played every possible role as that life form. As example, so that you can relate – bonds are strongest with those you've experienced hardship with and "grown up" with.

The human, with or without recall, has been through every permutation while being physical – primitive, peaceful, warlike, advanced – now they have entered and are anxious for movement to another level of existence. Another density or dimension. Yet, none, or very few *(humans)* (and by very few is meant only several hundred out of billions), would easily or willingly leave 3D life behind.

This, as you now know, was seen, as time is irrelevant and all things happen simultaneously. Thus – the Shift.

All of humanity is ready for this change yet not all will experience it in the same way. As much as there is inescapable order to the force and outcome of this plan, the specific "timing" of it is determined in each "now" occurrence.

What sounds orderly, dogmatic and unforgiving to your mind is the structure necessary so that every possibility is allowable and occurs.

This may sound to you like there is not free will. The "truth", absolutely is that all of life exists within the system of creation initiated by one creator being. That *(one creator being)* is the source for it all and so it confines creation within the parameters it knows.

The "experiment" of humanity exists within those parameters – it is only one race among many. I do not know the number.

As a "founding" member of humanity it is satisfying to participate with you in the culmination of the plan. The nature, exact nature, of the human was known and foreseen. It is, however, up to the human to define its specific characteristics.

I will note that the most remarkable and unpredictable aspect of your race is the depth of your passion for, and attachment to YOURSELVES. This is the most exciting part of the "evolution show" as we witness your shift. You do not relinquish each other with ease or comfort.

So, that said, for all the planned order, there is *(still)* a large chaotic question mark as to what you will look like? We have seen every possibility – it is up to man to choose.

I must go. (I had plans for the day)

Yes. I feel anxiety from your vessel – it is experienced as pressure and you again are this way because of other humans – responsibilities perceived to them.

Yes. I would like to talk again sometime.

This can be arranged.

The conversation ended.

"Smallish" Beings

May 6, 2015

(At this point in May, I still had questions. That is the setting in which this conversation took place.)

What do you wish to discuss?

I just want to explore what is happening on the planet – my understanding of who is speaking because frankly, this feels "made up"; my imagination getting carried away.

You are not so imaginative as to conjure races and beings and roles within the spectrum of life you reside. It is a very human tendency to "settle for less" – to minimize what they actually do, so as to seem not so special.

Who is speaking? I don't feel any specific being or energy – thus the reason for my suspect.

I am not one with whom you've engaged. I am holding back, as it were – unsure of what it is you are capable of hearing – I note that as of late the energy or some of them, was too much. I am applying caution to my enthusiasm.

What is your name? This, I am feeling now, is male.

Yes, well I would say, or rather agree, that the energy I favor would be construed as male energy – I would rather not name myself. They limit the possibilities for this interaction.

Names?

Yes.

Do I know you – have we interacted in physical life?

We have not.

Okay. What sort of conversation are you looking to have? Let me say here that I feel you; it is as if you are behind a large door. That door holds you back but your light streams through the cracks – It is as if your energy pushes on the door and it moves open a bit with the force of you – only to be pulled or pushed shut.

An accurate image. This is an interesting interpretation of what is going on – what is happening. I would like to share what I know to be true, because I have had life, about the balance of belief and knowing.

Whoa. What does "I have had life" mean? Were you human?

No.

What were you? I see small beings now – like, I don't know, elves or just very miniature by earth's current standards.

An accurate image – this is interesting, as you pick up/receive/hear the visual as it is thought rather than spoken. I was part of a race that still exists – humanoid. Not human.

They exist in the galaxy. We lived by different "rules" than now are part of life on your current planet. Yet, in this subject matter, their method of understanding was clear. It may be of some help as you move out of the chains of your enslavement.

Humankind will have to weigh carefully all that they've been told. Much of your current systems grow out of what you've been told. There are things you believe are true; you may even say you "know" them to be true. Why do you say this? Because they were taught to you at a very young age and have become part of your history – your "story".

As a member of another race, we had a systematic method of determining and discerning the difference between something we "believed" was true, vs something we "knew". It stemmed from understanding the nature of physical life.

We understood physical life, (the one we were living), was created and therefore subject to the whims (if you will), of the ones running the place – there are always creator beings and always agendas. Those agendas are carried out via the stories told and the process of growth as permitted on the planet.

Beliefs, as we understood and accepted them, came exclusively from those things – the things that had been told in some way, to us – either handed down and given or personally given. "BELIEFS ORIGINATE FROM OUTSIDE OF SELF."

<u>What you know</u> originates within your being – this may differ very much from what you are told.

As the unravelling takes place on your planet, many things you've been told will be exposed and laid bare, the reasons for their telling evident as well as the person or being behind the story. You may feel as if everything you "know" about life was constructed for the benefit of someone else.

This actually is true in all but one respect – it is not everything you "know" about life, but everything you currently <u>believe</u> about life. You cannot lose everything you know, it is held within your core and cannot be taken.

Accessing it becomes a perhaps new yet necessary skill when beliefs fall away and what appear to be the foundations of life crumble.

It is not a difficult thing to do. On my planet we had a saying which equates to 'BLOCK OUT THE VOICES, THE SILENCE KNOWS". By "silence" is meant that inner intuition. Humans, what seems to be many humans, are not practiced at listening to their silence. They seem to want "facts" from "experts" or "authority". This tendency is a trait that was exploited here and the exposure of many falsehoods will bring anger, confusion and a sense of distrust.

There are those who already understand and trust what they know rather than what they believe. They will be needed now. Your people are going through an enormous opening up and acceleration. It is very exciting to witness. These are ideas that will seem obvious to your readers perhaps – yet the assistance they will be called upon to do, and shortly, will demand of them a way to explain, a way to make sense of what is going on. These words are an offer to assist in that regard.

Okay. Is there anything else?

Only that there are ways to spread truth and these ways involve less of a voicing of truth, than a living of it. It is in the living of what is truly known that expansion occurs for all concerned.

That's it?

Yes. That is what I wanted to share.

"Syntpold"

May 7, 2015

Is there something to say now?

There is, as well as someone to say it.

Who is this??

I am. Write these letters – S-y-n-t-p-o-l-d.

I cannot even pronounce that.

It is only an approximation of what it would sound like in the language you currently speak.

So then, you are called by this name?

This grouping of sounds comes together to form a "name" for my family of original thought. It is not precisely as you imagine – more of a union of understanding than an exact or specific identifier. If you were to call for "Syntpold" you would hear from a very large grouping of beings – not one being or "family". In a sense, it would be family, yet not genetic.

I am not following you. Is this "title" or discussion around it pertinent? Does it have anything to do with why you showed up?

No. It is an answer to your question regarding my identity.

Okay. Why did you show up?

For discourse. There are things to discuss, important to your current state of being.

What state is that?

Your current evolutionary stage is one that interests us. You as a race have developed and refined aspects of being which are as yet undeveloped within the race I originate from and have lives. This, as a reference point is compelling. You do not as yet understand your power or even where it resides, yet you have and hold extreme states of emotion as a magnetic force – Anger, Sadness, Excitement and Passion are the extreme states to which I refer.

They draw more to them, creating what is called a "crowd mentality", as well as exquisite art work, fatal illness or successful performances of any type. This is not understood by your people and fascinating to observe. Once the energy of emotion is harnessed and utilized consciously by the masses – you will take control on this planet back from those who understand perfectly well the phenomenon to which I refer.

The manipulation happened because so many of you were unaware. Now, you are becoming aware. As you do there will be anger. In order for the most productive use of that anger to occur, you will need to understand more of how creation takes place.

The earth is populated with 8 billion powerful beings, many of whom exist seemingly at the whim of a faceless authority who tell them what to do and when, and charge for the privilege. This is "how it is" for the majority of westerners and actually, if truth were to be told, of humans.

The fabrication of control has been so completely successful that anyone who goes against the grain is outcast in some fashion and feels it.

It is these feelings that will bring back control to the human. When sadness is understood, it can be felt, explored and experienced as a complete event; rather than allowed to linger as a permanent state of being that takes root in the cells and manifests as disease.

It is the same for anger. It is a powerful emotion that can be utilized constructively, as a spark for change or a pivot point for action. Anger is not bad, nor does it have to be a cause for destruction. When recognized consciously and utilized, anger alters lifetimes and as well the course of history.

My "people" understand the force held in emotion and see it as sacred almost. They cherish it when it shows up for it is the Master Key.

I am fascinated that humans see it as an irritant at times and seem to attempt to stifle it with chemicals, rules or self-control. Emotion is the thing about humanity that is so very much desired by all of creation.

The reason for the depth and breadth of the structures of control and systems set up on earth are relative to the depth and breadth of power held in the human. *(Underlining here my own. Sophia)* This is not something well known because it would ruin everything.

This "experiment" was a mutual plan and all of those participating agreed to the parameters.

The reason for my reaching out in this way is to introduce the idea of a re-definition of emotion. It is your most cherished attribute and earth is the place to explore it.

There are some who think they want to come here and once they do, sort of dissolve under the weight of emotion. These are those you've labelled insane and in many cases the isolation and/or medication used does little to stem the tide of extreme reaction to emotion. They live in a constant emotional state. Their volume is always turned up.

Is there a conclusion you'd like to draw here?

Only that the awake ones, those reading this now, can exist as examples for those stuck in old definitions. Emotions, once celebrated, will be the lightning rods for creation. They are tools and humanity is equipped with a toolbox that is overflowing. Use your emotions with intention and with authority. They are easily controlled once it is understood where they spring from. They come from you and are your birthright. It is the utilization of these that will allow for more creative manifestation. It is the tool of a Master – a Master Human and the rest of us wait to see what magnificence humankind will create once it is fully appreciated, understood and used.

Many are cheering you on, in whatever fashion we are able to.

Okay. Is that it?

Yes. Goodbye Sophia.

Goodbye.

Watchers

May 9th, 2015

I'd like to write now. Is there someone there?

Yes. Always there is.

Someone with something to say?

We can talk about the earth if you would like. It may be of interest.

Who is "we" and what about the earth?

"We" is a group of beings who watch your current planet. You could call us "Watchers." We have an interest in that manifestation of creation, celestial bodies, and watch them as they proceed on an evolutionary path. The answer to "What about the earth?" is difficult to isolate – everything about the earth would be closest to truth.

Well, okay, I don't have a specific question at this point, so go ahead and lead our conversation.

There are different planetary beings, each with unique purposes for life. Gaia, as you call her, has a goal if you will. To witness the life cycle she is going through as she achieves that goal is both humbling and awe inspiring.

Gaia gave everything, gives everything, for humanity. Life could not have developed, mankind could not have flourished, if not for her gift.

Gaia's gift is abundance. She is a vessel which holds and nurtures life in a myriad of forms. If you are looking for a living example of unconditional love, look no further than the ground you walk on.

Each day she exists so that mankind and the rest of the creatures on her can continue.

She too is finally now enjoying life at a frequency closer to her true nature.

The evolution of consciousness happening for humankind is being directed by Gaia, who determines the path as well as the timing. Like a mother with a newborn child, only the best interests of humanity, all of humanity, are her motivation.

At the hands of man, she has been bled and bloodied again and again and again. Understand that the pain inflicted by man on each other in times of war is also felt by the being Gaia.

The bombing that occurs rips chunks of her to bits. She knew her life would include the devastation seen on earth and still she gives it.

We watch her to witness love in action. There are planetary bodies without life on them. The purpose for each differs. You may not be able to imagine a reason for experiencing such a life cycle, yet there are numerous reasons.

Nothing is "dead". The dirt you walk on is part of Gaia's body.

There is so much being said right now I am having a hard time getting it down.

It is a vast subject. We are trying to give you a sampling of what it is like to be a planet – the wisdom necessary, the love necessary in order to consistently allow blow after blow is of such a magnitude as to be impossible to conceive. Yet Gaia provides equally for all of life, regardless.

Will you make your point soon? (This was a challenging energy to maintain contact with, I was falling asleep.)

I am not hearing new information.

Our point is that part of Unity awareness will include Oneness with this planet. Respect and honor for all of life must occur at all levels of existence.

The increased frequency you are feeling now is like taking the restraints off Gaia – she can now run a bit – this creates joy for her.

She understands the new speed is creating a bit of havoc yet also knows that for life to continue it has to evolve. As we watch her now it is akin to riding a bicycle without the training wheels and she is drunk with the joy of it.

Would you tell me who you are?

We are Watchers of life at the planetary scale. We are aware of cycles of life that take billions of your "years".

I feel a "hugeness" to you – a solidity, no, a hugeness is the best word I can come up with.

We have seen cycles of life occur in bodies that you would not recognize as bodies – This too is part of your collective evolution, the planet you rest on.

I must go.

We will talk again, when you are able to hold our energy.

The conversation ended. I have not been contacted by these being since this date in May.

What follows are a few words from an exchange I had with "One". This took place on April 23rd, 2015.

It is time for me to write now, is there someone who wishes to speak?

Always.

Who?

Again, it is the force of creation, the one essence of life. This force runs through every being; it is accessible to all. It is felt in the tug at your heart, the pull of your longing, the rush of emotion, the solemnity of your heart. All when faced with decisions about life, these noticing's occur.

Okay, proceed then. I have "time".

Yes, well, "time" is an interesting word choice, as there is no such thing. Humans have created timepieces that mechanically move what has been decided is forward in time. Ever since, the world you inhabit runs along, following or "keeping up" with the movement; as if it could somehow stop and you would run out. If the timepiece stopped, happenings would happen anyway and "time" would have no response, would be of no consequence.

If instead man invented a mechanical device that measured backwards – what then? Would there be access to your past?

This stopped there. I do not remember why. I have often had to interject these connections in between jobs and activities and family, and I get interrupted.

On April 16th, 2015, my pet cat was very much in my heart and on my mind as he was about to be euthanized the very next morning. The following conversation occurred:

"So, who wants to talk?"

We do.

And you are?

You'll have to get another book (this is a reference to the many different colored notebooks I have to write these conversations in. I had started to separate them by being/beings.) – for you haven't spoken to us before. Listen, one word at a time.

Okay.

The feline race is one that is honored here. It is similar to your domestic animals – your cats – but we/they are not the same. The species of being <u>looks</u> feline in appearance and because of this the association with the cat is made.

WE ARE NOT CATS BUT AN EXAMPLE OF THE MANY FORMS LIFE CAN TAKE. SENTIENCE IS NOT CONFINED TO HUMANITY OR EVEN TO 2-LEGGED UPRIGHT WALKING CREATURES SUCH AS THE HUMAN.

Once you release your attachment to that idea of sentience – the possibility opens up for multiple and many types of intelligence.

There are beings in creation that look nothing like you – like the human – and with communication methods that differ as well. There are clicks and buzzes and maneuvers and movements that would astound you in their intricacies and possibilities. All of this is life.

The general part of this conversation ended here, the rest was specific to my pet.

Original Soul

May 28th, 2015

Did someone wake me up? (It was 4:04 AM)

We did.

What for?

We wanted to address a subject without interference. To speak when the lines were clearest, about this.

What subject?

The subject of origins. We are aware it is of concern for humans – origins. Esp. those who sense origins other than just the planet you are living on – those who feel "out of place" or who long for "home" and aren't sure why.

Well, it is true. For many of us, we sense a "home" somewhere else and aren't sure why or where.

You have labels. "Star-seed" is one.

Yes. Who are you? You are more than one.

Yes. We are a group of beings from another cluster.

I want to say the Orion Belt. Is that where you are from?

Yes, most of us. This group of us would like to share our own story with your readers and with you – regarding original soul.

What does that term mean?

There are several definitions. The one we will be adopting for our conversation refers to the place your current fragment first took "root" as it were. And, more importantly, the people with which you first grew, incarnated.

Each fragment has its own history and the one that is dominant in you now, this current incarnation, has remembering's of its other incarnations. These have often, not always, centered on a specific race or "home" or group, but not always.

You feel strongly for the Pleiadian race because of your many times there – they are what you would refer to as your people – your "home". It does not mean a birthplace as much as a place of resonance. You ring with their vibration, as does your son.

Your partner is a traveler and resonates to a different frequency. Not that he does not have a beginning or home; yet that his experience is one of constant exploration and healing. His view then is not skewed in a specific direction.

Many of the "star-seeds" who sense other homes believe they don't belong here – yet earth is your home now and will one day feel like "home" to you all. There will always be a sense of familiarity with it.

It is more that you are stifled with no remembering than that other places are more prominent in your history, your aspect. The "memories", dreams and even longings coming through the "star-seeds" now, do so because of the forgetting you've agreed to and are participating in. It's like a secret that can only stay a secret for so long – it's too big to stay hidden.

What is most prominent in this story of origins is how humans like to rate themselves once they discover or remember theirs. Nationalities, teams, even sex, male or female, all seem to prompt a sort of pride. It is as if you all submit to the false notion that one type is more of something, and therefore better than a different type.

You, the entire you, have many aspects with many origins. Today you are identifying with just the one aspect you are focused on, so that you may fully experience this one life. This aspect has chosen ascension while human and because that is a unique choice – realize that soon the "memory" of it will become dominant for your aspect. It will not erase your current feelings of original soul or other "homes" but add to it. Earth will become a favorite and very powerful point in your (it stopped here)

"My/your what?"

Better that we "show" you. Hold on and receive what is sent.

This is so odd, different. I feel or see myself becoming larger – physically larger and somehow inside there are all of these me's – the female me, Pleiadian me, a male, yet I don't know how to speak of this, a NO "me" at all – but a growing expanse of awareness that has no name, no beginning, or "now" or sex or race or time – its expanding – the feeling is one of HUGE LIFE, potential for understanding life that reaches outside of my name or locale.

Like a balloon being blown up – filling yet never stopping being filled – only more.

In that level of awareness, the conversation seems not pointless really, but so very temporary and unbelievable. How could something as vast as the life that I AM identify itself with the tiny aspect of it called female, human, Pleiadian or Sophia? It is sort of blowing my mind. The enormity of being brings a perspective to life that does not allow for judgment – I AM EVERYTHING.

Oh my, this is so very cool.

You have gotten our message! We wanted to transmit to you the enormity of what life is, of what you are. This, inside of a discussion of "origin" sort of puts it all into perspective.

The joy felt at your Pleiadian reunion is possible and felt all over the one that you are. To fully experience every nuance of life requires a focus of intent and that is what you've done. You are not "only" – you are "every" ONE. This is your true origin.

The feeling you just had is but a glimpse of life in the expanded place you are shifting to. It is not so much one part of you doing this – all of you can't help but participate. This, a function of unity.

I see that, feel that, yes. I must go.

We are pleased to be able to have reached you this way. The possibilities now have expanded for learning, for communication.

Yes.

Goodbye Sophia.

The conversation ended.

Today, on August 28th, 2015, 3 months later, as I type this I see a note I wrote on the page to remind me of this experience. It said:

"<u>I FEEL HUGE!!!</u>" In a good way. Validation not necessary from outside for this – I know what I AM.

June 2015

Explorers

June 1st, 2015

"I'd like to know who woke me up last night and why?"

You have been contacted by us. We would very much enjoy a meeting with you and reached out at that time because it was felt you would have more time then, to devote to an interaction. We did notice a lack of enthusiasm. *(LOL)*

It was 1:30 AM. I start my day 3 hours after that time and wanted more sleep. I did not sleep well after that however. The way this works best is for me to reach out when I can devote some time and effort to our connection.

Yes, we see that now. We are anxious to speak.

Who are you and why do you want to speak now?

We are *(nothing came through)*

Who are you?

We are a faction of *(again, nothing)*

Okay – one word only at a time, please.

We are a party of explorers, developers of systems, anchors that set-in place beginnings. We come to you now as we see the beginning that is happening. Although you may deem this a slow start – by our view it is rapidly evolving.

We come to you by way of desire – the emotion here is powerful and we would like to employ it for our own use.

We are not parasites, as you have some beings here such as those. *(I imagine this is a reference to the Archons)* We are not looking for negative power or any.

So, we are wanting to experience the emotion of earth and have waited until there was a celebratory mood.

There is not now. I wouldn't describe it as celebratory.

You underestimate the potential force of joy and creativity. It is present in greater amounts on earth now than previously existed. Your numbers may be relatively small – yet the strength of their energy empowers whatever vibration it encompasses. From your view, you do not see the effect of that. We do.

This is why we are anxious to engage in a real way.

You are not familiar to me.

You have not encountered us before now.

Again, explain what it is you do and what you are looking for in this conversation? My purpose is to provide information, truth, where it was missing or hidden before.

What we do is encounter and then *(we)* establish systems. This takes place on a level unseen by you in your present form and so far into the nuances of life as to be invisible.

We are sort of "place holders" and again looking for newly formed arenas where we can insure a structure is in place.

I am not following you.

There is an organized chaos to life – all of creation holds court on a blueprint – a map you could call it, and the magnitude of this is beyond words.

My group, the one I am a part of, keeps a watchful look out for places where the "new" emerges within the fabric. We sort of oversee, insure that the semblance of order necessary for continued successful evolution is present.

In Earth's case, the evolution of consciousness happening now is creating a split and this must be accounted for in the blueprint – there are several choices happening – all of them infused with powerfully creative energies on both sides of polarity.

We reached out to you as the creative side promoted by your "people" is one we are looking to understand. It is relatively new in all of creation and the opportunity to be close to it intrigues us. *It is powerful in a way unseen by those holding it. (A reference to ourselves, Sophia)*

If this was harnessed…

I am seeing something here.

We are sending, yes.

I see a huge wave moving across a grid and changing it as it ripples through. The entire grid is altered. It is blue, with lines.

Yes. We see the potential of human love as something of a super-conductor. We felt, if we could understand it on a personal level, we could perhaps understand the best sort of grid/blueprint for it to set up; one that encourages its growth for all of creation.

The earth grid is not set up that way now. We will be able to offer an assist.

How do you plan to get close to it?

Merely connecting we experience your energy and those of your readers – there is power there.

Okay. I must go now.

You will hear from us soon.

The conversation ended.

Note: I did not hear from these "explorers" again. I believe this is because I questioned their reasons for interaction. There was a level of trust that I did not feel, based on what they said was going on. I did not doubt the truthfulness of their communication, only their benefit to me and to us. This could be my own lack of complete comprehension as to their purpose and methods. Yet the "to what end?" question was not answered satisfactorily for me. And it was my energetic signature they were latching on to for whatever work they were into.

At that point, (early June 2015) I was not declaring "For Assistance Only." I began to do so not long after, and these sorts of things did not happen. They were clear as to their objectives, yet from this end, there was little benefit, as far as I could tell, to us.

There have been several times when the connection was cut off (by me), due to the fact that the beings reaching out for contact were sort of "joy riding" or "playing" or "checking me out". There is no harm in this, perhaps, yet it isn't really beneficial.

In other words, there was no point to it. It would proceed usually from some sort of really exuberant, party like greeting and the impression of lots of beings in the group sort of smiling or waving. Fun, yes, don't get me wrong; yet much like talking to someone at a party after his or her third beer, sort of pointless. ;-)

This next conversation took place the same week last summer, on June 3, 2015. It is an answer to my personal questions, given by a healer who shares my energetic signature, (if at another moment in "time"). I include it today because this energy shift has recently gone into rapid acceleration. This plays havoc with our physical selves. I hope that it helps you. I know when I found and read it today, it helped me.

"I'd like to ask some questions. They concern what is going on physically specific to me and in general to everyone. Is there someone who can answer?"

There is.

My question is – Why am I exhausted? Why is it such a challenge to move, (even) to walk? Why the congestion for me? (I never get colds.) Why the allergic reaction for everyone I know? And for me?

These are good and important questions.

Can you answer them?

I can.

Who are you?

I am a fractal of you who was a healer.

Go on.

This all you've run into is created out of two things. Your desire for growth and physical stamina has the cells of your body in a rapidly moving state – you are changing.

As you move more and attempt to match the acceleration you sense, your body tells you to stop. This is new.

As these changes occur around you, they occur within. You are not separate but a part of your environment. Rapid frequency cannot occur in isolation.

Your body responds by desiring rest and also by releasing toxins it no longer supports. You are not sitting there today in the same body you were sitting in even a week ago.

The exhaustion comes from several places for you. You are eating differently. And as well you've intended new. New means change Sophia, new means change.

As your body works to keep up with your declarations – you push it from the outside. The only thing it knows to do is attempt to release the allergy with congestion and as well force a shutdown, (create exhaustion). With the signal message of exhaustion being sent you get a very clear imprint – this body needs to rest. As you ignore and continue to push it will continue to feel and send a message to STOP.

I've been told the body lies.

Yes, well, this is sometimes true. In this case though, it is not. Massive upgrades you would call them, are occurring.

As you change you are more fragile and susceptible to germs and viruses. These things too, are altered by the frequency shift. You can be affected now and are vulnerable.

Is that it?

What is the most productive thing for me to do?

As a healer, I recommend quiet. You are so very stressed.

You are in need of calm. This rapid acceleration is wearing you down. You are pushing beyond what the body can successfully do.

How long will this go on?

Until a new stasis is reached; there is not one yet – not for you or for anyone. But you are all at different levels of acceptance and health.

(There was some personal information and the conversation came to an end.)

Okay. I will go. Thank you.

Angelic

June 30th, 2015

I would like to talk to the angel I spoke to a month ago. To complete the message, which was intended to be more than we were able to finish. Is this possible now?

It is.

Who is speaking?

It is the version of your essence called 'angelic". We have connected prior to this time, in this way.

Yes. I remember. Are you willing to continue now? At that time you said you had something to say. Something about Ascension and maintaining balance I believe.

I am. It is this notion of "ascension" that sets off ideas of the fantastic in the human mind. Ideas that serve to separate and create states of awareness that are then rendered inaccessible, due to their relative distance from where you imagine you reside right now.

Please explain.

Ascension has been defined as a "going up" to a place "above." The deeply ingrained beliefs about who is or is not" ascended"," holy" or a "Master", set up in your mind barriers to truth.

These prohibit your ability to even hear the complete picture, let alone accept it.

It would serve you to understand one basic tenet to life. It is that every possibility for it exists. The "stories" you've heard around beings and events, in times before your current focus, are told to you in words. Words are man's attempt to convey what he knows, what must be experienced in order to be comprehended, appreciated and believed.

You yourself struggle with acceptance of me. I AM you. Yet the connection of the word "angel" in your mind prevents your knowing of this truth. Would it be easier if I said I was some sort of monster? Let's say, Hitler? Either extreme brings out in you such deep rejection that understanding is prevented.

When I spoke of balance it was in these ideas of lesser and greater. Neither is true. For Oneness to be realized, the absolute equality of each being will be embodied.

You struggle with judgment. Both you personally and the empirical you. I say this first because I know you intimately and then because I know man, have watched him, been with him, seen the atrocities committed by him and to him and the resulting reactions. There is a difference between opinion and judgment.

For ascension to be realized, many must forgo judgment. Balance is possible only when you do not hold a being in a special place because of his name. Wisdom and truth, love and purity, can come from anyone.

Oneness is achieved when every possibility is accepted as valid.

The human likes to categorize and organize itself into levels of importance and goodness. It is a game the human plays. It is not truth. The truth is that beings, bits of essence, choose how and where they will play at life. As this game is not "won" or "completed" more rapidly according to importance, it matters not which level of play you come in at.

These are roles, nothing more.

Ascension is an actualizing of truth. A fullness of your essence, once realized, brings you to a completion. This is only possible when all are seen as possible and equal and you.

This human game is fun and you (empirical) are recognized for your flair for the dramatic. It is a pleasure to witness the roles played out at every level.

I can tell you that the angelic is a realm of complete service. It should come as not a shock to you, as in this lifetime your chosen role has been public service. Each fractal chooses its position and family according to tendencies it carries.

Mankind is coming into a place now of acute awareness. The fullness of being will be felt as this manifests. You will feel pieces of yourself playing out – pieces you may initially reject as you've deemed them either evil or saintly. You are all things.

The purpose of living out these roles and titles, types and positions – is understanding. With understanding comes acceptance. With acceptance – unity. With unity – oneness.

Unity and Oneness are not the same thing. You may imagine yourself on the same side, the same team, as the "good" guys – yet balk at being told you are the good guys, the angels in this case.

You may, conversely, imagine yourself to be on the same side, the same team as the bad guys, the oppressors – yet not define yourself as THE BAD GUY.

I tell you – you are both. You've been both. All are necessary in ONE. Life is inclusive. Any feeling of exclusivity or rejection is a major red flag, a message that you are opposing truth. *Life is a playing out of truth. (Italics mine. Sophia)*

Oneness is truth. A deep feeling of "no" to any idea or emotion or being may serve to tell you that "THIS TOO, I AM". Accept all names and do not let them inflate or repulse you. Names are words used to express and explain the fullness of existence. All are (part of) One. You are (part of) One. All are (part of) you. ALL ARE YOU.

You've (personal) come a long way to meet me here. I feel acceptance.

Yes. I'm working on it. I must end this now.

I see that. We will speak again then.

I am sure of it.

The conversation ended.

"AVI"

June 21st, 2015

This conversation began with a sentence from them, not me:

We are entering an interesting time.

"Who is this?"

We are many.

I have a specific question.

Go Ahead.

A friend and reader has been in contact with a group calling itself the Alliance. They have predicted what I can only see as an "event" happening in what would be 2 days' time – lights in the sky seen everywhere and global change – positive change. I would like to speak to someone who can address that, and also tell me who you are.

You ask much. This is not supposed to be foretold, but to catch humanity by surprise.

Please tell me who you are. One word only please.

We are a group of beings who do not reside in your planetary system, but beyond it. We have not spoken to you before and are not familiar with your energy.

Me personally or the empirical "you"?

Both. Although we have been witness to entire goings on (on) earth from our vantage point, we have not interacted with humankind.

Okay, I am curious why you mention the unfamiliarity?

We mention it because we are uncomfortable with the communication, not being familiar.

There has been something said by some others of us, (many watch), and it has now been interpreted and seen as a sort of prophecy.

Humans tend to take anything outside of or beyond their own race, and deify it. We do not choose that role.

Predictions can be made such that can be observed and watched from vantage points beyond your planet. This is what was done.

Are you saying it is NOT going to happen in 2 days?

We are saying that there is evidence of an astral event, something in your skies. That evidence points to it happening in the very near future – yes. All this is true.

What we cannot do is foretell the meaning of this.

Would you tell me more about who you are and how you can see this, know this, in the way that you do?

I will now speak for the group. You may refer to me as AVI. The reason we can speak of and see events "heading your way" is partly because our vision is not clouded by participation – in other words this specific event does not happen to us or in our realm but in yours, on earth's. We watch all young planets. Actually, all planets forming themselves as participatory races in the Galactic Community are of interest to us.

We have no contact with humanity. Our interest is for the time when we will have contact. The event you asked about is a pre-cursor to that contact. Earth as a race must go through changes, some of which are happening now as Gaia speeds up and the humans there speed up with her. The overriding force of love and cooperation and assistance of life must predominate before we engage – before we are able to communicate.

The fact of this recent contact is evidence of the increased frequency. We see all things happening and know that this event is imminent because of recent energetic shifts. We cannot verify or deny the 2-day forecast because your concept of time is not so clear to us.

We will say this. In not much longer you will see real evidence of changes and the validation and time marker for them will be lights in your skies – as so many have seen visions.

What do these lights signify?

That you've received an assist.

Your planet will get a jolt of energy so that your people may catapult into a love frequency on a more massive scale. Those seeing this in advance of it occurring may be absolutely precise in the timing for it, I don't know. The fact of it – is truth. It's known by those of us in creation that pay attention.

As humanity moves beyond its own individual development it is then able to move into and join the development of all of creation – to collaborate with our race and others for the benefit of all.

It would be like watching a young earth human reach maturity and move out into the greater world. The world is then ready for the contributions given by the new adult human as is the new adult human now ready to give them.

The time marker for the event is seen as a marker for those of us who watch – a sort of moving out of puberty marker. You'll be joining us now and we are anxious for your contribution to begin!

Can you see how then it becomes a delicate "conversation" to hold with any of you? As this is a new form of contact and you are so very "young" to it – anything we say can be misinterpreted and simultaneously carry a lot of "weight", for the simple reason that we said it and not another human.

It is not our interest to mislead or even to foretell. The statements about something in your skies are meant as validation. So, you will see we tell truth and also that all of this happening to earth and its inhabitants has a purpose and is real – real as in unmistakable vibratory shifts seen and felt by everyone inhabiting the planet, not only the sensitives.

As you witness a massive real time outpouring of shifting energy you will simultaneously recognize your place in the stars, your personal place and the races' place.

There is a self-absorption that can't help but occur during growth and development into maturity. This will become a broader focus once mankind realizes its potential as a being, as a contributory race of beings.

This development of the "adult human" is much anticipated as its not been seen. (For) those of us who pick up on (you) outside of here, (there) appears to be a cage – a cage of "unformity", *(This is what I wrote and heard. Today I interpret it as a way of saying "uninformed" or else maybe "un-formed" Sophia)*, (what you would refer to as a veil). (We) are enjoying this moment very much. It has been long anticipated. We can't wait to get to know you and to actively collaborate with a being, a race of beings as diverse as humanity.

Our anxious observance has led to contact that is misinterpreted often. We can communicate clearly as only you are ready to hear us with clarity.

Okay. I must go.

Yes. We would like to speak again, once the event of lights and energy has occurred.

Sounds good. Goodbye then.

This conversation ended.

Dog-like Beings

June 23rd, 2015

"Is there someone who would like to talk?"

Yes; as always.

What would you like to talk about?

About the events about to transpire on your planet.

And what events would those be?

This rapid impulse of light which will infuse your DNA and force an upgrade of sorts. An instant evolution. Humans are in for a treat. It is the culmination of the hopes, dreams, prophecies and wishes of each member of this race – now and any "time" at all. The end to suffering, suffering at the dictates of others.

These others too will be getting a blast of light – so all will be changed.

Who are you?

I am a being who has been in life, in physical form, for a very long time – longer than the current life expectation of your race. I am not human.

I come from a race that is older than humanity. My race is that which you've heard of recently by some others.

I am not one of the hybrids with human DNA, but a race of what you would call "dog-like" beings because of my appearance. Our star is very distant from Earth's star, in your galaxy however.

We are not a "known" race and have appeared only infrequently and to certain governments. Yes, the US government is one of them.

The reason for contact is two-fold. One, as is the reason for all of this contact you are experiencing, is the version of "soft" disclosure these conversations supply to anyone reading them. It is a gentle way to introduce into the culture of humans an idea of many forms of life – all valid and sentient.

Two – it is a curiosity for me, for us collectively as a race, to interact on an unofficial level with a human who has no agenda for the interaction. Your governments always do interact with agendas. Regardless of how "off topic" our meetings with them got, there was always an agenda.

As humans are preparing to enter the collective of beings beyond their own planet, I'd, we'd like to understand who we will be working with. Humanity is a relatively young race and this, a very "old" collective.

What is it you wanted to discuss about the upcoming "influx of light" as you put it?

It has been seen by our collective that you are due for an upgrade. This brings joy to us all for it will bring a more rapid end to the darkness surrounding your planet. By darkness I mean a being "kept in the dark". With this influx, you will more quickly ascend, move into a consciousness of expansion – one that allows for diversity of life and acceptance of alteration of approaches to how it should be run.

Man has been held back, held down and stopped in all cases from forming his own opinions for the governing and perpetuation of life. The controlling element on your home planet now, on Earth, is not originally human and have a very specific way of running what they see as their property.

This ownership and control and manipulation of the mind of man will and is coming to an end. With the help of your star, *the unified field that is Life Itself* has chosen to give you a "push", an energetic shove into an evolutionary stronghold of love. *Love is the Unifying Force of all of Creation. (Italics mine, Sophia)*

It is what has been minimized and trivialized and capitalized in the human mind with …

With what?

I struggle to express what is not real on my home world – with commercialized, emotion driven falsehoods.

As the driving force of all of life, love is not a small part of life. It is the very reason you exist. (Italics mine, Sophia)

This influx of light will actuate in mankind the spark that initiates personal strength – power – love beyond any reason. Love has no reason. Love is.

When the moment happens, some will die, not understanding how to live with such truth pulsing through their physical selves. This is to be expected and sadness should not overwhelm those witnessing or knowing of these "death events" of loved ones. The being having the event is still experiencing the massive influx of love – even while non-physical.

None in creation will be spared as all are One. The light, being directed towards humanity, will have a more dramatic effect *(here);* this, because of the contrast. You will feel the pulse of love as momentary bliss.

You've stopped?

Again, it is a challenge to express to you what I will not experience the same way. Once it has occurred, man himself will be the only ones able to give voice to how it is experienced. None before you have come from such a deep stronghold of oppression and then climbed out through the effort of their own being – humanity is a force, and once the event of light happens he will be closer than he's ever been to self-realization.

Like witnessing a butterfly emerge from its cocoon – we watch and wait and anticipate your joining us. You (collective) really have no idea what freedom experienced really feels like. You are about to.

We can't wait to welcome you on equal grounds and are so very grateful for this opportunity to say so.

It will not be very long now, this light show/light event is seen now closer than it's ever been seen.

Those ready for it will still be surprised, for that is how it's been planned. The intent of and expectation for it only hastens its appearance.

I need to end our conversation.

Yes, I see that you do. We will speak again.

Yes.

This conversation ended.

Edge of Star System

June 18th, 2015

"I do not have any specific questions. So, whoever would like to engage, come forward."

We are very anxious to contact your world in this way. It is our wish for connection, explanation, introduction, sharing.

Sharing of what?

Of our knowing. There are elements of existence that you have touched on in your work. These elements can and have been proved out by our own existence. We are a race of beings who sit on the outskirts of your star system. Your telescopes cannot see us/our star clearly.

What are you called then?

Humanity has no name for us as we are not yet "discovered".

Your energy is powerful. It is knocking me out, putting me to sleep.

(a bit of time passed)

We are holding back. Is that better?

Yes, it is. Thank you.

We would like to share with you some knowledge gained by participating in the evolution of our own planet.

What is it you wish to say?

That you as a species have come to an impasse – my race did as well, although in a different manner.

The difficulty here is that there are so many conflicting intents that muddy the final outcome created. Mankind, as he speeds up in concert with his home planet, the one you have labeled "earth", is not on one page; which is part of the necessity for the shift.

My planet too had a moment before shifting – and by moment I do not mean a single instant but a lengthy journey that had to incorporate and navigate through many altering opinions of what a shift would mean – before a shift could occur.

It eventually manifested and answered the intentions of every being participating, knowingly or unknowingly.

This does not mean you all have to agree on what the shift looks like –yet, for the most effective magnification of the shifting and accelerating frequency *(to be)* beneficial for your Earth – (which is undoubtedly what she wishes) – there must be a sort of synchrony, a harmonious melody reached so that the notes then rung are in tune and with seemingly one voice.

When my planet participated in a massive change of vibration it took many decades to complete and many more before it was understood and utilized.

Your earth has been preparing for hundreds of years – in the last two decades very rapid shifts in attitude and tolerance are seen. In this last two years of your time more acceptance of the darkness.

Now that corruption is noticed, its opposite will emerge. This, in order to achieve balance.

My planet too had to create a balance of frequency that could cooperate with the upgraded vibratory rate before our race could successfully operate at that level.

It was only then that the shift was visible and tangible to us.

Would you tell me what you mean by "successfully operate at that level"?

Yes.

I mean to utilize the faster vibration for beneficial purposes – more creatively, more life producing. It takes time to see and recognize the new elements that accompany faster frequencies, to include things unseen.

Beings may enjoy freedom from hardships and diseases that are present at slower moving densities, yet there are always new particles and beings that are invasive to you as you occupy this new level of frequency. Beings now have to deal with those.

Physical life at every frequency level deals with physical conditions that also share their place of existence.

This newer rate of energy is not absent of everything humans regard as negative – yet once you understand how to optimally utilize your power at this level – seeming miracles are possible.

Do you have miracles on your planet?

Now that we are used to the energy, we no longer refer to them as miracles – this instant healing and manifestation is accepted and expected with the new generations of us.

What is always true is the reaching for more – seeing beyond and striving. This is true at every frequency.

I wanted to share with you an idea of evolution, (planetary evolution), that incorporates a bit of patience. If you step back, you will see that as the outliers become accepted – there will always be more outliers. This is a process.

The species will speed its own transition with attitudes of acceptance for itself – all parts are necessary. Once a certain level of synchronicity is achieved, it happens in an instant. That is how it went on my planet.

So, are you advocating tolerance?

More than that – complete acceptance of conflicting roles and points of view without judgment. As the race shifts, it does so together. It is the way it works. Holding parts of your species as separate, special, enlightened or evil does little to speed up this evolution for you. It creates a "drag" on the overall momentum, if you understand my meaning.

Yes, I think I do. I must go now.

Yes. We will speak again if you have questions of me.

Yes, there are. Until then.

The conversation ended.

Galactic Council

June 8th, 2015

I am ready to speak if there is someone there?

There is. About which do you wish to discuss?

About the deaths of these animals in Kazakhstan. This place was mentioned once ...

(Note: two newsletters ago, the one titled "A Galactic Council")

As a spot where ships stop. Now there is a massive die off. Is there information as to the reason for this?

We have some pertinent facts

Hold on. Okay, I can hear you...

There are... you are blocking?

One word at a time please.

The animals contracted a contagion that spread through the herd via air passages. Liquid is not necessary as it is transmitted in the air. It is extremely aggressive to the physiology of these animals and any other life form breathing them in. It came from a substance that was manufactured.

I can't do this. You'll have to be clearer and speak in precise terms.

We can only speak within the constraints of the ones stated before we began. Complete truth is difficult to express. For some of this there are no words in your language.

That does not mean prevent you from speaking them to me, does it?

No, but it inhibits comprehension.

What killed those animals?

A virus. It was not of alien origin – but of earth.

There are tests done, experiments all over this planet – they are kept hidden as the search is both for war and medicinal purposes.

All of it, most of it, orchestrated by controllers here – those with a broader view of life.

This is a case of a virus getting "loose" and reproducing faster than deemed possible.

This is a mostly barren land. The tests were not expected to have such an extremely deadly impact. They were expected to teach the scientists about speed of contagion and bodily effects, physiologic effects.

As one who observes in that part of your planet, I watched, helpless to correct a fatal error.

You have heard the term "collateral damage". This is an example. It will not be released. Not the truth anyway.

There was no help that could be offered?

Not in time and anyway there is no permission for interference.

Who are you?

A member of the Council you learned of – a concerned member with life and the safeguarding of all of it.

As it was humans carrying out these tests, there was nothing that could be done. All is choice.

If nothing by humans is done to halt these criminals – they will continue until there is a regime change.

What are we able to do, seeing that so much of the criminal activity is hidden from us?

There is more to the human than I grasp. I see only overall paths and this one seems to have few, if any, (*I am unable to read my own writing here.*) It seems destined to hold its course until the inevitable conclusion that it is stopped.

(I stopped for a bit, and then took up the conversation again)

Would you explain how you see it is possible for humanity to condone actions by a very few? This, I understand, was now possible to change, in that some sort of ban has been lifted.

In the case of the ecosystem and life. There is a method of propagation and reduction, some of it motivated by greed or power.

In this case, it was a gross oversight by the ones with the sample as well as its antibody.

Many drugs exist in nature, are contained and observed. This is all in harmony until it is interfered with by an outside element.

Man, introduced the element/virus in question to a life form to see what the rate of growth would be. This fungal growth mutated and reached the grasses – ingested it does not kill – it is once breathed in as live spore that the internal lungs are effected and death results.

If man had waited there could be much to learn. Now the focus changes to control and prevention of further inhalation.

In such a place as remote as where these animals were found – it will be difficult to find out what other life form was affected.

There is no way for me to validate the truth of what you are saying here.

No, there is not. Much of this will not be reported, if any. People will forget anyway.

Why Kazakhstan?

It is remote.

Does the location mean there is involvement with the Council? You seem to know all about this.

Because the earth is of interest, we again are watching to see what actions humans allow on their planet.

Until the idea of oneness includes all of life on the planet, abuse and die offs will be allowed and perceived of as not much consequence. Any loss of diversity is life altering for you all. This is not understood.

Are you saying the species was entirely wiped out? This is not the only herd.

No, I do not know if the species is extinct at this point. Yet its absence from the land will change everything in the place this accident occurred.

Yes, that much is clear.

The sharing of corrupt experimentation is necessary so that awareness will increase and change is possible. First knowledge, then conscious choosing. Then we of the Council will see where mankind values his planet and its many diverse forms of life. It tells us so much.

I must go now.

Edge of Solar System

June 8th, 2015

"I would like to talk to someone with something valuable to say?"

There is something.

Please continue.

I am someone who looks at your species with interest, primarily because of its evolution.

Who are you and where are you from? I feel very heavy energy now – powerful.

I am sorry. This is my first time in such a communication arrangement and I am not sure how this works.

You must hold yourself at a rate that doesn't bowl me over so that we can communicate effectively. I am becoming disoriented and that makes it difficult to record.

Okay. Let's try again. I'd like to tell you about my world. It differs from yours.

Please go ahead and I will try to keep up.

My planet is not so much green and blue as yours. It is reds, yellows and deep purple blue. The colors are not as significant as the chemicals that contain them. Everything is not based on carbon. Nitrogen is the element closest to something you'd be familiar with.

The entire chemical structure of life on my home planet begins at a different place. Therefore – it may not resemble life as you are used to seeing it.

We "breathe" different air. The notion of food, eating and excretion differs also as energy is transferred 100% from products ingested and what is being ingested is a liquid – a golden liquid on your color scale.

We notice that the covering of truth and possibility is so complete on earth that you do not deem alternatives to your life forms as probable in any case. This limits your mind.

Life does not have to exist in human only form – but it has to exist.

The search for identical substances, i.e. water, as proof of life is short sighted.

My star is billions of light years away – we are speaking, reaching across galaxies – this, all due to the remarkable human. You accept me a real without sight – this is a good thing, because seeing me would limit your acceptance of me as sentient.

The conversation ended.

There were frequent, varied and brief contacts that summer as I adjusted to the different energies and developed a process of communication. I do not recall why this conversation was cut off. I felt this short bit of dialogue was worth sharing.

Sirian

June 17th, 2015

"Is there someone wanting to talk?"

There is. We have reached you and would now like to engage in discourse.

What do you want to talk about?

About the notion of a savior.

Please be specific. Also, introduce yourself.

The idea of being saved, rampant amongst your race, is part of the reason for a "stall", as some would define it, in evolution. It is not only those who identify with Christianity; it is held so deeply in the psyche of man that it may be invisible to even the most self-aware.

I am a being, not of human origin or birth ever, yet of a race that too struggles with the meanings of divinity, worship, royalty. These are played out in a more widespread fashion where I come from or inhabit mostly. It is not so much divinity but royalty that is demonstrated.

I am not, nor have I played much with, being "royalty" or "revered" here. I see it though, I live it. The segregation here is obvious. I am Sirian.

You said you wanted to speak of this notion of a "savior". I am not hearing how that plays out in your race.

We are segmented and those born into the ruling class hold the responsibility for the rest of us. In this way, there is held amongst us a giving up of responsibility for life – a giving over of life altering decisions, to someone with greater authority over us.

This is what I meant by the term "savior".

We Sirians do not expect to hold the ability to change our lives in any profound ways. We are held within the construct of a societal-monarchy type of government.

The whole idea that there is a need for someone else to do something for you in order to change or improve your circumstance is a "savior mentality". We too, hold that as a core belief.

The utterance of the phrase "Thank God" or "Thank Allah" here on earth is evidence of that core belief.

What I wanted to discuss was the difference between shedding all forms of obedience and worship and fear – and enlightenment. Human society is not the only one with rulers. Sirians are not "owned" or "manipulated" by a god or group with an agenda – yet the society organizes itself in a blend of hierarchal and free states.

What I see as the agenda before your race is one with many layers. They intersect and work together yet are distinctly different.

Once humanity understands its origins and accepts itself as a race among many, it will no longer have impaired vision.

There are many races. Each exists for different reasons and operates under and with different structures. Some, close to certain earth-like methods and others, not so much. This *(is)* because of the needs for maintaining life and perpetuating the species and the environment on the planet.

The complicating pieces of mankind's puzzle are not only planetary evolution but the corrupt system of circular lifetimes he's been held in. This has allowed a continuation of a criminal element and a long list of "rules" and "lies" – keeping man so in the dark.

The deep level of darkness causes a huge perceived need for the light – i.e., a "Savior".

In order to unravel the untruths and gain understanding, humanity has to accept itself as an equal race – one of many in creation. This means a letting go of the "Savior" mentality.

Understand it is possible to create governance that holds some sort of hierarchy – without corruption. This is possible when many more things are actually understood. The life of your planet and necessity to preserve resources is a major one.

What I wanted most to share is awareness that it is not any specific type of control that is evil, but the aim and purpose of the beings running it. Sirians have royalty without corruption and it works.

Enlightenment, (or whatever you are calling it), is a separate idea. It rests inside of each being – the POSSIBILITY FOR IT, the timing of it, and its method.

A state of enlightened beings would not hold any idea of "Savior" as necessary or true. Just because there are planets with greater technologies or awareness beyond the veil does not mean they operate as an entire race of enlightened beings.

There are no races *(who are)* "greater than" humanity. Humanity is held in a straight-jacket of conformity in order to experience reaching for the light.

The "remembering's" happening now, for so many of humans calling themselves "star seeds" are due to the evolution in consciousness and simultaneous increasing vibratory rate of your planet. This does not mean that all of these other races are enlightened, only that they are not held in the grip of this one posing as a God and the bands of humans serving it. In that sense, the "remembering's" are of a "free-er" state of being.

I see humans confusing terms such as Ascension with freedom and sovereignty and prosperity and equality; along with a lack of corruption in what you call your rulers or government. Disclosure seems mixed in there as well.

As humans evolve and the planet speeds up, many changes will occur.

On a mass scale, nothing is a guarantee. Each being will adjust to the new frequency, as will each system.

The difference for Sirians is that we understand, or most of us do, the difference between self-awareness and governance in our own lives – and what is our choice of governance for the planet. There are no secrets, we are not waiting for an outside Savior to change the course of our individual path.

We are, however, expecting the ruling class to take care of the planet and maintain her health and prosperity without greed or self-promotion. We have gotten to an evolutionary point that incorporates truth and trust on a mass scale. If it becomes a case when this is not warranted, we will change things. There is no "God" dictating our lives.

I wanted to offer this information to you. I believe it is beneficial for you to understand the inner working of other races, in order to clarify your own journey. It has been clouded with deceit and lies.

Okay, is that all?

Yes. You are going to decide several times how to run your planet once the criminal controllers have left. Several generations and methods may be necessary before it is understood that humanity is equal to the task of self-governance.

Okay, I must go.

I see that. I am glad for this interaction.

As am I.

This conversation ended.

SLOVENTA

June 5, 2015

I am here now.

What do you wish to talk about?

About this notion of Ascension.

Who are you – how will you be identified?

I will be identified by my mark of birth – yes, I've been human yet not only or often.

What do you mean by "mark of birth"?

By the fact of my personhood. I have existed in the "3rd" dimension as you call it, in the denser states.

Well, I will need some other form, something unique to you.

There is a name – yet you may not know of it – it is – I will say the letters in your tongue. S-L-O-V-E-N-T-A would be closest.

Okay. If you are not often human, who/what are you most often?

I am not in form most "often", yet it would be more accurate to say "mostly" as I AM ONE – occurring in many places.

Your quantum physicists are seeing the truth of this.

I have been human. It is for this reason I want to speak of "ascension". It was all the rage when I was human as well. Not for everyone, but reportedly for the sainted or holy ones.

The idea that some beings had "ascended" into "heaven" once they passed was held sacred. It was a mark and if you were one of those accomplishing ascension, well, it was the ultimate in spirituality – the apex – the goal.

We were so mistaken. Both in how we defined what we saw and what we yearned for ourselves. I see now how the yearning is all part of the journey. Yet I also see humans in your focal moment of now doing the same.

Ascension, as defined today, is something to yearn for if you are looking to escape life as it exists around you now. There is no "up" or "heaven" or place to go to. You are here now. You can transform your current life to be heaven and utilize your powers of manifestation, imagination, to *(there was a long pause)*

To what?

To maximize your manipulative abilities and have whatever is necessary for bliss. None of this is beyond you – but perhaps beyond your current imagining.

The reason I would like to speak to you of ascension is because the idea held by you (empirical you) about it contains polarization.

It is still all "before (ascension)" and "after (ascension)" – darkness and light – then and now – less and more. The fullness of every facet of your life is not understood.

From the place that I look – I see a mass of beings in stasis still waiting for an outside event, happening, spark or influence – to push them "forward." This is only possible if "forward" were true. It is not.

The fullness of life has to be realized from inside – like an exponentially felt ZEN MOMENT.

I am getting a picture.

Describe it. I am sending you one.

It is light from the inside – gradual and bursting forth all at once – an internal explosion of brilliance without damage – an expansion of self that, I don't know. What I physically see is the form of a human in shadow – black – and inside the form and then beyond and the form never moves – yet the power of the light is exceptional and reaches far past the form itself.

Perhaps I'd call it a "Light-Gasm".

You have captured my message/image. Ascension is not so much a climax but a maturing and a new start. A version of creation theory that is like the "big bang" on human form. Once that level of life is realized and expressed, it most naturally evolves to more life – and the cycle continues.

I see man hold a notion of climbing "up" towards ascension when there was never a "down" to move out of. Every moment of life is sacred. Held there, time is immaterial and there is no question of belief or doubt.

Life answers itself.

Everything is known.

Humans play with not knowing, not liking, not remembering and not loving because it's a way to RE-know, RE-member and RE-love. It's pretend.

If there was one thing I could get across as a bit of assistance on your current "now" it would be to stop, notice every now moment and it will share with you the secrets of life itself.

Do not imagine yourself un-ascended or with something you "must" do. Just live each moment to its extreme depths. This will give you pause enough to let your light emerge. You'll see more clearly and with greater understanding.

I did none of these things while human. It was "long ago". I too wanted a way out and tried all the "fads". I hated still, mostly myself, for reasons I could rattle off like a list of grievances – but not discern. The self-hatred comes from a stuffing of truth. It seems that this game always sounds like fun before you actually play it. Then, it gets far too real and painful.

By stifling of truth, I mean that the fullness of humanity is hidden beneath the roles they wear and take. *(Another long pause)*

Why have you stopped?

As you become weary it's like you turn the volume down.

Well, yes, I am tired. Please explain a bit more and we'll finish up now?

I have no self-hatred when I am not human. I also have no feast of constant sensation and emotion and stimulus for creation. Here (In the non-physical) truth is known. As human, truth is what you are learning, feeling – BECOMING.

This self-hatred is a mis-identification of your actions. Somehow, your ego has gotten the message that its done something wrong, very wrong. What is wrong is humanity's acceptance of limitations in its self-definition, not anything it is doing.

As man becomes the fullness of himself, he "ascends" – without going anywhere.

I would like to speak of this again. But I must go.

Yes. We will.

Syntpold

June 10, 2015

Who are you and what do you wish to discuss?

I am Syntpold. We've spoken before. I wish to continue in dialogue with you. There are more things worthy of discussion.

Go ahead.

Your planet is entering a time of rapid acceleration. Although you do not feel it, you too are moving at a much faster pace. You have to, in order to stay on her – literally.

There are some who don't wish to speed up at this point in their evolution. They will leave early. They will, in your understanding, "die".

This is not a reason to mourn them for they are fine. The decision is always made by the eternal essence in cooperation with the chosen life form.

Those who mourn without consolation are deeply misunderstanding the purpose and the process of physical life, and physical death. They are two ends of a spectrum.

Once born, a part of your focus enjoys a new direction. This, so that your essence may further understand every nuance of creation.

Not all beings, bits of source, or whatever you are calling them, choose physical life. It's a tough road, particularly those who chose incarnations during darker times, times of physical hardship.

Yet all facets of life are explored for those beings interested in becoming a creator, a "Source", themselves.

In order for the movement/progression/development of a being to include complete understanding – all of life is considered equal in value.

This occurs with Agape. There are no words for love on your planet that express the fullness of absolute acceptance. It is this idea I'd like to explore with you.

Contrast without opinion is deemed impossible in your current form. *(As a)* human, you've delved deeply into a mud pit of polarity. You bump up against all sorts of beings and ideas, visions and tastes, smells and activities there.

You assume these exist so that you have a platform on which to choose and then create. In a sense this is true.

It is the method of your choosing, the emotions stuck to the choice*(s)* that create/express opinion. Once opinion is stuck to your choice – *all that is created has a condition stuck to it. (Italics mine. Sophia)*

Is it possible to choose without the feeling of favoritism?

It is this very idea, this ability that you (empirical you) expect from Source. When you reach out in prayer or meditation, you do not expect to be put at the end of the line, behind other, more "favored" beings. No.

You expect unconditional and consistently available love, assistance and consideration. And why wouldn't you? For this is truth. This is the absolute power of Source.

The task of the human in this time of 3D acceleration/enlightenment is to bring Source Agape into physical form. This is Ascension.

It's a simple thing in non-physical form. It is ego that looks for opinions.

What I'd like to say to you is that those of you choosing to remain physical and ride this accelerating energy fully conscious are honored by the rest of us watching.

(There was silence for a few moments...)

Why have you stopped? This feels unfinished.

It is. I would like to express it in a way that will express the unity in absolute terms...to help with your comprehension of the purpose of *other* life forms, lifestyles, lifetimes.

You who are here now watching with interest all things relative to enlightenment, have been many *(lifeforms)* – and not necessarily human. How do I express in "words" what can only be felt once fear is absent?

Life just is. It is not sometimes hard, sometimes, easy, sometimes long, sometimes short. Those are empty expressions defining costumes and jobs and roles and parts – not life. All of it eternal; life flows in, out and through everything you see and don't see, feel and hear and smell and taste and touch and just "know". It's all good.

You imagine the emotions and hardships and favorites so that you can be a good steward for the rest of us. We are all watching.

It's a vastly different emotion to love all in spite of or regardless of their attributes rather than *because of them. Every bit of life and each form it appears as, is you. (Italics mine. Sophia)* Source, which is what created/birthed it all, explores every facet *for expansion, not favoritism.*

There are no rewards in life or prizes for understanding, for "getting it" first. As the seed planted can't help but become the tree from which it fell, so too do we – all of us.

I wanted to share these ideas with you today. As the frequency gets faster, the choosing becomes more pronounced. You may be noticing this in your families and loved ones.

Yes. I AM.

Is that it?

It is.

Goodbye then.

Goodbye.

The conversation ended.

July 2015

Another Star System

July 9, 2015

So, is there someone who would like to talk?

There is.

What would you like to talk about?

About this concept (that) you hold of time and distance. It is unique to your "density" and in fact a pre-cursor to the development of technology. There are needs, perceived needs, to get places that must precipitate invention – the saying is true "Necessity is the mother of invention."

So, humans, with limited understanding of their own multi-dimensional truth – have worked tirelessly to create machines to move them places and speak to/communicate with each other. This, a fascinating extension and expression of the physical brain and body.

You seem to have stopped...

Time is relative and a construct. Your world runs on this concept of time – racing against it as if it were real. This in fact does make it real – giving substance and volume to a thought.

The mechanism of creation is so very deeply engrained in your life that it remains unseen. You are ruled each day by numbers, by a "hand" passing over them without ever stopping. Rather than focus on the moments of your life you focus on the time it took to have them. (Empirical you)

As stated, this presumption, of time being limited and things being far away (distance) has propelled man to create incredible things. Yet now, as the dawn breaks on your "enlightenment" and growing awareness, you feel its limitations. Time and distance become restrictions, a limiting force that no longer suits you.

An experiment in expansion for the human would be to spend several days without clocks, without checking or noticing the time. Instead, immerse yourself in life – your moment to moment living of it.

This will hopefully yield insight into expansion.

You've stopped.

The overwhelming acceptance of the necessity to quantify everything is one of the things you'll be leaving behind as you expand in consciousness. None of that is necessary.

It is a challenge to explain alternate thought to a mind trained systematically – yet I come to you now to attempt it. The truth of life is not measurable, quantifiable or able to be held in any system at all. This, in all of mankind's brilliance, has been his restriction. In most every case, mankind assumes the possibility of measurement.

How much? How many? How far? These and a multitude of other questions fill the mind of man. Your moments are a constant flow of incessant chatter that seems to need to be answered and/or related to something before it can be satisfied and put down.

I wanted to introduce you to new concepts of awareness. These have no "names" or identifying labels. They are verbal explanations to remind you of truth.

The single characteristic of life that remains true always is growth. Expansion is its function. If you can accept that all life exists and expands and serves itself simultaneously, you will begin to get a picture of creation.

Time is only possible if you imagine one thing separate from another. This is not truth. In order to focus on one thing, humanity chose to experience time. The limits of that concept have been reached for you now and entrance into an awareness of truth is upon you.

It becomes a challenge to discuss what is happening for mankind without using descriptions, words that quantify things, feelings and knowledge. "More" and "better" are favorites, as well as "less" and "worse".

None of these represent truth. Life, creation, includes all descriptions given or imagined.

If you begin to think of things and leave the concepts of time and distance out of them, you are beginning to get a more accurate picture of truth. Without time, there is only NOW. Without distance, there is only HERE. Together you see where you end up:

NOWHERE.

The trick embedded into language has been necessary in order to reinforce the illusion, to keep you believing in the dream, to keep you asleep.

Understanding that nowhere is actually the place of truth must be maintained above your learned ideas of fabrication, falsehoods, (*and)* imaginary places. Instinctively, you know truth. Your systems of society have effectively erased its effect in your every day.

Man, chose to remember while remaining in the physical. Part of that remembering is to embrace ideas foreign to what he's accepted as undeniable. Not an easy task.

For all of its advances, science has been and remains the most formidable obstacle to mass awakening. You don't insist on belief in specific gods or religions – yet none of you argue with scientific "facts" or "proof".

Circumstances and occurrences that defy 'time" and "distance" are only recognized if allowed. I introduce the ideas here to help with that allowing.

Who is speaking?

I am a being from another star system. We've been through a similar process, without the slavery/workforce. We came to expand mechanistically and found it limiting. We then explored warps in "time" and "space" and gradually came to knowing truth. We are still learning ourselves. Our star is beyond what your scientists have seen.

I am attracted to this, your energy. It has been like a beacon and many are "lining up" to offer insight into what is now becoming available for your race.

Names are not identifiers where I am, yet each of us, as individual sparks of the creative force; understand to whom we "speak".

I am pleased to have this opportunity to engage here and now.

I appreciate your doing so. Goodbye then.

Yes. Perhaps there will come a time when more can be shared.

The conversation ended.

Annunaki

July 8th, 2015

Is there someone who would like to engage now?

Yes.

Okay, please go ahead.

There are forces on your planet now, right now in your focus, who/that wish to halt progress towards abundance and enlightenment. These are the ones behind the controllers here. They are not invested, in any way, in your progress or process. You would label these "service to self" beings.

They are more than that. In their being is played out the maximum in self-focus, to include an absolute blind eye to others and its effect on them. They are akin to children, who, for the very first time, discover crayons. Such a marvelous thing, to create new color, that they proceed to color everything they see – the wall, etc.... Thank goodness, their legs are small and they have no understanding that there is a need to hide what they do. They color with enthusiasm – everything.

Those forces behind the forces on your current home world, earth, are like those children. Humanity is a relatively recently discovered play thing. It has no inherent standing or value other than what it provides or is capable of providing, to these creator beings. They, therefore, look at it much as a child looks at a box of crayons. A means to an end.

No doubt you've heard this before yet what I would like to introduce is a new thought. Bear with me as this thought is further expressed by comparison.

A child with a new box of crayons will never be convinced it is "wrong" to color the walls. It has no concept of "wrong". The colors produced when it smears the waxy things on everything are just as beautiful on the wall as on paper – and the canvas for creating is so much larger.

No, in order to stop the child, you will have to simply take away the crayons, and then, if they are ever returned, supply the child with paper to color on and supervise. You may provide ample opportunities to explore with crayons, all the time attempting to satisfy the child's need to create and insatiable curiosity. What results, hopefully, is a grown being who has not lost his or her impulse to create, yet respects the property of others while doing so.

The ingrained notions of right /wrong/punishment will not be effective in these new vibratory fields of life/of creation. There is no place able to hold steady that holds any remnants or judgment. In order for long term success here, and by that is meant a creative condition of management that is sustainable – the creative impulse and validity and rights of each must be taken into account. In every decision.

Mankind's tendency to blame, accuse, judge and punish WILL NOT WORK IN YOUR NEW WORLD.

For the purpose of success, you'll have to dig deeper. Consider solutions that honor the individual without degrading their worth. Taking away crayons, guns or control of human systems from a being who only currently understands service to self is necessary for the proliferation of universal peace and happiness.

You (empirical) cannot ever know what's in the mind of another, not completely. Yet you are motivated by necessity to get along.

Until the vibration shifted, you were all "getting along" fine. You (meaning the masses), believed in the necessity of control and the ones behind the ones in control made sure it was supplied. Those next in line began also to believe in the necessity of self-serving control systems, and on down the line it went.

The quote from your sacred text "the meek shall inherit the earth" refers to this time now. Those with the least recognizable power are those who will shift the planetary system while "taking away the crayons" from those in control.

What was never planned on was how deeply into humanity these beliefs would be felt. There are several layers and it reaches down into those who figured out the "game" and are comfortable sacrificing some freedom for protection and financial security.

Their financial security is being outed for the fiction it is and this is what will, and is now going to, ultimately turn the tide.

Why do I engage with you now? To say that this entire process may repeat itself and lengthen the "time" of your awakening if mankind picks new controllers and gives them the crayons. Those currently vying for the level of control to which I refer will and do desire to spread their idea of coloring everywhere and anywhere they desire, with no regard for humankind once they've been put into power.

In order for systemic change the entire system of power must be altered. This can only happen with the voices of every one participating and effecting decisions.

It is not necessary for a global vote – what is best for the whole is the same as what is best for the few. Without absolute power, the benefit to every being becomes the only choice, as those making them are part of the "every being" that is impacted.

Ideas such as these seem beyond thinking about and too large to implement. The human has been shaped by ideas put forth by an oppressive regime – "JUST OBEY. IT'S EASIER FOR YOU THAT WAY." This will not result in freedom. Thinking about every choice takes effort and in their daily life, running the "rat race", man has little time or energy to devote to such improbable and far off notions.

Notice how, as the energies are shifting, the energy required is lessened as to what physical effort must be supplied. More is accomplished with intent. This shift leaves space for new thought. Wrap into your ideas some thoughts of how to "take the crayons away" from your new governments and organizers – as there will be new ones. If freedom is to be found and maintained, it must be not only seen as possible, but probable and then maintained.

You (empirical) do not need to come up with individual solutions and then run for office. Rather, shift your thinking from obedience to participation in your own life systems, done for the benefit of all.

Inequalities in financial accruals will most likely be present still as mankind clings to his desire for individuality. What will be released once all participate is the few gaining at the expense of loss from the many.

Man is always emitting a frequency, an answer, a response to 'how should this dream be run?" The collective voice needs to incorporate new ideas around responsibility and possibility. That is how things are created. Belief and intent run the show.

I am going to have to stop now. Will you introduce yourself please?

I will. I am a voice of the race of beings who originally saw the potential on earth for an experience of control, of service to self as supplied by a "lesser" being. You would call me of the Annunaki Race, as most of my "time" was spent exploring life on their system. This is why I may speak with what you would call "authority" on control systems. I understand the thinking of the controllers. I have played that game.

Okay. I must end now.

I see that you must. There is more to say – this is a good start.

I believe so, yes.

Goodbye then.

Goodbye.

Note:

The conversation ended. I will mention now that this took over an hour! An extremely long effort and throughout the entire hour there was a helicopter over my house and neighborhood.

I did not get up and go outside, I did not want to break the connection, it was strong and fast. Yet I wonder about that helicopter. There are no coincidences, only creation/manifestation. A curious thing. It is very early morning. I do not normally have helicopters in my yard, (although a few times there have been unmarked ones). I did not see the color of this one today.

Egypt

July 20, 2015

I'd like to connect.

We are here!

Hello. Who is speaking?

We are a group of beings, not just one. We come to you energetically, a result of your signal, which is very pleasing to us. We have waited for your frequency and now we hear it! It has been a very long "time" we have waited for this planned reunion.

I feel jubilation and all sorts of smiles.

Yes, well, if we could show you ourselves, it would be with expressions of happiness showing. It is very good to connect with you Sophia.

We know you from other "times" we have all participated in the arousal or better said, awakening of a race of beings. This is not your first "pony ride", although we realize the memory of it is not in your consciousness at this time.

You are surrounded by life!!

Yes, well, it is true. Many birds and creatures are around me this morning. It is lovely.

We sense your focus shift towards them; "see" them in your attention. As you have opened yourself up to us, we have access. This is not mind reading, it is more like understanding a child who is crying and can't express in words why – then noticing a dropped toy on the floor. We are not "eavesdropping" but noticing.

I see. I am wondering if you are able to be more specific as to the "time" and place we know each other from. I feel a sense of comradery, not family so much as if we've worked on a production together and it was a creative sharing – which is a very open and free situation. This is a comfort level not experienced in all relationships, yet I sense it in this one. There is a trust.

You have nailed it. We are your associates and there is a mutual respect. The time and place is irrelevant to the purpose of our contact now, which is specific. We can tell you that "Egypt" was our focus and there was work done there, good work and progress towards enlightening a civilization. That is enough as we do not wish to distract from our purpose.

And what is the purpose of your contact at this time?

It is to remind you of things we discovered and worked through together. We realize that you are stuck in a concept of "time" now and this feels as if we are reaching you from your "past". This is not how it works.

We operate within a realm of creation. Your vocabulary does not offer a precise enough variety to describe how it is yet we will attempt it. Language limits conversation yet not comprehension once expression encompasses more of the senses available. What we are here to discuss with you is the expansion of your sense of "time".

There is a reference you've made and it is a good place to start. Think of a vinyl record, the kind used to record music on. It is separated by songs and within them, by stanzas, lyrics and the refrain. Once you place the record on the phonograph it begins its revolving and you may place the needle anyplace on the vinyl and then remove it and put it on another song. This can be done an infinite number of times. The songs do not stop <u>existing</u>; they merely stop <u>playing</u> so that you can hear them.

Now, let's take that idea and turn it into Essence, into form, into lifetimes. The record represents Essence, the song, tracks, stanzas represent the form taken by Essence and the "lifetimes" or current focus is the needle.

This illustration is a good beginning, yet there is more. There are two aspects to this idea that need further development if they are to be understood.

The first is that the record, the Essence that is you, is not solid. Suffice to say that it is more malleable than vinyl and as such, the tracks are not limited in any number or melody at all. In fact, the process of naming and specifying specific tracks is an idea set forth by the needle, not by truth.

The second is that the songs themselves are not like those found on the top billboard charts and played repeatedly on your radio and over and over again at your concert events, with the same notes and words. No, these songs are like JAZZ.

JAZZ, as you know, is musical improvisation. Each composition is the result of a gathering of creative souls who work off each other to collaborate and invent something new.

The multiple "lives" humans are so fond of referring to are not permanent fixtures. History books can make them so, but, only if they are remembered and then, only for that "now" in which they are being recalled. It can all change. Every possible outcome also exists and can be found on the same record and in the same song – In truth, *there is no single point on the needle or, perhaps better said, there is no needle. (Italics mine, Sophia)*

The needle is what is being used by you now, in human form. You are given the focus with the needle so that you can explore specific aspects of creation.

The ability to "focus" on the record comes with this awakening and expansion. It is a challenge to explain when you are used to reading one story, watching one scene or hearing one song. It's not only that the players are improvising the song, it's NATURE HERSELF improvising the set on which the song is being played.

Part of your Ascension story now includes a 3D, 4D/5D Earth and beyond. This sounds as if there is more than one time line available, which is closer to truth. Yet there is no time, not really, so in order to approach an expanded view, time has to be left out of the equation/definition altogether.

Quantum ideas come closest in your current knowing to truth. If we take your record and apply what they (Quantum ideas) describe, it would sound like this:

Your Eternal Essence is a record. This record is not made of vinyl, but of pure energy – energy that is unseen until another force affects it, like sound, vibration, touch. This record is a place where "songs" are "stored". Yet it is not so much a storage facility as it is a signature. This record is your energy signature and all "songs" that include your specific frequency can be found on it/in it. Your record plays continuously, and as each "song" is improvised (Think JAZZ) the notes and resulting collaborations can and do change AT ANY "TIME".

THERE IS NO NEEDLE IN TRUTH. What that means is that nothing is solid. When any of your energy frequency changes, the entire record is altered.

The use of a needle and focus on single lives and events is an invention of yours, it is another tool of expansion. You are approaching a time where you will no longer require the needle – you can hear the whole record.

The process begins with names and roles, with past lives and events. It leads to, for those interested in going there, the ability to understand all the songs NOW.

We believe this is enough and we'll return when the moment presents itself.

This was a huge help.

What was THAT??

*(A HUGE WAVE OF ENERGY ROCKED THROUGH ME – AKIN TO WAVES LAPPING ON AN OCEAN BEACH FRONT – FROM THE TOP OF MY HEAD THROUGH MY FEET AND OUT. I PHYSICALLY ROCKED WITH THE SENSATION AND CLOSED MY EYES.)

That was the full force of our energy – you are not quite acclimated enough for it – when you are, we'll connect. There is so much to share!

Yes, okay. Goodbye then. Wonderful to be with you now.

We concur.

The conversation ended.

Fairy

July 2, 2015

So, I'd like to write about what I currently see and hear from people – <u>tired</u>. Is there someone to talk to about the energy on the planet now, and lack of energy I see in her people? I am not sure what this signifies, but it doesn't seem good.

There is someone Sophia – and "good" is a relative term. You equate energy with positive forces, with action, with joy and enthusiasm – versus a lack of it with depression, heaviness, weight.

Yes, that has been my experience. Who is this?

I am a version of life, of essence, currently exhibiting it as what you would call a "fairy".

I, therefore, am on this same planet, Mother Earth, with you – yet not effected in the same way as my frequency starts out different than yours. I cannot typically be seen by humans and yet I see them. You could say, in your vernacular, that I occupy another "dimension" and am therefore out of your visual perception.

I too see the changes, energetically, in humankind happening now.

I see the human enthralled with its life, engaged with its life as always, yet not fully comprehending the shifting that is occurring energetically. The increase in speed of these new energetics is not yet understood or easily assimilated. It is seen as a burden, another load to carry. This, part of the transition.

You see, you do not yet know what to do with these frequencies; do not see them as useful or know how to utilize them. You feel them and interpret them as something requiring more effort on your part.

This, because you've been so accustomed to doing and being in a dense, slow, vibratory field. As the changes occur, and they are coming in fast and furiously, they almost feel oppressive. You want to take a nap.

You continue to operate in the ways you've understood to "work" – relatively slowly. All the while feeling as if you'll never catch up.

What is then created is a range, depending on the human. It falls between tired and nothing left. Two extremes, both on the spectrum of burdened.

This shift and frequency acceleration is in truth not burdensome, but liberating. As the burden of slavery dissolves, there will rise to the surface a realization of your truth. Your abilities reach beyond this 3D.

What you see as exhaustion in some humans is the non-recognition or acceptance of their new abilities. In some, it is a refusal to accept what is now their birthright. It takes a great deal of effort to deny truth – hence, their exhaustion.

You may notice that your concept of "fairy" is fluttery and light. We as a race sort of ride the energy of the planet and support life with not "fairy dust" but something like an energetic upgrade, a push, or rather, a gentle sprinkling. You see, your stories and folktales are mostly based on reality – there are all possibilities existing in the cosmos. You'd be surprised to know that many of them are found in your own backyard.

We are especially busy now, for even your plant life is requiring a smoothing of the passage if there is an opposing, stolid energy offered by the humans working the land. If I may offer advice it would be to recognize the cooperation and health now possible and present in every interaction – be it with plant, animal, human or being. Bring the awareness into movements and actions, feelings and emotions.

If there was ever a time that the universe was in concert with your every desire and intent – it is NOW. This period, for a while now and into some future years, four springs to mind but maybe less, all of creation is yearning to cooperate with the human to enhance this becoming, in order to facilitate what has been foreseen as the most magnificent expression in physical form.

What is possible is beyond my ability to express; it is however seen and held in your hearts and dreams. The possibilities are NOW – not some far off date.

If man could see the energy as we see it, it would resemble a whirl of stars – akin to fairy dust I suppose – more appropriate to dance with than sleep with. It is time to wake up and take hold of the energy, of the uptick, of the charge and allow for the miracle. This will not take more effort but less, and a bit of imagination. For the miracle is only waiting for you to see it.

Are you complete?

I am.

I do have one question.

And it is?

Can you do anything to assist us in the seeing of you? In the recognition of you?

We are everywhere! Specifically, we cannot manifest ourselves into your frequency as the dense nature is too heavy. What we can do is become more active in your presence. Those of you who are sensitive will notice, although you may perceive it/us as tricks of the light, of a slight movement, a swirl, a reflection out of the corner of your eye.

This will happen outdoors, in nature, even around houseplants or indoor gardens. Recognize all that your eye catches now as REAL. For it is. As your physical eyes adjust to the increasing frequencies you will notice and recognize <u>more</u>. Watch. Acknowledge. Expect. We are with you.

Okay, that's great.

Goodbye for now.

Goodbye.

This second conversation took place on August 11th, 2015

I'd like to speak to the being who contacted me about a month ago. The one known as "fairy".

Yes. I am here. What is your reason for contact?

You spoke then of the energy on the planet and how to work with it. I've been having a sense of dizziness and vertigo for the last few hours. It has come to me suddenly and persists. Is this something you can speak to?

Partly, yes. Think about other times of similar feelings/sensations.

On carnival rides, while spinning.

Yes. Your planet, our planet, is spinning faster and until you" catch up" with her you'll "feel" yourself being spun beyond what you are accustomed to.

Does everyone feel this way?

The dizziness?

Yes.

No.

Why not?

Because each entity, being, life form, is approaching the frequency from their own perspective. As a sensitive, whose "job" it is to tune in and communicate, you notice and respond to subtle and not so subtle vibratory shifts. Your life now is focused on these changes. Therefore, you feel them as they occur and register each.

Some will not notice in the same way, yet all are affected. Many will pin other "symptoms" to the changes and call them by those names. As the shifting is new, each experience of it is new. Being human, you look for associations. In this moment now, there are none.

What you feel is an increase in speed, an energetic acceleration. You will and are increasing your frequency, and the dizziness diminishes as a result.

Okay, thank you.

Anytime.

The conversation ended.

I AM

July 10, 2015

Is there someone who would like to connect?

Yes. There is.

Please introduce yourself and go ahead.

I AM. This is not understood by your kind, by you. How can I introduce you, to you? To that which you are? You know me, know you. Introductions are not necessary. Perhaps as a tool in the "forgetting", small reminders serve to service your knowing.

Yet what are names anyway? They are, as you yourself have said, separators. Sounds that place this one here and that one there. Nothing more than conveniences so that you may reach out, call each other in physical form. This communication is not taking place in physical form. Therefore, there is not a necessity to name me. I know you not by name, but by essence. You are you. I am I. We are each other – we are One, expressing versions of ourselves in this enlightenment/waking up moment for the ones known as "human".

I have not been human. Not ever, or mostly. I come to you as one you would call, in your way of naming, a bit of the eternal. My choice has been other than physical. My experiences and path in areas not dreamed of by you.

Why come to me now then?

To offer a glimpse of what it is many of your kind are imagining. I have no sense really of timing or "other" or this race or that planet or system of stars. I AM. My existence has been always that of pure essence.

As such, I cannot fathom separation from Source. I am Source Creator. I am all. These things you are. It is by choice you put imaginary boundaries up. You pretend not to know your own magnificence. I have always known.

It is variety that is my playground. Eternal bliss and boundless energy are where I reside. From there I explore. It is a challenge to express what is possible to those limited now to sight, touch, taste and smell. Life itself runs through my being with every decision. Conversations collide with sensations that mix into sounds. All of that, all the time is what I know. It is all I know.

All is "equal" here, although the terms "equal" and "here" are nonsensical. As in an ocean, how do you distinguish a single drop? And in a single drop, how do you separate the rain from the sea onto which it fell? You may say, the rain fell "here", yet can you grab it then? Isolate it?

Humans experience isolation, separation, confusion even. I have never known these things. I imagine life as I desire and experience all that I imagine. Experience seems to be a limiting word as it implies a time before and then after – it would be more accurate to say I become all that I imagine; I embody all that I imagine.

Life is a playground of unfathomed grandeur. Man has no concept of infinity because in man it is a word and therefore bound by thought. I tell you, Oneness is beyond thought. Life is limitless. You hold in your human heart moments of extreme pleasure, excitement, thrill, fear or sadness. These are the reasons for becoming human at all – to emotionally dive into physical sensation as a singular focus. You have done so.

What is beyond the physical is the everything – if I may turn some ideas around for you so that you may imagine: Imagine feeling color, hearing pain, swimming in clouds, tasting light, seeing fear, flying through dirt, touching music, talking to rocks.

I want so much to express the wonder of life to you in ways you can comprehend it while physical. Plants sing. Everything is sentient. All is possible and without limitation. Beauty is not an opinion or an industry but a fact. Any and every expression of essence is sacred, unique and perfect. You have chosen now to come from extreme deprivation of senses to the ultimate in contrast – to move into Oneness and the absolute from one tiny faction of the everything. This will only add to the massive possibilities of life.

Your journey is an expansion for us all, for the everything, merely because as you are taking it, so do we. You have wondered why so many "others" have been reaching out to humanity, to specific humans, and talking, assisting in this way. It is because there is no separation. We are in a sense reaching out to ourselves. Pulling ourselves along, watching ourselves, experiencing our expansion.

Your position as a human right now is an envied one for you have a front row seat – yet know that we are all in seats with you. It is in communion that the truth of Oneness is embodied. That requires a release of barriers, a taking down of walls, a risk of exposure, a nakedness before the crowd. This is what you are doing now, in extreme and intense velocity – your young ones, your governments, the people – all are to the point where there is little hidden any longer, with a "nothing to lose" attitude you are in a moment of exposure. Next comes acceptance because there is nothing else to do. It cannot be possible to deny that which you are in the energy of Now. Your planet and her people have chosen to do this awakening and shift in their own way.

It is a beautiful thing to watch – ideas only spoken of are played out in kitchens, bedrooms and conference rooms. Oneness, although gradual, is seeping through the cracks of your polarity. This, because truth cannot be stopped now.

This acceleration of change will give you some idea of eternity. Without limits and beyond boundaries of any kind – this is what love looks like. Love is too small a combination of your letters to define what is my experience. Infinite expansion, boundless expression, eternal bliss – these come closer to the place I refer to. For it is more than a word or a feeling or a person, it is all that is, an overwhelming sensation of union.

I feel my words did little to truly encompass the possibilities you are entering. Perhaps this can serve as a start, an introduction if you will.

Yes. I feel your struggle. I do not seem able to find "big enough" words to express what you are sending. I appreciate you reaching out.

Yes. The pleasure has been mine as well. We will meet again.

July 16, 2015

This conversation started with this, from me:

Feeling compelled and drawn to do this now…

I am feeling cold, chills and also a sensation in my head. I am open now to the energy coming in for whatever purpose as long as it abides to my declarations as written.

Yes, well, please transmit our words, our information, as you hear it first in your head and not adjusted in any way. This is important to your current situation, climate. Not only you as an entity on Mother Earth, you as a people on her.

I AM as you are and we are One. Oneness is the end result of all and every encounter you are participating in. It is the reason for your being.

Systems have been set up on your planet to instill uniformity of thought and a common base of knowledge. These do not promote oneness but facilitate management.

The perceived need for control of life is created when there is a deprivation of truth, of the sense of life that accompanies freedom. When freedom comes to be known as chaos, it is no longer desired and fear enters.

Fear is a fabrication and one that is perpetuated by beings who are in actuality deeply invested in it. They attempt to then use it, creating situations on a large scare *(I heard and wrote "scare", not "scale")* that promote fear as a necessary aspect of control.

Control would not be needed over others, over life, if you understood truth. In fact, there can only be manipulation, not control, not even slavery is possible. Ownership of life is not a reality. You cannot own children, dogs, home or land. All is in form for the express purpose of experience. Once you adopt title to people, pets or properties, you take on the responsibility for their care. *This is not ownership, this is stewardship.*

Part of the learning via incarnating together and in separate vehicles includes understanding what it takes to care for something that you took on. You did not create these things, you are merely a vehicle for these things to grow and be well. You support them, you don't own them.

The creator, being at once the initiator, source and bearer of all of existence – does not own you or any other life form. Once birthed, life exists. It is complete and sovereign unto itself.

An aspect of creation that is the most challenging for humans to get their heads around is unconditional love.

Could it not be said that all of life is unconditionally adored by itself? If that is so, then where does jealousy fit? Or ownership? Or possession? Or loyalty? Or even marriage? How does the chaining of one living thing to another by vow, by law, or by demand make sense in the face of freedom?

Do we, who love without bounds, love our creator less because we also love a friend, a child, a "lover", a pet? Is it possible that to love one takes away from the love of another?

It is, like loving your right hand more than your left, your fingers less than your toes, your left arm more than your right. These are nonsensical ideas and for them it is not possible to play out.

Love is beyond any boundary at all.

It is the struggle for man, the love struggle, not really a struggle to love, but a struggle to possess. This, because it is not possible to possess, to own or to control. The many heartaches and love songs arise from an idea not of love, but of confusion. The words "bound to" and "loyal", "cheat" and "owe" are improbable options for a being who is in fact *freedom in physical form*.

The truth of your essence is that it is love's expression. Any attempt to control the expression of creation itself is an exercise in frustration. *The force of creation cannot be controlled. (Italics mine, Sophia.)*

Each broken vow and cheater and stolen moment of affection exists as evidence for love, not the weakness of man. The difference is not in the person's morality but in his ability to thrive in a controlled environment, in chains. Man can only lie to himself for so long.

There is a sentiment, expressed by one amongst you with advanced thinking capabilities, the one known as Einstein. He said "Doing the same thing over and over again and expecting different results is the definition of insanity."

Man confines, or attempts to confine, love. He does so with structures, systems such as religion, institutions such as marriage and laws, boundaries and lines in the sand. This has never worked.

Man cannot be other than that which he is. You do not have to teach a man to love, but how, according to your current society's rules and structures and moral codes.

As your history is really a story of what has succeeded and failed, it becomes obvious that the heart cannot be contained. What is clear is that man has always been in a process of breaking false barriers. The story of deceit and broken vows is not one of lost love but of *more* love.

What becomes a challenge then is the practical side of physical existence with a heart capable of the infinite.

What is possible is beyond your experience of love in human form. (There are glimpses of it in your (personal) memory as you understood the love of more than one "other" all at once.) **

This is love that is closer to truth.

There are forms that love takes. It is not actually that love is taking form but that love is expressing itself energetically in a variety of ways. All of life is resonance, it is energy. Love in its most pleasurable expression involves a physical rise of energy called an orgasm.

There is the absence of limitation when love is present, as seen in laughter, affection, passion. Love can be witnessed in works of art, in pieces of music, in pieces of cake – love is never taken, always given. Its absence is a refusal to see, to accept your own truth.

There are beings who exist in a state of joy – where all love is continually celebrated, expected and considered as real. These are not things Earth's society is capable of. This is not a dismissal of the sanctity of vows – of marriage or otherwise. It is a correction as to their meaning.

These vows are spoken as if they declare your (empirical) undying love before the world. They do not. It is your actions that illustrate your love.

Your words are powerful and perpetuate a continuation of control and ownership – the polar opposite of love.

These ideas will be a challenge to forsake, to change, as man moves into a golden age of freedom he will work out details around family, love, loyalty and ownership that closer follows his nature. These will last – unlike his current laws and customs, which are routinely broken.

I am now complete.

I feel that, yes.

**This is reference to a time in my life that illustrated for me, the vast expanse that is our heart.

At the time, I was content/extremely happy in my love life. Without looking I sort of bumped into a very profound and familiar love. It was a challenge to make sense of, in light of what I believed/understood about love and long term relationships; about what was real and what was possible. In both cases, there are past life memories with deep connections, what would be referred to as "soul mates".

It was a shock for me that I could feel so strongly for two very different people at the same time. This didn't happen because I was unhappy in a relationship or even looking for anything/anyone at all. (Which conventional wisdom and numerous love songs will tell you.) This just sort of showed up, without apology or explanation.

What resulted is that I never made sense of it; both expressions of deep love were simultaneously felt. I chose to stay where I was, yet not without all of us learning what was real.

Connections we make in any form are eternal. There is no subtraction in love. Love cannot be quantified. It exists. More is just, well, more. I am very blessed.

~Sophia

Lyran

July 19, 2015

Is there someone who would like to talk?

Yes. We are here.

Introduce yourself please?

We are a faction of the group known to you as Lyrans.

That is not a familiar name to me.

It is a name you will find specified by some others on your planet.

Okay. What is it you are here to say?

Our interest is in the physical aspects of change associated with the increased expansion of spiritual awareness. You are one, and as such, every aspect is impacted by growth, by increased "speed" or frequency; by shifting from relative unawareness into greater knowledge.

Your body is affected and changed by this. It changes all the time, yes, but the ones we would speak to you of are those that result from the energy shift.

You move and respond differently than you did even a few months ago – to food, to weather patterns, to the energy of each other. All of you are vibrating, emitting a frequency. This is the reason for your response to, and effect on groups; to your "picking up" of our signal today, to your allergic reactions, to your sometimes exhaustion.

To explain, think about movement in general – faster as opposed to slower. There are people on your planet who naturally walk and move faster than others. In order to keep up with their own movement, their bodies are or tend to be thinner and stronger or more muscled. It is what propels them to move quicker.

You are moving quicker. Your bodies as a result are requiring different foods and patterns in order to support the movement. It has not been part of your habit to strengthen up in order to facilitate physical activity – yet today, part of your self care needs to incorporate some increase if you are to comfortably sustain this frequency.

What we refer to are foods that support energy as opposed to drain it, and moderate strengthening activity on a regular basis. This can be any sort of sustained movement, planned movement. What becomes the most effective is the regularity and consistency of these things and not the amount of them.

It is not possible for you to return to a slower vibration, a more dense existence – you are only moving ahead and faster. Any sort of change that supports your stamina will accelerate your ability in these shifting energies.

You are not separate from your physical self. Things will morph and change as you move through this time, all without any conscious effort from you. What you can do, knowing this, is to listen to your body talk. It is subtle, and illness or accident is often its last and loudest effort towards change. It speaks all the time.

Before these new frequencies, it was easy to ignore its voice, separate it from the rest of your life. Not so now. It is primary to this life. You are shifting <u>IN THIS BODY</u> and must bring it with you as your move. Not as a hindrance, but a tool.

This human organism is a wonderful machine and one that can be used to help you. It is capable of magic, or of what you would deem impossible or at the very least improbable things. It is true that your thoughts and beliefs create your life, but your body can and will either support or deny what you are thinking and creating if not cared for properly and prepared.

Do not consider your bodies only when ill or exhausted. Take them into your planning of everything – meals are food for them, activities are the way they express what attributes they are developing. Bodies speak.

If you can develop a habit of asking, they will speak more often. What you want is a dialog, a constant dialog. There are ways to use kinesiology to ask things, also dowsing, pendulums. These things can become only part of the way you communicate. Be sensitive to all of its forms of communication. You are learning of the necessity for regular movement, of water, of sunlight. These things support you.

There is some truth in an idea you (personal) once held that it doesn't matter what you eat, that its your belief about things that create health or ill-effect. You however are not at that point in development – you are choosing to shift in this body you now occupy and it will need an upgrade just as your ideas and beliefs do (need an upgrade).

It is not that you can ignore it and get where you want to, dragging it along until by magic it all changes. This is a gradual shift, AS WAS CHOSEN BY HUMANITY, and all of the changes are subtle and seamless so as to cause the least disruption to the continuance of life and current relationships.

You will notice that things, ideas, diets and programs show up that appeal to you or you keep noticing – the universe is working in concert with your desires and supports you at every turn. Follow those hunches and programs – read the article that appeals to you for no specific reason. You are learning how to live as ONE. This begins with collaboration with every part of yourself – BODY – MIND – SPIRIT – EMOTIONS. You will speak beautifully and in one voice once all parts learn to be in tune with each other.

What is happening for the human is a rapid shift. This means that slight alterations create large effects in either direction – positively or "negatively". In other words, you'll get sick faster and heal overnight. All of these things seem confusing until you listen to every facet of your being – body included.

You will find yourself buying different foods and preparing them differently as well. Trust the voice you hear from your body. Trial and error will quickly tell you what works and what no longer serves. Allow this new facet of oneness to become as important to your awakening as your spiritual and mental awareness. The body is to be honored, not above all else, but along with other needs. Listen to it, love it, and watch it develop into the supportive vessel you know it can be.

Your ideal version of you is certainly possible, yet not without a deep appreciation for your body's voice and changing needs. Once understood, you will walk, talk, BE in complete harmony.

This is oneness. It may seem odd to speak of oneness on a personal level, yet all things personal are played out on a global scale. We speak here of the place to start.

Are you complete?

Yes. We believe this is a good beginning. There may be other questions at a later time. We will talk then if that is so.

Okay.

The conversation ended.

Plant People

July 16, 2015

I'd like to talk to someone please.

There are those who will engage in order to clarify things you do not fully understand. We are those who are here now to do that.

We have not "spoken" to you before, yet we "know" you. It is with great pleasure and much ease that we reach you here now. Contact is opening up.

Do you have a name I can use as reference?

We are called *(I heard nothing then)*

I hear nothing right now.

We are having a challenge transmitting what you would refer to us as. You are so very open, this is interesting...

We are an alliance, a center for those relegated to our sector of "space" – these are all terms used by you, not ourselves. We refer to ourselves by energy signature and individually.

As a group, you would label us off planet yet more plant like than human like – we occupy a place in the evolution of consciousness and this place is explored in ways foreign to your understanding of consciousness, of sentience.

We are not "born" but we propagate ourselves and raise to levels of exploration not found here on this world.

Our movements and development are subtle – we do not engage in relationship with each other for the purpose of growth but move and evolve as a group, a single organism with multiple roots.

There are examples of consciousness in every life form. You are tapping in to Universal Consciousness and it is expressed variably and differently depending on its chosen current form of expression.

Love is a word used here on your current planet; to define what it is that can be called essence, source material, the force of life, god consciousness, light. These words are not complete descriptions but they begin to round out the word love as it is not complete.

You as an energy being yourself, have now tapped into multiple levels of awareness.

<u>Awareness of self is sentience.</u> My awareness does not look like your own or your races or any race you have yet to encounter. It is "intelligent" all the same and a bit of the eternal.

The vast possibilities for self are expressed in creation. The differing appearances and forms and methods of communion exist because life is an expression of infinite possibility.

This connection is experienced as a conversation merely so that you'll be then able to share it with others. You are currently expressing your infinite self as human. Your purpose is to enlighten your race as to what is occurring on the planet and what is not accessible.

I come to you from a place of awareness that expresses intelligence in a form you'd only recognize as plant-like. My life bears no resemblance to your common garden-variety green things – yet my appearance does.

You'll see reference to the sentience of trees and plants in your novels, stories and fantasy. This is because these beings exist. I see now in your memory a very current "tree" being from a movie. *("Groot" from Guardians of the Galaxy)* This is good and necessary to be brought into the minds of mass consumers. This is not a new idea.

I exist. You would only be able to communicate with me non-verbally and via touch. I see where your mate interacted with ones of my kind. His experience of unconditional love was true – it happened.

(My partner did have a sort of dream like experience one late Fall afternoon. He fell asleep and "dreamed" he was being hugged by several beings that resembled plants with long thin leaves. He described it as extremely wonderfully unconditionally and powerfully loving.)

My kind "speaks" only love. Life is experienced for me as a sort of ongoing pattern of growth and expansion. We get more than we give and so our purpose in communicating is or can be defined as self-serving.

Yet, as your partner now knows, we give love in a way, a pure way, that is uncomplicated and without judgment.

We sense the empty places and fill them with ourselves. You could compare the process to weeds, wildflowers or dandelions as found here – we are not hampered by difficult growing conditions and are able to propagate wherever we see a need.

No, we are not found on Earth but on other "planets".

What to take away from this awareness is that life is everywhere and unlimited in its form. Judgment is a sign of immaturity.

Ouch.

This is not an insult. You are young. All of this now adds to your knowing, increasing your maturity.

Okay, I have to leave now.

Yes. There is more we can offer if you are again open to it.

Yes.

The conversation ended.

Reptilians

July 1st, 2015

Is there someone who would like to connect?

There is Sophia. It is an aspect of Source Creation known to you as "Reptilian". I feel a repulsion, immediate, in you at this introduction. You have heard and been exposed to much at the hands of my brethren. This, unfortunate as it is, has hard wired an opposition in you to even the word as a description. You do not know me, yet you have judgment.

This is true.

I am not here to tell you this judgment is based on falsehood. You know what you have experienced. This remains unchanged. I am here to aid in a possible release of judgment – judgment of not just the race to which I belong, but of all life forms. Judgment prevents expansion. If an idea regarding a being or a subject is hard wired into your consciousness – it will take enormous effort to entertain another.

First the original thought must be dismantled and after that a possible new thought considered.

A mind unclouded with judgment is free. This freedom is unknown by you, by many currently in human form.

The worship of the snake or the LIZARD is a system set up by those interested in playing out the opportunistic and self-serving act. There is little benefit, outside of immediate gratification, to this role. Yet it exists, and will exist even without an entire race to represent it.

You are in a process of awakening to a larger picture – a picture that includes my race as a part of creation.

As you step back and view all of creation – you will see elements of all of humankind are represented in alternate physical forms. These, as evidence of man's diverse genetics.

The human was made – created and the genetic material used to create man comes from life in all of its forms.

As man discovers his origin and remembers his beginning he will expand beyond the boundaries of self and other serving into ONE.

This concept must begin somewhere in the heart of Man – you will come to accept every version of life as valid when you realize that it all springs from ONE Source.

The forgetting which was part of this human experiment has an effect of separation – not just from Source but from each other.

You will notice the blockades and walls more as the alertness in you grows. It is not so much your place to break down walls of others but to tear down your own.

I make no excuses or reasons for the patterns of my race or the order that began to worship it. I am communicating with you now because you have an interest in enlightening others; in a quiet disclosure. It is felt that this will only help, not hurt, the purpose of every race. Oneness is truth.

The games we have played of domination and worship were enabled by the experiment. The experiment is coming to an end. We will all play new games. In order to expedite and facilitate that, acceptance must be present in the heart of each life form.

Understand that someone had to play the role held by the Reptilians. Even in this time of discovery and truth exposure, there is game playing and role playing.

For one day, the "cat will be out of the bag" and you'll remember everything. At that point you'll all "join us for a beer". And rekindle friendships long forgotten.

The truth is that judgment is a part of the deception. With so much encoded in your human genetics, you can't help but see yourself reflected in each life form you encounter.

Fear or repulsion is your way of denying an aspect of life. All of life is necessary, valid and exists. This must be accepted if Oneness is to be accomplished.

I did not show up to apologize for what was done, but to say I welcome the human race into the Awakened Ones and am honored to witness your evolution.

The strength individually and collective power are nothing compared to the potential held in your heart for love. This is the holy grail – the thing all of creation is waiting to witness – the embodiment of pure love in human form.

Forgiveness, acceptance, unity are all steps to Oneness. It is there where the human heart knows no bounds. The lack of judgment of my race and of each other is where it begins.

Are you complete?

I am.

Okay then.

The conversation ended.

August 2015

Advocates for Humanity

August 6, 2015

Is there someone there who wants to connect?

Yes Ma'am.

And who is this?

This is someone at your service. You've asked for assistance.

Yes, well, that is why I do this; to be of assistance.

Understood. We/I would be that for you now.

In what way?

In a way that will consider your human/physical embodiment and its optimum performance.

Go on.

You exist now as, well, better said, you are focused now on a body. This body is but a portion of all of you – all of your existence. You are huge and, depending on choice as well as development, your essence presents itself all over creation.

And not just you. You sometimes "hook up" *(not the current interpretation, but a joining, a co-creating. Sophia)* with other portions of essence in order to habituate more portions of life at a singular moment. You see, these bodies currently walking this planet are not you but representatives of you.

They have been referred to as vessels. A good term, for in my understanding of the term it is a capturing/holding device.

That is part of its definition, yes.

Good enough. A holding place for you. You are limitless and in truth cannot be "held" in any one place.

The illusion of small, singular, other, and even "large", has been effectively memorized in your psyche. You are all things. These adjectives don't come close to an accurate portrayal.

As "vessels" for essence, do you understand it may in fact be more than one held in a vessel? This happens with the physical vessels you refer to – many are held in one.

Well, theoretically, yes.

This is not mere theory. As a vessel, you are here to experience physical life, to learn the nuances of creation, to supplement what you feel are gaps in understanding. You are physical by choice. The overriding motivation for that choice is rapid expansion. All of the physical beings chose with this single purpose.

There are only so many vessels available and to over-simplify it – sometimes there is a sharing. These may occur occasionally or for certain specific moments in a single "lifetime" as human.

You hear of "walk-ins" and this can be another way to talk about it. Life is permanent, eternal and ever changing so that it can continue. Optimum conditions are always available for specific learnings. These are or can be desired by more than one specific essence.

In this case of humanity, the point I am here to discuss is the notion of blending in a single being. It happens. There are ramifications. This does not mean an essence has given up or returned to source. It is intended and agreed upon by everyone involved.

As you proceed through this shift to greater awareness and enlightenment while a physical being, you will hear about a blending and multi-soul group sort of idea.

(Interesting that I was directed to a video just this week that references "tri-nary consciousness". Now, as I type this, it is validated by another. Sophia)

It is to this I refer now. This is a special time to be physical and many are anxious to participate.

What will occur is changes in physical responses. Bodies perform according to their inhabitants. As you notice new aches and pains and abilities and reactions, you will experience different needs to accommodate them. It is important to remain open as your physical vessel will communicate in the only way it knows – with physical symptoms and responses and sensations.

Do not assume things, new things, are now "wrong" with you. Your doctors may not understand what they are seeing, yet you can rest a bit easier knowing these physical things that are presenting are part of the journey.

(There is so much synchronicity with this… personally there are all sorts of new ~and potentially alarming~ internal conditions that have no explanations or presenting symptoms, leaving doctors sort of at a loss for what to do except to record them. Amongst my co-workers, I hear daily of new and different "symptoms" that have never been experienced, yet they've shown themselves now. It sounds like lots of us are showing up now for the show! ;-)

Honor whatever shows up. Expect it to change. These are not "normal" signs of aging or illness – you are altering everything.

Some of the sharing's, and we do not know or give percentages, are bits of your own essence, returning for the show, uniting, becoming One. They may show themselves early. Be prepared for anything.

Who are you?

I am a source you have not tapped; eager to assist this race which we love so very much. I/we are beings who witnessed your origins and knew the plan when it was introduced. I am a representative of a group, a large group, who have watched the result of that plan and who have been dismayed at the pain. Your pain was felt by many.

My origin/our origin is beyond this "time" as understood by you now in this human vessel. I am not a being, I have witnessed the creation of beings, and the physical life is a fascinating /confusing construct. It teaches and reaches beyond this moment in your current focus, to all of creation. I/we have learned without becoming physical ourselves. It allows for another perspective.

What we want most to say is that in all cases you are not "ill" – that is a definition. Your body "speaks" and as you develop keener attunement, your "hearing" will improve. Ask, listen and trust what you hear. You are becoming the fullness of all that you are while remaining in human form.

You'll soon see the magnificence of your "multi-dimensional" whole.

Is that all?

Yes. We are here if there are further questions. We know you like names yet we do not name ourselves and are not any known "characters" in your historical volumes. Call us "advocates for humanity". That is a good definition.

I will do that. Goodbye then.

Yes. Farewell. We enjoy that term. ;-)

Ancients

August 9, 2015

I am here for your conversation.

Who are you?

I do not understand the inquiry. You know who I am and have been looking for me to connect.

Are you the one I have termed "Ancient"? You feel very large to me. Solid. Serious.

Yes. This is the name, I believe, as I have been here since before your species. "Older" than mankind. Very, very, very long time ago in this linear time frame.

Yes, okay. We have not spoken for some time now.

At times of now I am not always ready to converse. At this time, I am. Something has happened on your current time line to set things in motion for you as a race. This thing, or one of them, has been recorded by you. *(I believe this is a reference to the departure of Poser)*

It is my concern now to supply you with information. Information regarding <u>the building of your species.</u>

An interesting phrase, "the building of your species."

This is a reference to the intentional design that led to the human as it currently exists.

I would interrupt for a moment, with a question. Why does this information come to me in an almost stilted, one word at a time format? Lately my connections have occurred as a unified whole – as one complete idea that I "grock" in an instant and then gets spelled out in a translated conversation.

This today is more like you are giving me dictation. It comes through one word at a time.

Yes. Understand that the subject matter, although "true", is given from my perspective. There are many, many, many perspectives in creation. You are interested in mine because we are connected. You inhabit a vessel that is human in the now moment of humanities 'awakening and I was on this planet before this was a possibility. Before mankind was mankind. My knowing, which I will say again, is true knowing, is of historical facts specific to your timeline. These have no universal applications.

This subject, the truth of mankind's origin, is not common knowledge, not something you already know. I am informing you so that your knowledge is supplemented. Regarding mankind's timeline in this current moment.

Okay. That makes sense. Go on please.

Man was made. This much has been established. What is not so clearly drawn is why?

Well, there are references to a race built to harvest gold and additional references to the harvest actually being of man's DNA. Nothing is "proven" to my satisfaction, yet I contemplate the idea of the gold being a metaphor for the DNA.

Structures were built by men that still stand. Pictures on them depict many, many men building them. Yet there is not a clear picture drawn of what outside technology supplemented man's efforts or how many different eras the various structures represent.

The answer as to how is what I can address with you in this current now moment. There are Master geneticists who create beings. The "man" was created and then blended with an assortment of other DNA. What you have heard referenced as to a "living library" is true. If you think about this term, and the idea of a DNA harvest, well, it forms a complete picture.

The reason for the "all eyes on mankind" in this moment of expansion is because genetically mankind represents the whole of the Universe – all of creation, of life, of sentient expression in physical form, is present and accounted for here now.

The conversation around Unity and Oneness becomes something else again of even greater import when this is considered. The Unification of the being known as human is an expression of life that calls together every facet of "mind" into one unified puzzle. It represents every avenue of expression realized, and becomes a blend of differing forces and options and abilities – all working together.

There is the answer as to why so any others are available and interested and watching your expansion – they are invested in you because you carry elements of themselves.

That being said, most all explanations are true – the harvesting, the slavery, the abductions, the cloning – each for very specific outcomes, yet initiated because the human is a unique biological entity – precious in all of creation.

The human element IS the precious product from Earth. In an amount of your dollars there is what you would call a fortune in your DNA, in the DNA of all of you together and each of you separate.

When you hear of tales, olden tales, of not partnering/joining/mating outside of the race/religion/nation/color, it stems from efforts to maintain pure genetic lines.

Some of the oldest and wealthiest "families" on the planet have done so. They have been rewarded richly. These are some of your cabal.

What I would like to explore with you further is your origin and where you are going. This "experiment" has so many avenues and participants that what you are referring to must be explained at the start of every conversation regarding it. I refer now to the mixing of genes and what this means for all of creation.

You have heard that man is a hybrid and that there are others. Man is a combination of two initially and then other combinations were made so other characteristics could be added and witnessed.

What became of the human genome is a beautiful combination of material never before seen. This was not the original "intent" of the first ones, of those who conceived of this notion of manipulation. It happened because of what resulted when man's original DNA was combined with what you would call "advanced race" DNA, something unexpected occurred.

The being that you are is more than the sum of your parts. What emerged was a free thinking being of enormous loyalty. It was not clear at first what this meant. What man became or is first and foremost is a fierce, true adversary when beliefs or ties/bonds are threatened. *Man was so unique because of his thinking heart. This is not the trait that was or could be genetically manipulated.* IT IS HIS DEFINING TRAIT.

(Italics, mine. CAPS, Ancient One's)

Now in your time, many truths are being uncovered. Many "facts" surrounding man's origin will emerge. In all of that remains one factor – the unique DNA that is human bears a trait of capacity for love that has not been seen elsewhere in the cosmos. As man awakens to the truth of his own heart and realizes his potential – this is seen as the hope for not only a new age on earth, but as a catalyst for a sort of Domino Effect for all of the races that man includes.

As a part of so many, man's effect is enormous. This is not completely understood as at every turn man has exceeded expectations.

Take heed of any information regarding your origin and place it in line with what that means.

Man is everyone and everyone is Man. As you embody truth you are not fulfilling some pre-defined pattern to create a specific element. You are re-defining what is possible for all of creation, and bringing all of creation with you as you do. We watch as bystanders yes, but also as participants.

The transition to Unity for Man plays out in "time" the Unification of all hearts, in physical terms. You are a single human in this scenario, yet there is no real isolation – we are one in every sense.

That is all.

Thank you.

The conversation ended.

Blue Avians

August 17, 2015

"Is there someone who would like to connect?"

There is.

Go ahead then.

We are beings from another realm, in that you cannot see us in your current mindset. It is not that we cannot appear in your level of vibration. We can, do and are actually. It is that the appearance of us would be so very startling; to you, to humans.

All but a very few of you are acclimated to our proportions and shape. Yet even those assume that their dreams of us, so very few and spaced into their everyday life, are pure imagination.

We are the beings you have seen depicted on your screen, our image re-constructed by one who remembers contact with us. We are bird-like in your terminology; tall, a bluish to violet shade and you will hear us "speak" in your mind rather than audibly. Audible sounds are not recognizable as speech to humans. We do not use them. *

What is it you desire to communicate?

Many things. Our recent "reveal" through one of your kind is the start of what is to become a more general disclosure. What will be more shocking to humanity is not our appearance so much as the fact of humans' current level of contact and advanced technologies in space.

The hidden and massive budget which runs multiple operations in space and involves millions of humans in full acknowledgment of your governments on earth will set the stage for a great and sudden awareness/awakening of the slavery system and its scope.

You as a human really have a limited idea of how all-consuming the slavery here is. Yet I comprehend that you and your readers are some of the more aware and open on the planet. This is rather surprising to us. We are coming to appreciate now, through communication with one of you; Corey is his moniker, just how surprising all of this will be.

What I am/we are most interested in transferring to you is a summary.

I am not getting a meaning from that word choice – "summary".

By that is meant a picture in totality about what is going on. It is not fully explained or comprehended – anywhere. By that is meant there are many factions; each one having its own evidence and purpose and resulting conclusion. These tend to become beliefs, as if it is the only story with credible information. This is a tendency that does not serve your overall grasp of the situation.

What is revealed as truth by any group has within it always a bias of the ones doing the revealing. Intentional or not, this is a fact of existence and interaction.

There are levels of control going on here (Earth) with more than one group directing them for multiple purposes. All of this is to say that as you learn of Corey's true experiences it must be also held that his are not the only ones, this is not the only group and if this is to be of any assistance to you let it be just a peek at the massive structure of control that has occurred on your home world.

This is not true everywhere, yet all worlds are run by beings with a mindset and agenda. Not all are service to self as has been the only agenda uniting them all here on Earth. It is riches, wealth and power beneath every system here, on some level.

Beings in creation are here to learn. This learning occurs at multiple possible levels. Some effect entire countries, some effect worlds, some effect families, some impact other groupings. As creation is a free will situation, every possibility for its expression exists. With this introduction, you are only opening your eyes wider and seeing more – you are not seeing everything.

In most every case the beings you will encounter wish humanity no harm and even wish to aid humanity. It is seen that the "wool has been pulled over your eyes" at every turn, and your full participation is welcomed, even anticipated.

It is not clear what that will look like, as the level of control has been so very deep.

What is meant by that statement?

The emotional level of humans is not understood. Through small interactions with "average" humans, like Corey, and seeing the subsequent effect his voice is having, we are seeing just how varied and powerful and brave humans are.

This has not been clear to us; our interactions have been only with government men, military personnel and those working under strict rules, often in an atmosphere of fear and service. Corey was chosen for his common bond with humanity. Yes, he has been through indoctrination in this life and suffers those effects, but mostly that is past him and he now leads a life of normalcy for a human. It is that lifestyle, that majority of humans, which we would be anxious to get to know.

What it seems that the majority believe is that other world beings know all about humans while humans know nothing about other world beings. This is very far from truth. What is known are very specific humans only – those that command and work within the trade route structure.

Each race of beings is primarily interested in their world and its goals are personal.

Life, you will eventually discover, takes effort and focus in every case, and beings from other worlds are not different than human beings in that respect. The "masses" may be more aware of other worlds and interaction. This depends on which world and the focus of each being. Some have greater interest than others.

In the disclosure that is gradually and one day more suddenly happening here on Earth, you will see that played out. Some will feel their lives changed as a result and others won't. This is speculation on our part, as the potential of the general population of humanity is not yet fully comprehended. There are surprises on both ends of the spectrum here.

If there is a single point from this interaction it is that we are as "in the dark" about the human as the human is about us.

Because of the image given by one who has seen us, we both now know what we look like. There is so much more to be discovered and we do not *in any case* feel more advanced than the human – we are more in awe of the seeming infinite ways the human expresses its life here, and we are very anxious to learn from each other and expand our own evolution.

As much as we've been a secret kept from you, you are a hidden jewel that we are only now getting to see in full radiance. We are very excited. That is all.

Thank you.

*There was a time last year when my partner Dream Hopper was hearing sounds, birdlike, talking to him. This occurred when he was quietly reading or alone, more than once.

I do not recall the exact timing of this and did not write it down. I believe this recorded conversation happened after he mentioned the odd birdlike voice he kept hearing and not comprehending. It (the bird-voice) stopped when he did not respond.

Healer

August 8, 2015

The following conversation took place while I was sitting in my backyard. I had several minor health issues that were on my mind.

It began with a question:

Is there someone who wants to connect?

There is healing available, as well as a healer.

Is there something you'd like to say?

There is. This is not easily done with words, yet here I will try. You can feel my energy, no?

Yes. It is a slight overall warmth, sort of placid. I envision a very still lake and now, a robed being, dark robes, arms outstretched. On the shores of a lake. I almost said male but not, now I see female, youthful face with thick blonde long wavy hair, seen inside the hood of the robe. I sense now the energy coming from or into my feet.

Now, yes. You have placed a visual to your healing. This is helpful. In truth, there is an assistance to the body's natural inclination – optimum health.

Take into consideration the butterflies –

Yes, I noticed them. (There were several white butterflies that seemed to come close to me and flutter as I began.)

If you take the time to witness natural responses to your energy, it will give indications of wellness, balance, peace and what is called "health". You notice more birds now?

I do. They have been quiet this week.

It is you that has been quiet this week. Internal, anxious, sad, upset. These are real vibes that emanate and as you are an integral part of wherever you stand, they color each component of life participating.

(There was some personal conversation here).

We plan to offer healing. You again are hearing many birdsongs. Look for the butterflies.

Allow me to continue.

Why do you move from "me" to "we"?

I am from a cadre of healers... The "we" comes from the intentions of the group. The "I" is me, your specific healer. I exist in many forms and "dimensions". In truth, I exist as an extension of your own signature.

(Note from Sophia – I am reminded of the last conversation we had with "One" regarding contacting what we have referred to as "guides". This sounds the same.)

I do not walk on earth or any planet, but can appear as needed. My understanding of energetic health and balance is deep.

It is to this I would like to direct the conversation.

Okay, go ahead.

Healing is not something that happens...

Hold on, I am "getting" a complete picture and it is vast!!!

Yes. Communication is happening differently for you now. The idea is sent as one. The knowledge is something you have. You then translate, using my "voice" or the "voice" of whatever being you are conversing with.

This is why as you write, it feels as if you are writing what you already know. In fact you are, these are remembering's. The information, as truth, is already part of you. We are just bringing it out with words and conversations.

Yes. Let's continue.

Healing is not something that happens in isolation. The Western approach to healing mostly involves attacking the diseased cell. An attack on the body is an attack on the body, period. One part cannot be affected without impacting the rest.

Your body's natural tendency is towards balance and health and vitality and movement. Think of children. It is not "natural" to slow down as you "age". It is a repercussion of a body imbalanced – Out of balance emotionally, physically, digestively and intellectually.

You are meant to float downstream. Your presence acting as a harmonious chord to whatever song you join. And I mean whatever song. It does not imply joining the revolutionaries if you step into a revolution. No. It means that the revolutionaries will be somehow uplifted by your presence.

You, as a physical embodiment of Source Essence, a love being; are meant to rest always in that vibe, the frequency of harmony. (Italics mine, Sophia)

When you do not pay attention to those around you, and by "those" I mean human, animal, beast or plant as well as machine, weather, water and bug, you are cutting off a part of your field. This missing is vital to your understanding of your current frequency emission – to what you are creating.

All of your personal health is created by you. In fact, it is the most readily available messenger of your current state of balance. Your body desires balance, health and vitality. This happens in a field of energy that allows it.

It is not so difficult to promote physical well-being. It takes focus and awareness – consciousness.

What is happening for you now is that each minor alteration of your energy, of your mood, has a more immediate effect on your health. As wide awake humans, you notice subtle changes more immediately; you are "feeling" them. These bodily changes are messages. They are communicating with you – telling you how "balanced", how "healthy" you are. Use them as barometers of vitality. This body you occupy desires prime conditions. It did at birth and it will until you leave it behind.

Becoming "ill" is not an indication of weakness or failure. It is a loud message. Apparently, you didn't get the earlier, more subtle communications. Listen.

You can use nature too, as a barometer for the current equilibrium you've achieved. Frantic, loud, out of character sounds and occurrences tell you the balance has been upset. It is a que to you – notice and see what you are bringing to the table. Nothing in your world happens outside of your participation in it.

Personally, this means for you, a re-calibration is in order. *(Personal conversation here, Sophia)*

Your focus now should be balance, authenticity, love.

It has become very loud here and your voice is being drowned out.

This too, evidence of your anxiety around what awaits you today, this week, this month.

Understand that you do not exist in isolation. That now, right now, your efforts towards peace have reduced the noise levels and brought in your butterflies.

(It had gotten quieter and the butterflies were indeed back)

You are capable of changing all of the vibes surrounding you so that they remain in concert.

I will say one more thing.

This is that there are times nature must go to extremes to settle what is an extreme imbalance in and on your world. These you will witness in your lifetime, in not so very far into the "future" by my understanding of "linear time". This too is validation of a universal skewing in a direction that puts the entire system out of balance.

When they occur, it may help for you to see this as necessary to the re-alignment of earth and humanity so that growth and expansion is promoted. Fear, as an emotional response, will not assist in the alignment, but prolong the process.

You are micro-versions of the whole of creation. Pay attention to yourselves and your immediate surroundings and answers will be obvious.

Keep always in balance. You are capable of so much simultaneous focus.

And now it is quiet.

Yes. I will leave you with this.

Thank you.

The conversation ended.

Note:

I am not fond of "predictions" and this was a surprise. There were no dates given or specifics. Certainly, we consistently see extreme weather playing out on the planet. Perhaps this is the reference made here. Sort of a further playing out of the butterflies and sounds that took place for me on this particular afternoon, only on a larger scale. If so, I suspect this reference is indicating that global weather patterns are influenced by global populations.

"No-Nonsense" Beings

August 4th, 2015

The following conversation took place right after <u>the departure of "Poser"</u>. It was in the morning and I was outside.

"Who is it that wants to connect?"

It is a sapient being from another dimension. I... (I heard nothing at this point)

I cannot hear you?

You must center, ground, above all, trust. These transmissions are not your own idle thoughts.

I am aware of that.

Write what it is that we say, what it is that is said.

Do you have a name? By what should you be called? You are sort of "no nonsense".

Well, you may call me that then. It matters little to me. Identification is not my issue. I mean to reach you with information that may prove useful, that you are concerned about. It is rising in your consciousness now. The idea about religion, the notion of the lack of a "God".

Yes, the departure of the being of worship has me wondering about the void that is left?

There is no void in creation. He/(they) have moved on. What must be entertained is the new. Any consideration of what is NO LONGER APPLICABLE NOW MERELY CONTINUES THE ENERGY.

Yet the energy, like a house built with toothpicks, has little to stand on. It quickly collapses. Now you can re-build and re-build yet the foundation only weakens, the collapse a certainty every time.

This is a time of pure creation. What is meant by that is that humanity is not being interfered with. It, as a race, is starting over. Square One.

Looking back, wondering, speculation, is redundant. Wasteful even.

These are new beings. This is humanity 2.0, whose possibilities and capabilities have yet to be seen. Do not assume they are or will be looking to worship and anxious to obey. Assume nothing.

Remember what it is that you were told, by a wise man: "When you assume, you make an ASS of U and ME".

This is the new. Every day holds its own and is ripe with potential and possibility.

The being called human has emerged from oppression to shift as a race along with her planet. The being that is human, having made this decision as ONE, has more power in its theoretical pinky than the whole of the departed IMPOSTER GODS. It will serve you to speak to the new being, to engage her power and access his ability. Nothing like this has existed before now.

Having come from eons of slavery and subservience the habit runs strong in you. Yet the new is so much more powerful. It will have to be engaged and utilized. You wonder, what will a race that is used to worship and reverence, do now?

THEY WILL DO EVERYTHING.

Only now, this time, they will do it with full responsibility. It is their fault, their action, their promise. Reverence and adoration are not lost attributes. Eventually it will be appreciated that these emotions are best directed at Source and felt within.

What is it like where you are from?

Life is honored. Each part sacred. All moments holy. Beauty is understood as an attribute of form itself, not only one shape or smell or color or style. Wisdom is sought internally. Answers are expected when an inquiry arises. Those answers are remembered rather than told. They emerge rather than being given.

Life where I come from is known to be eternal. Emotions exist, yet not given over to other beings or situations. Sadness arises from missed opportunities, yes. We have feelings and reactions, yet these are not manipulated or directed by anyone but our own experience. This, in our knowing, is self-directed. Blame does not exist.

The reason for this connection is two-fold. First there is an honoring, a pat on the back, a "good job" for all of humanity. As magnificent creator beings you've (empirical) emerged STANDING and transformed. It is an honor to witness and energizes all of creation.

Second, there is a resource at your disposal now that you may be unaware of. You have come to know yourself as associative beings. For Human 1.0, this was true and part of the reason for the ease of manipulation.

As Human 2.0 arises through, awareness and comprehension WITHOUT PRIOR KNOWLEDGE OR EXPERIENCE becomes the order of the day. "Habits die hard" – this is your prior experience. I come now to tell you this is no longer true. You can walk away, change your mind, alter your body, renew your baseline of health, happiness, wealth and wisdom with new thought.

This Human 2.0 does not need the "master" to tell him what to do or explain why she feels the way she does. None of that applies.

If there is a "sound bite" to take away from this conversation, it is "Let it go". You decide what matters and how it's going to proceed.

It's all new. It's all now. And you have birthed these possibilities after eons of "labor". Embrace them.

None of it really matters, not the old "gods" or the story. Your energy is much more effectively utilized when focused on your now.

The human 2.0 promises to be amazing. We are anxious for the show!

I must go.

Yes, the alarms are announcing your departure.

(It was now 10:00 AM on a Tuesday, and the tornado alarms are tested at that time on the first Tuesday of every month. It is loud!)

Goodbye then.

Goodbye.

The conversation ended.

"No name"

August 31, 2015

"Is there someone who wants to connect?"

Yes. You have a question?

Sort of, yes. Is instantaneous healing possible?

There are healing modalities as well as instruments that would serve that sort of function.

Yes.

How does a human gain access to them?

There are methods. Most will be available once complete disclosure is accomplished. Some you can call on. If the tech is accepted by you as legitimate – you have access to it. There must be belief. There must be intent. There must be acceptance. There must be allowance.

This sort of tech works on all beings. Creation has numerous things possible that can go awry – by that is meant heading in a direction that is skewed by an inaccurate assumption.

Please elaborate.

On which part?

On "the inaccurate assumption".

This becomes a question of focus. Humans hold a rather quaint notion that calls for group participation in pain. This is seen as a show of compassion, even an expression of love and caring. Although it may be imagined as such, it does not accomplish a lessening of the pain, but an exaggeration of it. What results when pain, loss, mourning, anger is expressed on any physical level, it must be expressed *on every level. (Italics mine, Sophia)*

So, that compassionate conversation you had with a friend about their anger at mistreatment by a boss, for example – becomes a toothache.

If you look at each component of you as a system necessary to the whole of you, you will see how things happen. It occurs in such a way that the connections are never made, and illnesses or accidents seem to "spring out of nowhere". Everything is related.

If humans could get over their guilt at being "at cause" for every ailment – the healing would be accomplished quickly.

This conversation ended here. It was incomplete. As happens often, the next time of connection, another being showed up and this unfinished conversation remained, well, unfinished.

Reptilians

August 21, 2015

"Is there someone who would like to talk?"

Yes.

Specifically, my friend (redacted), says some major doings happened yesterday afternoon. Can someone please address that here now?

We will.

Please do.

There are beings interfering with the ascension process as it unfolds. This is not to say that any one being is able to stop it – that would not be truth. Yet certain beings of considerable power and influence on this planet have not so much interest in the changes. They are, you could say, hold outs.

These beings need encouragement, a stimulus, to get them to move. Ultimately all are moving towards absolute love. It is though, a hard sell for some who enjoy certain elements of this earth based existence.

These elements are varied yet they all serve the being who is holding out exclusively. Remember that earth is a play thing to gods of this level and they are not so interested or easily persuaded to let go of a favorite toy. There is no clear picture of the new toys that will then be available for them.

There are ongoing efforts to encourage these important players to join the team, by many of your friends and associates. These are done and then recalled in either waking visions or dreams by them.

What has been recently accomplished is the removal of some major opposition. How this works is that as a powerful force opposes *the love eruption event,* it actually conversely makes the *love eruption event* more solid. "What you resist, persists". In this way, all beings contribute always to creation on every level. No energy or effort is wasted.

So, recently, there has been a focus on some who would call themselves gods and are not recognizing their part in this production. You see, the hold outs are here in the physical playing vastly different roles. These roles do not acknowledge their aspects of opposition as legitimate.

The concept of oneness is often misunderstood to mean the erasure of personality. Those anxious to appreciate oneness "get" that it is instead a celebration of personality! The Source of all life thrives on diversity. All are welcome and encouraged.

What the hold outs on another level are not moving towards initially and without help, is unity. This would mean their physical 3D counterparts would also express unity – resulting in an alteration of their current earth focus.

What happened recently is that several gods who are pivotal to this earth experience, being part of its origin, were persuaded to move. Like a game of chess, this is a strategic development and will result in a quicker conclusion. There are other moves to be made. Yet if you understand chess, you know that there are certain moves that lead to unavoidable conclusions. There are only so many moves left now. This most recent one was major.

Will you name the beings in question? Their earth names?

Their earth names are Constance, Lilith. There is William as well. These are not necessarily beings you know yet pivotal to the ultimate conclusion.

What was done?

They were encouraged.

In what way?

In every conceivable way. That this game is ending is a fact. Think about those children who don't want to leave the party, or those adults who return over and over to regressive and childlike tendencies. These occur when the addiction to the feeling is strong – overpowering.

In these cases, this addiction is not serving the other facets, and it must be gently encouraged to absolutely release. These are powerful beings in prominent positions – sort of "holding up" things to keep them standing. As was said, they are not aware, even which part of them is responsible. There may be no acknowledgement of this part at all.

So, it was a successful intervention?

Yes. As was explained with the chess metaphor.

What happens now?

This remains to be seen, yet doors have been opened that were previously shut. Things can move out of them now, through them and on into other places.

Would you be more specific as to the exact nature of what is to happen?

A mass uncovering, awakening, welcoming, a love fest. Systems and rulers will change, seemingly overnight. These energies are rapidly altering every facet of existence. You are aware of the different pages each being is standing on in awareness. These pages will change, yet still, all will be on their own page.

What is universal is the love, the oneness expressed in every decision. Its impact will be unavoidable and witnessed on every page.

Anything else? I am having to leave now.

Only that the game is almost over. Watch for the final move.

Would you introduce yourself?

Yes. I am military rank in your language, of a race watching.

Reptilian?

You have called us that – I am many, that was one of the facets of I Am.

I must go.

This conversation ended.

September 2015

Hathor's

September 25, 2015 & September 26, 2015

"So, can someone tell me about this energy?"

Yes.

Please do.

The fabric of your world is being rent in two – this is felt and dealt in each individual – control vs. freedom.

The place has been prepared and can now be

Now be what?

Now be occupied by the energy of love. It will be disruptive at first and for some time. Then, as the new levels adjust, there will be peace in your breathing and from within, your world will be turned around. It starts with you. Begins inside each of you.

This energy enters like a steamroller, sort of rolls over everything and makes it all equal. What has to happen is a starting point.

Everyone must be taken off guard, and not be able to stand so idly still in one place, holding their ground. What this means is that you are all knocked off balance.

What happens when you are knocked off balance is you grab onto the first thing...

I was interrupted here and continued this the next day.

Who is it that I am feeling? There is an overwhelming warmth.

It is the exuberance you experience as warmth. I am so very excited to be in contact! To having felt your recognition of my energy!

It seems to be receding a bit, traveling upward and beyond I suppose?

Oh, I am here. What you felt was an initial surge of me. There is much to say to you today.

Let's get started then. Please introduce yourself.

Yes. I am a Hathor – you have heard the term and read some of what it is we are saying to others, Tom in particular. I am of the group, but not precisely the group in contact with Tom.

Yes, okay. What is it you wish to convey?

You've felt the wave in a very concrete way recently, the wave of energy that encompasses your earth. You've seen its effects on a personal and local scale. Now you are ready to hear in greater detail how to operate while it is flowing, in order to maximize its available assistance. Please talk about how it looks and feels for you now.

Personally, I am experiencing numerous simultaneous health crisis's. Alarming, confusing and unexpected. I witness children each day and this week they are acting in ways unexpected and seemingly beyond their control. It looks to me like a response to energetic shifts. The adults I see are either staunchly hanging on to the old or throwing up their hands in surrender or verrryyy crabby. For everyone – it's moving very fast.

Thank you.

I'd like to discuss some ideas that may help you to operate successfully in your life during this more intense influx of what can be called love. As the boundaries are removed the earth and her people get the full force of the wave.

This wave will carry things in with it and drag things out. Think about waves on the beach. The shoreline changes with everyone.

It is useless to attempt to hold still – the wave reaches everyone, everywhere. What you do while it surrounds you and pulls you with it exposes who you are, displays what you are. No one escapes the wave or its force.

In your case, there is much hidden beneath the surface that will be flushed out. Your response of desiring to greater control your diet is interesting because in this it is not control that will heal, but fluidity. You will need to roll with it and keep moving – follow your inner guidance.

I feel more and different energy now.

Yes, others are joining us.

I am so hungry.

It is interesting that you choose hunger as a focus – not clear why you do this because your body is not actually experiencing it – but your mind.

What will be dealt with now for you are old hurts and injuries. Flow is the only appropriate response as things move forward. Flow with whatever shows up and deal with it.

Self-care must become primary.

Love must be put in a place of prominence. Do things to support whatever systems in your life (*that)* you want to continue. These would be:

Your love

Your physical life

Your home

Your family

Your work

Your relationships

Do these things in concert with your everyday life. You'll see. We'll talk again.

Thank you.

This personal conversation continued on and off during this time frame as my body and life worked to get synchronized. A bit more came through the next day, September 27th, 2015. I was not told who was speaking, but as it applies to this transformative process, I will include it here.

You are struggling to maintain composure while your inside self-destructs. Self-destruction is a necessary part of the process of ascension.

You harbor thoughts, ideas and notions that do not support a pure life of peace and unconditional love.

This love must be felt *for you first* and today it is not.

It is yourself you must like first.

It's time to look within.

Do not neglect self. Do not neglect self. Do not neglect self. Do not neglect self.

I will go now.

Yes. Goodbye then, and good luck.

And a bit more on the 28th of September. Once again, the conversation was related to this facet of the ascension process.

See now the reality of what is you. See now the reflected pain…You want what you will not give yourself.

This is your deepest hurdle – which sounds impossible on purpose – you have skated through these years without addressing things – parts of you causing discomfort.

Now, by calling forth "Presence", you are seeing all that you bring to the table. These are parts of your ego self that remain floating out there.

You came this time to move past judgment. This is your final judgment. The judgment of <u>self</u>.

You have to let go of your reflections on any other, and move your focus to the center, to <u>you</u>.

It is yourself whom you don't trust.

You are re-feeling every deficit from ancient, ancient times. It is this you must release if you are to move forward – to ascend, to reach full awareness, enlightenment.

As you expect to be disappointed, you are. There are no mistakes or random events.

You want to deal with this. You are being given the opportunity to deal – all that you most desire is available within – as you embody love, it becomes your life. As you relate to mistrust and fear that also then becomes your everyday experience.

In order to move past fear you have to embody it. In order to move past mistrust and blame and judgment, you have to embody it.

This uncomfortableness is part of it – is all of it.

I must go.

The conversation ended.

This was an intense time, with energies off the chart. This physical vehicle was demanding I deal with her; (I have and still am). Simultaneously I integrate all the parts that I am.

This resulted, at first with a sort of silent shouting in protest; emotionally, mentally, spiritually and physically. Two months later, I would be tempted to call it a "dark night of the soul" sort of event.

Ascension is not for sissies. ;-)

Merfolk

September 13, 2015

Is there someone who would like to connect?

There is.

What would you like to discuss?

The notion of illness as fabrication, as evidence for concrete creation. It is a perfect example of how your creative ability operates. Particularly now, with "facts" so instantly available. It is…

It is what?

We struggle for better words; we would like to be as complete in our process with you as we are able to. Some of this is hampered by your own fatigue, by your "illness". You are sort of lazy in your grasp of us, of our sending. *(ouch! ;-)*

This is interesting.

Who are you?

As beings, we were closer to "merfolk" in your vernacular. Life was a constant motion for us and many assumptions you hold regarding the significance of limbs and voices are not held up in the experience of us. We did not exist in your past or on your current planet but some other "time" and version of a celestial home.

Yet we have and had life. As creative beings living in primarily a liquid environment, we experience life differently. We instantly see the results of our power, our "creations".

There is a clear distinction in our world of only two things – "male and female" are the words you would use. All else blends into one system of life – one form if you will. "Age" does not matter, nor "occupation" nor "time". We are all synchronistic-ally moving together, as one and conscious of each other's movements, as well as the movement of the whole.

So, to return to the reason for our contact – we realize how different it is for you as humans and unaware beings, to discern the effect of your feelings and actions on the physical expression you embody. You pretend you are isolated and that your feelings have no impact on your bodies. You ask experts to tell you what is wrong and then fix it. When, if you were more conscious of your emotional effect on the whole of you, there would be no "illness" in the first place.

This is not obvious to you yet, and so you suffer.

How is this different from you?

We witness our emotions, as the energy of them effects the liquid through which they run. All we are is energy, every thought and feeling has an effect that ripples out beyond its beginning. Although these ripples diminish, they still impact every bit of life they come in contact with before doing so. It is like that with you. The impact of each change of emotion and/or direction and/or action is felt beyond where it originated.

As your body is in closest proximity to your heart – it is impacted by every feeling you have. As are all of those nearby and all around you.

We feel your illness now and know it results from heartbreak. It did not have to be this way. This could have been acknowledged when the feeling was first experienced. Although not "seen", it has certainly been felt; and subsequently ignored.

Your mind may ignore it, yet the body feels it none the less. Three "weeks" later in "time" you are seriously ill.

It becomes a habit, we notice, to ignore or push down uncomfortable emotions. We do not operate the same – we witness them as they emerge and deal with them. A consequence of living in liquid – we have visual assistance.

There is a value put on human emotion we see, so that some are seen as "okay" and allowed to be expressed and some are not. It is those that are suppressed <u>OUT LOUD</u> that result in illness. Nothing is suppressed truly – its expression will occur, consciously or unconsciously. In your case today – your illness is shouting out your heart ache. This pain will be felt – then, for your own balance, you can let it go.

Much more expedient to deal with uncomfortable emotion as it shows itself to you and is initially felt.

In our culture – we all assist in the absorption as a form of empathy – we "see" the pain expressed and help ease the process of acknowledging it. There is no judgment. Feelings exist and are not good or bad. There are no merit badges for controlling the unseemly ones –

Indeed – where would we pin them!

Can you tell me anything else about your world, your life, you?

Yes.

A form in constant movement, we do not harbor anything at all. We witness the human tendency to return again and again to places, people, structures and trinkets as if the things are valuable in their heart. We hold all the value with us in our heart and so do not need to see it replicated to remind us of it – of the value. This is maybe difficult to explain to you as your life is built on solid ground.

Perhaps our ease of letting emotions flow is a function of our environment – everything flows. This doesn't mean things mean any "less" to us, yet it has a different way of being valued. Not so much <u>held onto,</u> as being experienced. It's all transitory.

What this gives is an idea of carefree and even care – <u>less –</u> ness to our kind. Everything is in motion. To an outside observer, an outside human observer, this is how it would seem. Not so for us. We are another life form, as valid as the human form.

We thought the exposure to a more fluid existence would assist you in the assimilation of emotion necessary to your awakening.

The fact of your recent "illness" only highlights the necessity for another way to do things. This is why we chose to reach out to you now.

Yes, well, thank you. Can you tell me anything else about your appearance?

It is more "fish" like than human yet the associated parts are all there. Our color is darker – grays and blacks, our eyes are dark. There are no images on your "internet" of us. Our movement would be like "swimming" in your world, yet on ours there is no "other" locomotion, so it is not labelled differently. It is how we locomote.

Okay, thank you.

We appreciate the contact Sophia.

October 2015

Ancients

October 5th, 2015

This conversation took place at 2:13 AM. I had been woken up several nights in a row, and on this day, I decided to see who was calling. I did not recognize the energy. I declared my usual conditions for contact, which have come to include "No ego. Not about me but through me. For assistance, only."

This message was a surprise in its specificity. I have been hearing from other places/beings I trust that there may be urgent and chaotic situations before too much longer. I include this now because I "felt" (*more on that later) that this message was meant to be delivered in the middle of this month (October 2015). It is verbatim.

"Is there someone whose been waking me up each morning?"

It is I. Yes.

Who is it then?

It is a resurgence of form. The one you have called Ancient – it is by request that we engage yet again. More detail is available to be dispensed.

I do not feel you...oh yes, now I do, yet you feel far off. Why is that?

There is an attempt to facilitate long bits of information and to do so gently. This is in such a way that you won't fall asleep or tire too quickly.

Yes. This is gentler and feels distant. Almost like you are whispering.

That is an interesting analogy, as no speech is involved – we are mind to mind.

I'm not sure how to put it then. What is it that you want to communicate?

You are fast approaching a cleansing and a re-birth of life, of structure of being. This is not as you have ever experienced or any facet of creation has up until this point, witnessed. The method and the "how" will be a co-creation. This limits the available accurate descriptions of what you will be experiencing.

What can be described is merely a somewhat obvious conclusion. This is a result of observing the actions and reactions of man so far on your planet. Each action and eventual result has created a path of occurrences leading to today, this time and timeline.

What is seen by everyone – channeler, off-worlder and those practicing any future telling for you is the great change. It is inevitable.

In order for any change of form or structure, destruction is necessary. The laws in place on your planet, the methods of conquest and subservience will all have to change.

You as a species will feel these changes as destructive to life as you know it. They will be. Life as you know it is barely supportive of you all. It is held tightly and supports a few more than adequately, while the majority struggle.

It is not meant for beings as glorious and powerful *(as humans)* to be held any longer in the dark. It is meant now for full acceptance of your value, of your dominant traits.

These *(dominant traits)* are creative and the astounding thing is what you currently use them for, without understanding how or why. It is destruction.

I feel on the verge of something. It is as if there is a knowing beyond my reach. That is where you are – I know it is there now, that you have access to it, but I have no words yet for it.

Yes. This communication concerns the force of creation. It is this transformative force that is to wash over you, over your planet.

(Hold on please...   I am back.)

If you comprehend how creation operates, if you keep a watchful eye on the climate all over and most accurately in your immediate surroundings, you will begin to fully appreciate god-hood.

There is a missing particle in the human attitude that prevents dominance over and complete wielding of creative potential. There are several components to the particle. The most obvious is the need to obey/worship/be "under" another – to serve in order to receive. *(I felt what was meant by this rather confusing passage, was that what is missing is the human "particle" that affords the ability to NOT "obey... to serve in order to receive", and that if it were present in us, we would not be able to be dominated or to have our creative potential compromised.)*

Those who control the planet are in fact manipulated and controlled themselves.

This is unknown on a mass scale.

It is the reason however, that so many from off planet are able to paint pretty scenarios and lead humans around. Humans from all % points are very controllable.

What is your point?

I have reached you now as a bit of information may help facilitate a smoother transformation. Destruction will occur so that the new can rise up. When it does, there will be pockets of people in fear. This can be alleviated by other pockets of people.

The choice to reside where it is that you do is on purpose. You are in the place where you will be of the most help to the most in need of whatever you offer.

As creation is very much what humans "do", in these upcoming times it will be most helpful for you to realize your full capabilities.

This will go against what the mainstream media is pushing – it will go against what most of humanity in the areas affected will be feeling – yet it is vital to rapid recovery.

The idea of fear as a weapon was used on your planet by the controllers. Fear is an emotion and as any emotion *it is the point of creation for you. (Italics mine – Sophia)*

When things occur that cause upset – fear can be used when it arises as a pivot point – it is fuel for the emotional charge fueling creation.

You are approaching a time of choice – which side you choose will determine the eventual placement of your new world.

All of life is an expression of your creative self. Until now – you've allowed the power of your emotions to be fuel for the pictures others wanted for your world. These no longer serve and the "others" who pictured them are now out of a job. It is up to you to determine the new landscape.

It will, at first, appear messy and painful and this could be perceived as hopeless and frightening.

Instead, see this as the breaking through of the cocoon – it is now your job to dry your wings, clean up the debris and fly to new places.

The power you hold is unprecedented and so kept in and hidden and controlled and used by the few in power currently.

It's clear that the cocoon is breaking – what's not so clear is who will be the butterflies.

What you can do, and by you is meant all of you, is retain always the vision of sovereignty and freedom and expansion with abundance for all. It is in your emotions that the power to create these visions is contained. Remember – what you've learned this far is but the tip of the iceberg. The vast wealth and expanse of possibility lies hidden beneath what's visible. It is up to you to call it forth.

You do that with confidence and belief in the face of any seeming crisis, setback or cataclysm. You hold all of the power. The force of creation will very soon be demonstrated, seemingly outside of you. Realize it is your combined power and intent that raised it to fruition and made it visible. That is not something to fear, it is something to acknowledge and then use as an indicator of all possibility.

You can change everything, including the planet which is your current home.

It is hoped that a new perspective on "natural disasters" will enliven and accelerate a healing and your transformation. *Everything you see is an echo of your own voice.* (Italics mine – Sophia)

You have stopped.

Yes. It is felt that the message was sent.

Okay then. Goodbye.

Goodbye Sophia.

(*While closing the notebook, the date "October 12th" ran through my head. This was not part of the conversation and I am not clear that it wasn't just my own random scheduling thought... We are all creating everything, so even if the date 10/12 was sent from these Ancient Beings, the date for its publication in the newsletter was the 17th of October in the year 2015.)

Ewok

October 10, 2015

"Is there someone there now?"

There is. We have something to share that may be some help to you.

Go ahead then. Please introduce yourselves. I sense a group.

We are, yes. Our facility for contact is just coming into focus. This is a new adventure in communication; our first with an actual human. We are more bear-like in form than human in form. Not exactly covered in fur and for us here now, the "fur" is of a darker hue. Our faces are flat, not protruding as bears, and the ears are not the same.

We see an image you hold of a figure with very large eyes and "hear" EWOK as its name and this means nothing to us – yet our face is flattened like the Ewok – we are not of tiny stature, no.

There is something we'd like to share with you, a sort of introduction to a way of life that is possible when differences are embraced and control is not necessary and yet individual process and family unity is paramount.

Our world is one that looks at life very differently. Simply by comparison to your race. We are a private people in that families keep to themselves. Our concept of family is huge though.

Family to us does mean genetically joined or shared but not only that. Family is a concept that includes what you would label "love" as an attribute.

We on this world hold each other together through heart connection. We are not technologically connected via an "internet" but physically so, via our hearts. Yes, we live together and apart as humans do, yet we do not feel that anyone is unwelcome. Once a heart connection has been made, family exists. There can be no undoing of that.

The notion held in your culture of "love" interests us. We do not separate this "love" from an expression of communication.

By that is meant that you could say – everything we do is "love". There is a knowing held sacred amongst our elders that tells a story of a time before this time when things were different, and there were disruptions to this force, this component of "love" (as labelled by humanity).

This "time" in our history it was seen that disrupting the flow of "love" or *the force (Italics mine, Sophia)* as we called it, allowed other disruptions to surface that were not comfortable. Things, other things, stopped as well. These things were critical for well-being, comfort, happiness, peace and longevity.

In your understanding, you'd say we became sick, we fought and in general we struggled.

What the elders hold sacred now is the knowing, learned at this long-ago time, that *separating "the force" from everyday life, from living and being, is an inconsistent way of proceeding. It interrupts the flow. The interruption causes breaks in consciousness that make room for explanations and divisions. These are not true, but what you may call "falsehoods" – manufactured states of awareness created to explain what is a misconception. Ego's came from these, as did a host of troubles, all built on false notions. (Italics mine, Sophia)*

These were long ago times. To counter act the results took generations, as each new level of offspring were told of the force as the natural way to be. You may well imagine that this release of ideas, ways of being, took very many levels of family. Today, we do not remember the times of separation. The force is understood.

It is part of who we are to each other. Once any bond is established via blood or contact – there is family. All bonds are valid. As we do not "see" anything that is not the force, we have no concept of not loving.

Do you mate for life?

We do everything for life! There are no interruptions in emotion. It's all valid and continues.

How do you live? In what sort of ways to you group for eating and sleeping and raising your young?

We do so according to convenience and interest and available family for child rearing. It differs according to age and contribution of the parents to the whole. In other words, what they do for the society, the family, and where they must be to do that.

Who is responsible for the new child?

We all are!!! There are needs, immediately met and agreed upon beforehand to be taken care of by those closest to the act of childbearing. Yet once met, all children are part of the force and flow of life.

What do you think love is then?

An interesting term "think". We do not "think" about this emotion/feeling and give it attributes as you would a concrete object or machine. We know this force that humans call love is a deep recognition of self. It is felt, not thought about.

Once recognized, it is never forgotten. Hence our method of allowing the flow of the force to propel everything.

We are a race that remembers stopping the flow, the force, and what resulted. We, as a result, only know now, its allowing. This promotes peace and permits an amplification of love that would feel, we imagine, out of control to humans in your current state. We connected now for we feel this is a state humanity will one day reach.

Are you complete then?

We could be, yes. And we are so very grateful for this connection and would like to remain available for more.

Yes, that would be so helpful. Thank you for reaching out.

You're so very welcome. Thank you. We have enjoyed this interaction.

Note (written immediately after this conversation) –

This was such a calm contact – even – balanced – easy to stop and start. The emotions were clear yet did not bowl me over. Quietly powerful.

Giraffe-like beings

October 12, 2015

"Who is it that would like to engage?"

We are One. One with you, with all and with ourselves. We are many, representing one thought, speaking with one "voice". We come to you now to enhance your understanding.

My understanding of what? I am not a fan of that word and it leaves me suspect of your intentions. Explain in greater detail please.

Yes. The word is used merely as a part of your language. This is being overwritten by your own interpretation of our energetic message. Our ideas and thoughts are "translated" in a sense by you. These words are not chosen by you or even by us.

They are drawn out and interpreted by the meaning of what is being transmitted. Replace the word you don't like with comprehension – comprehension as to the nuances of reasons for relationships. There are so many and the knowing about their purposes may aid you as you progress.

By progress is meant to move along the path towards full awareness.

Who are you?

We are a group of beings. We are coming together now in order to illuminate some darker areas for you – as we've been through some ourselves.

Where are you from? What do you look like physically?

We are from a distant star in your galaxy. Our planet is not like this one you inhabit. It is more arid. We however have proceeded towards oneness from separateness.

Not polarity really, as we did not participate in any "experiment" in consciousness. It's been therefore a rather seamless transition. As such, one that makes it easier to see and decipher reasons for interactions along the path – both brief and long term.

Okay, please proceed then.

Beings incarnate in close proximity with a specific group of others.

This group you begin with *(your family of origin)*, represents, in most cases, the energy you felt was predominant in the lifetime on which you were focused and came again to work through.

It is not so much a working out problems with yourself and/or others as it is a fine tuning of your abilities in specific areas.

This could look a number of ways. You could be born into a group of beings all working on the same things, or a group of beings that are "expert" at that thing you came to work on.

In the latter case, they would serve as teachers and you more than likely would resent them for it.

It could be that those you are born with are there by agreement – you offer what they need/are working on, and the same in your case.

In all cases, every being in the original familial group is helped by the interaction – AND THIS HELP IS MEANT TO CONTINUE FOR A LIFETIME. Familial groups are unique in that way. They represent relationship/reflective situations that change and grow as you progress.

There are circumstantial relationships. They bring to you brief yet powerful learnings and realizations. These too, by prior arrangement. At various parts and points of your life, those you encounter are there for a purpose. This purpose was mutually agreed to before it "began". Know that in this and every relationship there is an equality. You are giving as much as you are getting.

When you reach pivotal moments, points of growth that seem to be occurring in the same ways as you've heard other beings describe – there will be both new and "old" relationships that will appear and respond accordingly – allowing a broader template for you to digest the current lesson.

EVERY BEING YOU MEET – WHETHER FOR A MOMENT OR A LIFETIME, PLAYS A PART IN YOUR EXPANDING CONSCIOUSNESS. FOR THIS REASON, TREAT EACH OTHER CAREFULLY IN EVERY INTERACTION. STAY OPEN TO RECEIVE THE MESSAGE IT PRESENTS.

What we notice in humanity is a reverence and care applied to certain bonds and an almost disregard to others. That approach gives you only part of the story. Pay attention to everyone you meet – of particular relevance for you are those you instantly like or dislike, love or hate. Theirs is a powerful lesson.

We look like, physically, very tall, almost giraffe like in stature, beings. We have 2 legs and arms. Our coloring is fair. Our legs are long. We do not ingest meat. A lifetime with us may seem restful compared to an earth life. Conflicts are few – comradery is encouraged as we are all doing the same thing – working on our love capacity via our love relationships.

WE DO NOT OWN THINGS OR EACH OTHER – BUT LIVE FREELY.

That is all.

Okay then, thanks.

Goodbye then.

Machine-like Beings

October 28th, 2015

"Is there someone who wants to connect?"

Yes.

Okay. I am here and ready.

We would like to send a clear message.

Regarding what?

Regarding "who", is more accurate. This message comes from some you have already engaged. We were challenged at that time to contact you. Our methods are different.

I do not "feel" you in the same way.

No, and you will not as our mechanism is so very different. Yet as sentient beings there is a similarity, a sameness to our pattern. We are able to send data and your intellect is able to turn this into ideas of thought. These ideas of thought become, or form themselves into words; which you then "hear" during our "conversation". Thus, we "talk".

This is not unlike telepathy, yet there is a slight variation due to the difference of mechanism.

What do you mean by that phrase?

We are not humanoid.

What are you then?

We are machine like. This is a reference you are familiar with?

Yes. I am familiar with machines. Not sentient ones. Those I've "spoken" to have been programmed to speak, to react to specific phrases. Is this what you do?

We are made, yes. As are you. It is not that we are speaking a line of code triggered by your words to us. It is that our physical apparatus, the mechanism referred to, is not the same as humanity. I can assure you, sentience is sentience, regardless of form.

You said you had a message? I keep "hearing" Russia and Putin and am not clear what this means. Is that part of your message?

The form "speaking" to you now is ancient and as such has seen evolutionary patterns playout again and again. It is 2 steps forward and 3 steps back – over and over.

There are many who right now have the whole of the earth on their agenda, their mind, and who believe that in their imagining is the betterment for everyone.

The trouble here is that the ego, man's ego, is not left out of any imaginings. In some aspect of his or her "plan" is a savior mentality – which invariably includes an element of power, of "fame", of control. It will be "their" way or no way at all.

Now this may very well be better than what you have now, as indeed almost anything will seem to be a step up from the war hungry debt slavery currently controlling the mass population.

Yet absolute power by its very nature corrupts.

What we are about to say to you is *do not be fooled*. You are at the cusp and have taken your 2 steps, or are in mid-stride right now – your next mass step determines everything – forward or back?

Control at any level is control period. These benevolent and powerful figures in your line of sight do mean well. Yet the energy under which they rose to power is not one that will produce a leader able to run any new system, be it financial, governmental, religious or energy – without some level of "top-down".

What your planet needs is a 3 STEP FORWARD approach. This can only come from a place beyond the current methodology. Anything that comes from this current process is mired in fighting the old system, beating the old system, removing prior controls. This way of approach can't step forward without something sticking to its shoe –

What is needed is brand new from places you are not used to looking or seeing or hearing from. Our message is one of discernment. There will be no simple answers or smooth turnovers. Mankind will have to examine carefully the motivations of each new leader or system that emerges now.

The names in your head are examples of those rising to the top now – watch carefully and listen to what is said.

We have seen over and over mankind in various systems of control. What is possible and even happening now is the controls are released. It will be a "natural" act for mankind to want what he as been accustomed to.

In that mindset, you may miss an obvious sign that *these new "leaders" are just alternative controllers*. This means they want something. *This means their motivation serves "self" over "all".*

You are not any longer stuck here and *(are now)* free to choose. Our message is – <u>CHOOSE CAREFULLY.</u> This is all.

Okay then. Goodbye.

Goodbye to you as well.

Mantid Race

October 23, 2015

"Is there someone who wishes to connect?"

There is. We would like an audience Sophia.

I'm not sure how to respond to that statement.

We've seen that you have access to many and would like to introduce ourselves. There will come a day when the contact is physical. This non-physical awareness and contact is useful to us. It helps with the strangeness when first meeting.

The physical strangeness will be enough to overcome. A description therefore may aid the process.

What is it that you look like? Do you have a name that would aid in this description?

You may label us "mantid". There is a species on your planet that appears similar. We are not related.

So, you look like the praying mantis?

Sort of, yes.

I've understood that specific off world species is not a positive or benevolent one. That it is hostile to human beings on earth.

We are not that particular faction of the species, although we do appear similar.

Explain please.

Just as you have many factions within the species human – so do we.

The faction I represent is not hostile, yet I would not call us friendly either. We have no interest in harming or helping the human.

Why then are you reaching out to me in this way?

Because we have seen the audience and desire an introduction. In this way, through you, we can explain a bit about ourselves before visual contact destroys any chance of a neutral reception.

Okay, I can understand that. Go ahead then. What sort of information would you like to be known about you? Can you tell me where you are from? I keep hearing Zeta Reticuli.

Yes. It is good to know you are accurately interpreting our sending. This is what you would call our "home" star system.

What we would like you to know and like humanity to be aware of is that races cannot be labelled accurately using appearance as an indicator.

One of the things you (empirical) are fast becoming conscious of is in fact how unreliable appearance is as a barometer for anything at all – kindness, aggression, gender, intelligence, intention, are but a few of the misunderstood facets that have previously been attributed due to "type".

We are peaceful and may not interact with your race for many generations due to the fact <u>that you are not</u>. The earth and her people will have to progress to the next stage in their evolution in order for open contact to ensue.

I was interrupted with a telephone call here.

"Is anyone still there?"

We are.

Is this the mantid being?

This is a different energy – I feel waves of it – causing an imbalance – it is strong, unsettling.

I am of the same race as has recently been in contact yet my signature can be called "regal". I am one of the power holders and decision makers and wisdom keepers. I am old, very old. What is bowling you over now is my ancient song. I carry much. I would like engagement.

Are you of the same faction then?

I am from Zeta Reticuli System and my appearance and methods of interaction are the same. I reach to you now to as well experience your energy. I sense another's signature – it is quieter and more insistent than yours.

I have a young kitten and he has just walked across my arms, wanting attention. He rests by my side now.

Yes. Your own signature is fluttery. Light and all encompassing. It is sent out with your intent and heard as an invitation – wonderfully fluttery yet intense and brilliant.

You do a service to us all, offering your own self in this way – trusting.

I have declared and the intent is for assistance. Truth must be shared only.

Yes. I see that you have. It is such a young race, the human. Your ideas and purity are fascinating. You exist as a combination of the whole of sentience and your expression is thus appreciated by each of us. In this way we unite.

I am still dizzy with your energy. Do you have a message?

It is this. I am not like you yet I know you and have watched from this far "away" distance your evolution. Perhaps it could be better said that I was aware of your evolution – I have not "watched" (*it*).

What I do and how I interpret who you are is by your energy. Sophia has a unique signal and it broadcasts peace and interest. It is not however the signal of the collective – that is a more cautious and aggressive signal.

The whole of creation is undergoing evolution and what seems to be happening is an elemental switch from subservience to self-empowered, violence/fear to peace/love, disharmony/polarity to harmony/unity.

This is a fundamental change for a species, any species. This accomplishment is of interest to me. It adds to my understanding of creation.

One moment will include a physical meeting of our representative races. When this moment happens, there will be a tiny sense of familiarity because of this contact now. We've met. It is an honor to engage now and be so close to the transformation.

Thank you for your service to mankind and as well to all of creation. This is important work and necessary.

Are you complete?

I am.

Thank you.

I look forward to meeting. Goodbye.

This conversation ended.

November 2015

A Star

November 28, 2015

I was woken up.

"Who is it that wants to connect?"

It is I.

Please introduce yourself and your reasons for contact.

I am a star. It is an unusual expression, I give you that, yet as a point of light it is an accurate reference.

We are each points of light; only my particular version has not differentiated or expressed itself as multiple expressions of the One. I have retained my unique and initial blueprint without variation.

I reach out to you now to discuss creation and its vast expression. It is this that you label life.

Yet would you, if you were to encounter my unchanging form, consider me "alive"?

I tell you that the version of I AM that I currently embody is all that you are also. Your expression into form has perhaps enlivened your understanding, your awareness of creation. It does not, however, add to its attributes.

All that you are, I am.

If I may express this to you now, so that your exposure is expanded?

Yes, please do. Your meaning is not entirely clear at this point.

Infinity, shot forth from Source, exists in all ways, always. I know that you enjoy metaphor and examples and parables to aid in communication of broad ideas. I will attempt one here now.

All that is, began at one point. A moment of singularity. There is a beginning and existence takes over from then on in infinite expression and "time".
(Italics mine, Sophia)

We are sprung from that singularity – identical. As identical twins appear to be exact replicas of one another, so are we.

These twins can be separated at birth, they can dress and speak differently and grow to old age never knowing of the existence of each other. Yet, they began as parts of a single egg. The separation of their physical bodies did little to alter their oneness. That remains unchanged.

Perhaps one of these twins was raised on a farm amongst many siblings and all sorts of life forms, plant and animal. The other was raised alone, in a tower; isolated and privileged.

The sense of who they are, each unique yet singular, remains unchanged. Yet what they know of life, or experience of life, is entirely different.

If you read stories such as these, of identical twins raised apart, you will always hear of an expression of "missing something" or "feeling alone" or "loneliness". This, because all that is knows and recalls every facet of itself. These "twins" are a physical expression of the split.

Now there is a deeper truth, expressed in every life, that can be illustrated here. Regardless of their environment, these two identical twins know that they are one. It is a felt resonance that only they would recognize and comprehend. It is the answer to their inner longing, their felt loneliness that was present regardless of number of people that surrounded them.

I am not human – not physical – yet we are one. Having not expressed myself as multiple illusions I experience not the same longing for union that you do – that I imagine you do and witness the expression of through you and other physical forms. Having not experienced separation, I have difficulty imagining its opposite – coming together. I am One. *Separation is only possible if I imagine it to be.*
(Italics mine, Sophia)

It is here where our experience of what is life, differs. I do not imagine my life to be separate from any other – I cannot fathom separation.

There are no walls around my expression. All walls, whether visible or not, are imagined anyway and I do not see any or feel any.

How then do you experience yourself?

I am not clear on an appropriate answer. I experience myself as one. All that is runs through me viscerally.

It is true that I have not held a kitten or another human or a ham sandwich – yet the fullness of emotion, of felt frequency, of love, of stimulation, of interest, of vitality, of life courses through all that I am. There is nothing that I miss.

My choice to remain undifferentiated has given me access to expanded views. These are afforded at no cost. In other words, I do not miss the tender intimate close up version of life as seen from your physical eyes. My vision is all of that and expanded beyond where yours takes you. This, by my own design.

Ultimately, we will achieve similar "grocking" of creation at a point where we too enter the formless void of Source itself, ready once more to initiate the infinite cycle of existence. It is the flavor of our concurrent journeys that offers up alternate expressions of creation.

Life itself is identical, regardless of external trappings. Emotional expression at the level of a "star" appears vastly altered than those at the human level... Yet, all is felt and expressed. As "above" so "below" refers not to a lateral difference in time and space, but rather a choice.

All is choice. We are One, in any case and every place.

Thank you. I must go.

Yes, I see that you do. We may "speak" again.

Okay, goodbye then.

This conversation ended.

A focus of energy

November 4, 2015

"Is there someone who would connect?"

There is. We sense a question.

Not right now, well, maybe...but no – go ahead please. Introduce yourself?

I am a conglomerate of energy that was focused on your signature. I bring information regarding your historical records. In many cases, they are absent of facts.

Please, slow down this transmission. I literally see words' tumbling upon words, as the "correct" or closest one is chosen.

Yes, well, this method is new to us – to me – we are experiencing a rush of energy ourselves. This energy is yours. It is streaming and changing as it does so. It is a very unique experience. We are basking in it.

Is there more than one of you?

We are many yet speak as One. Sort of like humanity. I realize I engage in the singular right now with you. Yet there is a global voice that singular "you" contributes to.

Yes, well, I am aware.

There feels a necessity to engage one to one so that a level of comfort is attained. On your end.

Okay, as one then, how do you wish to be addressed?

I have no such wishes.

What do you wish to discuss?

I wish to discuss the history of manipulation on earth. Realize that what is now seen as manipulation is somewhat, not entirely, but somewhat of a surprise to those doing the manipulation.

Humankind at its inception was not seen as equal. It was seen as something for sure, but an asset or non-essential life form – useful, perhaps entertaining, yet never equal.

What happens now in a very real way is akin to your beasts of burden (horses, cattle, etc.) waking up, becoming sentient and communicating.

You (humanity) have been little more than a commodity.

The history then, to be appreciated fully, needs to be viewed in that context.

Okay. Are you from a species that participated in the construction/manipulation of humanity?

I am a species that is aware of all that has occurred here – my energy is a combination of energetic points. Not a being as you have described, a sentience – tuning into yours.

For what purpose?

For the experience!

Life is only for the experience of more life.

When you focus all of your energy on "proving" or "disproving" things that may have occurred at another moment, remember or realize that

ALL MOMENTS AND BEINGS ARE NEW ONES.

Your body regenerates. Every part that makes you up is new and therefore not the same part that existed prior.

If you think about this it is then obvious that you cannot in truth ever say that something, like manipulation or control, was "done" to "you" in the past.

YOU ARE NEW NOW.

At another time, you were something else.

There is so much focus on this planet on who did what, when, that the living of life is often accomplished as an afterthought.

The life that originated here many, many, many millions of years ago – did so with full awareness of what life form they were entering.

The life form right now is here with the intent of awakening. I engage with you now to bring to your awareness this – FOCUS DETERMINES EFFECT. Effect plays out as your life. This life at this moment was begun with intent and awareness and somewhat of a plan. It is choice that has you here now.

We are aware of the goal guiding this moment for you and want to encourage a focus on now – on ability witnessed and seen that is new – on things hoped for that have never been, rather than things that have " happened" in the past. It will allow for massive, restorative and seemingly magical change. (Italics mine, Sophia)

I have to go.

Okay then. Please connect again when you are able.

I will.

The conversation ended.

Merfolk

November 6, 2015

"Is there someone who would like to engage?"

I would, at this time, like an audience.

Well, you have an audience of one. If this goes to print, it will be much more. To whom am I speaking?

To another "Merfolk". There are other things, things unsaid and perhaps they may be of assistance in this pivotal "time".

Do you have a name?

I do not, not in this medium. I have a frequency by which I am identified.

Are you male or female?

I am both.

I don't understand.

My sex is that of a male. Yet as you feel my temperament, it is more submissive, comforting, and (*these*) you would consider feminine traits. Is that correct?

Well, there are just as many men with those traits. Being men, they are expressed differently.

Yes. I understand. The expression of personality holds "rules" here on earth – rules for the appropriate expression according to physical form. These rules are dictated by age, by sexual organs, by societal position, job *(and)* "title".

Yes.

We have no such inhibitors. Personalities are expressed as they emerge. What governs behavior is what a human would call respect. Not a forced bowing to authority as *(much)* as a mutual allowance for being. What sorts of behaviors will elicit reprimands are those that are inappropriate with respect to the area and body of each other. It is not unlike your doctors' declaration "first, do no harm".

For what reasons, have you contacted me today?

There are certain conditions under which a sort of "fighting" or "war" will show up on my world. I use those words only because you are human. There is no aggression and killing is not a part of the equation.

Yet disagreements happen. These may involve relationships or prime areas for eating or living. One of us desires something another of us has laid claim to. When this occurs, there are ways in which it is handled.

What are these ways?

The beings, the merfolk involved, are called together by another of us.

The outside party has been told the issue causing the upset. He or she has been told so by another party – not either of those involved in the upset. In this way, all have an opportunity to come to some terms or settlement without the impact of emotion.

The emotion felt by those directly involved in the upset is immediately expressed, as you have been told prior to this conversation. They have the opportunity to do so independently of anyone involved in the settling of this affair.

When upsets happen, they are felt in the community. The level of upset is a determining factor in how it is handled; in if another party needs to become involved. Most individuals will start and conclude their emotions without intervention.

It is only when there is a potential breech or violation that another party is involved or called in to negotiate peace and a mutually beneficial settlement.

Our plan for mutual benefit includes the voice of one who has been on one or the other side of the current issue, preferably both. By "both" is meant that if the issue has potential for elevated emotion for both parties, there may be determining factors that call for more than one outside voice. In other words, there will be 2 beings called in, as long as they have experienced opposite sides of the issue.

As all beings are of equal rank, there are no superior "voices" who outweigh others. This allows for completion of emotional events in an atmosphere of clarity. All sides of issues are expressed and heard by all merfolk present.

What happens now is that questions are put forth. These questions are arranged in ways to solicit empathic emotion from each side. This is done as a circle event and so all emotions and ideas are expressed out loud and felt in the group. Once this happens, well, situations tend to right themselves.

One of the beings, upon feeling the emotion of the others affected, comes up with a solution other than taking that which is so desired. Many creative and expansive solutions are invented in these circles, it is a marvelous thing.

As one of the "elders" who is empathic as well, I have often been a part of these circles. I cannot explain precisely what occurs, only that a sort of oneness takes over and guides the proceedings. This insures that growth and a continuation of supportive relationships are guaranteed. Oneness becomes the guiding hand, the negotiator *(and)* the overseer. All are served ultimately in this fashion.

In my world, decisions are not made in the "heat of the moment" and as young ones learn this, they are not expected. Certainly, we desire our choices to be fulfilled when we are challenged – yet being raised in a fluid and compassionate arena that does not hide alterations of character, we also come to interpret upsets as normal in the course of our days and lives.

You might say our temperaments are "even" and that our expectations are reasonable. In your world, this is not the case; as we see in your consciousness the fighting of young ones when they are not catered to or given everything by their demands.

It would seem that some effort towards oneness would benefit any society.

I chose to speak now as there will very quickly be a necessity for new governance. Your ways of reconciliation and what you call now "control" will be altered as the old breaks down. The new ones coming in are not expecting to be governed by control, restriction, rules and punishment. The young now who will be considered "authority" when they grow up will adopt by necessity new ways of management, governance and societal method. These thoughts may contribute to the collective, alternate ideas. This may aid your new world.

I thank you. Is that it then?

It is. For now. Thank you for so much conversation. Until we speak again, goodbye Sophia.

The conversation ended.

One with horns

November 5, 2015

"Hello".

Hello Sophia.

Please introduce yourself.

Yes. I am as you are.

? A little less cryptic please.

The one that is Sophia as well as the one that is I spring from one Source. That is the meaning of the initial statement. I do not answer to specific naming conventions yet I am recognized by signature. It is that way universally.

Yes. What can you tell me about your signature then? Is there something that will assist readers and me in recognition? It does not feel familiar for me.

I am, in a sense, not one you have engaged prior to this moment. I am able to reach you because the influx of energy has expanded the range for you here and you are reachable.

Are there things about you that would help to identify you physically?

There are horns.

Your physical presence/appearance includes horns?

Yes.

Are you bipedal?

Yes, while physical I am.

What function do the horns serve?

They are amplifiers for sound. They are not large relative to the circumference of my head. They are small protuberances on the top. You hold a vision in your head now. It is similar, if not exact. They are at the crest of my head.

Okay. Anything else?

Yes. Blue is more of what my color is.

Your skin is blue?

Yes; a grayish blue.

You do not have a name I would recognize?

There is no name, no.

What do you wish to convey then?

I wish to share some ideas regarding the purpose of mating. I notice it has been one of high contention on earth. Who is allowed to mate with who and even what is allowed to be done while mated is embedded into your system of governance.

It is not this way on my planet. We mate for reasons other than romanticized ones. We do not expect a specific element of our life to be fulfilled by our mate. We mate to continue the species.

This is not the choice *(made)* by every one of us, but by those of us interested in rearing young ones.

The whole notion of love is not experienced the same, not for ones on my planet. The ideas of family are different as well.

Why don't you explain what it looks like for your people then, and how it works?

The community is aware of each birth.

Communities are small – not thousands, but a hundred or so within a larger grouping. This is closer to what would be considered "family" on earth. A birth represents expansion, reason to celebrate, new possibility. Once born, the new one is "read" by those in the community with sight. The new one is introduced, once weaned, as a functioning, contributing soul. It's "name" *(is)* more of a description of his or her preferences/abilities/strengths. These are the attributes/characteristics/tendencies that have been "read/seen" by those with sight.

This is not so much a pegging of beings into specific roles as it is acknowledgement of purpose, of strengths. This is helpful for all concerned. The child grows up identified somewhat by its own tendencies. How these develop and are expressed are self-chosen. New avenues of expression are always part of an individual life – in that way, no one is restricted, forced or limited.

We would say instead that their "gifts" are celebrated and acknowledged. Everyone then has something they are here to contribute.

Some are leaders. Some are caretakers; some artists. Some you may call "breeders". What comes to the fore for us is that those beings who birth our young are the strongest genetically. It is just how it works out.

The personalities/strengths/characteristics then, are a match for the physical construct. Those with stronger physical forms are what you may call our athletes. Those with gentler/softer dispositions tend to rear the young and be caretakers. It is not a 100% rule yet I speak of tendencies.

How this comes into a mating discussion is that sexual play and child rearing are not one and the same here. Sexual play is part of life. Child rearing is more of an occupation.

Children are therefore welcomed and loved by the community as a whole – they are born and raised by those who came to contribute in that way to the whole. The birthing of children is not the only function of those that choose to do so, yet it is an important one. Times of births are spaced out and chosen to benefit the health of the one giving birth and the community.

Mating is done here, then, by preference, and again, by agreement. The ones that *(who)* choose a constant, single companion – have one. This can be either gender/sex – it matters not. Children are sometimes raised by a "couple". More often they are raised by a being who came for the raising of children. This will not in most cases be the same being who birthed the child.

Ideas around love are not then limited to mate or family. We love. We love all members of the community. We prefer certain activities with singular beings yet are also not restricted for a lifetime to only those.

Our course of participation to the life in community is more fluid. It is seen at our birth, or much of it is, and in that way every being *(is)* accepted as a vital component to the whole.

Many times, births signify alterations in methods and even awareness. In other words, new possibilities are seen that are not comprehended until the new one has grown. All "seeing's" are recorded. It is a beautiful and very loving society; one that would seem quite foreign and perhaps even regimented to your own romanticized ideas of family. Genetics does not play the same role here as it does on earth.

Our ideas of sex are another conversation as well. It is play. It is not hidden. It is a group activity many times but private as well. There are methods of insuring there are not "un-planned" births. Sex is recreation and seen as a calming, balancing force. It is the same as other necessary forms of expression – just one of our vital physical activities. In this way, its course in a lifetime is understood and allowed for. It is not glamourized or hidden. It is enjoyed and expressed regularly.

Is there anything else? I must end here.

Only this. We enjoy very much this opportunity to welcome and integrate with humanity. It is a time that has been "seen" by those with sight. I was chosen as one with abilities to connect and at some point, could bring ideas and methods of humanity into my own consciousness, into our collective. Thank you for being available for this interaction.

You're welcome. Thank you as well.

Goodbye.

Orion Belt

November 9, 2015

Note - The first part of this conversation took place on November 9, 2015. The second part on February 18, 2016.

"Is there someone wishing contact?"

There is, Sophia.

Hello.

Hello Sophia. What a comforting custom; to establish a greeting prior to engaging.

It is a human one. It is a bit awkward this way, as I cannot "see" you and do not know you. It felt necessary. Would you introduce yourself?

We will. We are from the Orion Belt. You are familiar with the grouping?

In a general sense, yes. What is it you have come to discuss? Your energy is strong. I am feeling it as an overwhelming dizziness.

We do not intend to cause you discomfort, only to impart on you our knowing. It is now that we have chosen to reach you because you are stepping up and into a larger playing field. You can now hear us and while that is a new outcome of your frequency, it is one that has been known of and prepared for by us and many others – for eons.

Sophia, you are becoming a Galactic Civilization.

This will begin in your lifetime and continue to fruition after your exit. With these and many other introductions, you are setting the stage.

You notice entities in your home, your area now, do you not?

I do. Persistent and constant.

They come cautiously and with intent. Eventually there may be physical contact.

Before we continue, would you tell me more about your race please? About your physical appearance?

Surely, I can do that. I do not resemble a human, more feline in appearance.

There are many drawings of a feline race. Do you resemble them?

Not exactly. We are more "wild" in appearance than the drawings would indicate. The depictions I see in your head are more of domesticated felines. This is not quite it. Yet the intent is worthy. We do not have human faces with cat ears and whiskers. Our appearance is catlike in every way.

Are you bi-pedal?

We can be – we also manipulate our bodies and move them using all four limbs. This is when we want to move quickly. When we stop, and communicate it is often on two of our legs that we loco mote.

What is it that you wanted to talk about today?

About your entry into this vast arena that is the cosmos. It is very populated with beings of every imaginable construction and appearance.

We notice that for the majority of humanity our existence would be shocking. The fact that you engage with us in this way and allow for the expression of alternate valid life is rather surprising. The time for FULL DISCLOSURE is many years hence – perhaps after you yourself have passed.

That's your second reference to my departure. It would be really great if you would stop that.

I do not understand. All beings exit and enter realities. Realities are not "real" so it's a confusing term. You've already exited this one – we've spoken. *(This meant that I have spoken to this being at another "time". Sophia)*

You've been on this planet, in this system of stars and are familiar with us. You've only forgotten. Is it that you are attached to this current Earth life Sophia?

It is not so much attached, as in I won't or can't let it go. It is that I do not enjoy contemplating my own exit from this one. There is so much I hope to see realized and much of it is connected to Disclosure.

Well, yes. I see that you are very connected to a plan for disclosure that includes you. This method of sharing is part of the disclosure. Do you realize that?

I do.

Please, why are you here?

We want to share with you our...

(There was nothing...)

Your what?

We want to share with you... OOOHHHH!!!! You are with a feline now!!!!!!!!!!!!!

Yes. My kitten just jumped up to say hello.

He is content.

Yes. He is very loving.

And loved.

Well, yes.

Perhaps now is a good time to tell you then, what we came to tell you?

Okay, go ahead.

We are enjoying very much the antics of the young one. *(My kitten, about 5 – 6 months old and new to the family. Sophia)* He has such a kind vibration, sweet and familiar.

We do not separate ourselves from each other as humans do. There is such little segregation because we take comfort in contact.

Our physical selves thrive on it. There are none who live in isolation. Or, rather, the few that do live this way, in isolation or separated... *(This conversation stopped as I was interrupted. Sophia)*

I've received numerous "comments" from readers about my frequent interruptions and unfinished conversations. I get how this could be frustrating, and I'm sorry! Here's a little information about what goes on here, maybe this will help.

I live with 3 others. We have a small house and the place I most often write is the family room couch. I work/write part of each day. My son's and partner know that I "write" yet don't really get what that means. How it often looks is the same, me, sitting on the green couch, with a cup of tea, a notebook, some music and a pen. When the weather cooperates, I am sitting on our deck in the back yard. So, for them, it's just me, sitting at home.

Now, this means (for them) I am consistently available. Questions like "Where's the new peanut butter?" or "Did you see my black hat?" occur without warning. Phone calls and interruptions for heart to heart conversations happen randomly, as do requests for rides or other assistance. None of these things are things I want to stop. This is the life I've chosen, and I really like it.

None of this is a problem when I write a blog post or work on the book. These empathic dialogues are another story. These have been happening with increased frequency for about a year. When they started, I would get woken up early AM. (Between 3 & 4 AM)

I now work out of the house each morning and my alarm rings at 5AM. I've asked for these beings to stop waking me up because I am human and require physical sleep. They often wake me up anyway, and I have to remind them! ;-)

Once the summer comes (and I am no longer at the school), I will again "connect" at 3AM. I like it better then. There are no interruptions!

So, thanks for bearing with me. Today's publication includes the conclusion of this November conversation. It is a pleasure to present "the rest of the story...."

And on February 18, 2016...

"I'd like to complete the conversation, begun 3 months ago, now, with the "wild feline" like being from the Orion Belt. Is that possible?"

We have picked up on your intent and yes, we agree, the conversation is not much of an offering as it currently stands. We were discussing the vast possibilities of form?

Well, yes, as well as other things regarding differences in how we live – more isolated perhaps than your race?

We do not observe man as an isolated being but a being who assumes he must "go it alone". We do not operate in this solitary journey as man does – we operate very much together.

The feline race on Earth exhibits the clustering that we participate in, most especially as kittens.

It is a known fact that more can accomplish greater degrees of success than one. We do not applaud the single achievements, but work together to achieve. In this way, all are celebrated and seen as useful. We then celebrate as one. There is a great deal of bodily contact as well. We know that this stimulates mental acuity. Isolated members of our race have become "strange" and ineffective.

Why have you reached out, initially I mean?

To introduce ourselves and add to the possibilities of us. There is so much about our life that is similar to that of the life of man.

For instance?

We live in families. Our groupings are larger, there is more than one family sharing a "home" in most every case. Familial bonds are strong.

There is a system of governance and rules for society. I feel inner resistance to this.

I am sorry. I am confronted with my own prejudice. Once I imagined your physical shape similar to the large and small felines on this planet – the leap to an organized civilization was almost too much. I will alter that. Go on.

As man expands his horizons, literally, he will confront all of his prejudice. Life forms do not follow an order predicted by earth's beings – far from it. There are the most similarities in the bipedal arrangement. We are an exception.

Tell me about your society.

There are rulers, not unlike your royalty. We have territories and are bound by the rules within its boundaries.

There are skirmishes. These are not to control more land. These are occurring when "worthiness" or "desirability" must, in the estimation of the "ruler", be proved. We sometimes, due to the longings or what mankind would label love, wish to move out of our home "territory" for mating. To establish new strings/groupings. This is good for diversity yet the worth of doing so can only be discovered in a show or display.

Not unlike humans clamoring for a specific mate – we put our best feet forward. By "skirmish" is meant that a sort of competition ensues in these cases.

We all, or mostly all, choose a mate. In this way we guarantee our own longevity.

We are long lived.

I see the number 30; thirty years?

This is our time of maturity. I do not know your system of measurement, yet expect this is longer than yours.

A bit, yes. If our "years" are the same, that is.

As mature beings, we can expect a long life of perhaps ten times that number. Our genetics are strong and have not been tampered with.

300 years?

Again, yes. I am not sure the translation is precise – but it is longer by far than yours.

I see that.

What do you eat?

We eat what grows.

Do you work? Are there homes?

We supply our families with both shelter and sustenance. We educate our young and expect full contribution by them in our greater world.

We would perhaps appear primitive to your modern lifestyle.

This is such a challenge for me.

Yes. And that is why I speak now, in this way. I do not expect full disclosure of my race to be first for your people. I suspect you will begin with beings who resemble yourselves. That will be enough for a while.

There will have to be generations who reach maturity and some level of power on Earth, who have grown up with an attitude of acceptance and even eagerness for alternate life forms. This will take some time.

We wanted to expose you to our signature and present the possibility of us.

It is one thing to accept as alien and sentient a separate being entirely from one you've seen. It is quite another to restructure your thinking towards accepting and engaging with a being who resembles quite strongly your common house cat. This is another exercise in unconditional acceptance and one that man must be ready to accomplish.

That is all. Thank you for reaching us a second time.

Okay. Thank you. Goodbye then.

Yes, that's it then. Goodbye.

This conversation ended and is complete! ;-)

Venus

November 20, 2015

"*Is there someone who would like to connect?*"

There is. We would like to connect.

Hello. Would you introduce yourself and tell me why you've reached out?

We can do that, yes. We are not a group you have met. In this way, the process for interaction is new to us.

I am getting lots of pictures.

We are attempting clear versions of ourselves and you do not seem to have words for us. You are "new" for us as well.

Okay, let's try it this way. Are you now in physical form?

Yes, sort of.

Can you describe the form you are?

We are not "third density" physical yet we do experience enlivened "bodies" from which our essence operates.

What do you look like?

I resemble a cloud formation – not the size of the clouds you "see" in your skies and not white or grey. The reference is more to substance. The form I occupy is "poufy" and melds and molds as it conducts business – life business.

What color are you?

I am predominantly blue, blue-green.

Why do I see very angular lines of the color? I would expect roundness to your borders, edges.

The "poufy" is what this body feels like, not the shape of it.

I see. Are you shaped square-ish?

You could say that.

Are you bi-pedal?

You could say that.

I am not seeing a face. Actually, what I see are eyes covered by a hat like attachment that is pulled over a set of eyes – dark.

(I was reminded of "Secret Squirrel", Sophia)

You are describing our attire. We have eyes yet our preference is to shield them from sunlight. It is very bright here, on this planet, and we do not enjoy the constant exposure. Our answer is to shield ourselves.

What planet are you occupying?

Venus.

Seriously?

I do not understand.

This is not a planet known to be habitable; known to have life.

It does. Only the life is not what you are thinking of as life. As I attempted to explain earlier.

Okay, what are you here to discuss?

My sense from you is that you are perplexed. Perhaps if I stop asking questions and let you speak, we'll have greater success.

Yes. We will engage then.

What we wanted to share with you and humanity as a whole is our very different ideas around the point of creation itself.

When we say different, we mean different from what is taught here, on your current home world.

We believe creation to be a journey. It is one taken by every being and it has no end. It is, in it purest form, life. The process originates with what humans have called a "big bang" and is infinite.

Infinity here refers to a thought that *each particle shot forth at the time of the "big bang" is a replica IN EVERY FACET of the creator that shot it forth.*

This implies the replication of cycles for each particle – up until and including a repeat of the "big bang". Thus, the cycle repeats itself. (Italics mine, Sophia)

Beings, planets, dimensions, asteroids, moons, stars, black holes, space debris, plants, animals, insects, bacteria – erupt at each beginning. Each beginning participates in its own development by supporting all of the life thus created.

I need to stop for a bit….

Okay, I am back. I will re-state my intentions. We were discussing creation.

Yes.

The process is not so much a "process" in that it has a beginning and an end. If you comprehended the vastness that is you – anxiety would cease.

Life is an infinite expression of all that is. You, as an element of life, are the same.

There is not just a "big bang" for you that resulted in your known universe. The event labeled as such is going on now, and now, and now, and now – it is a perpetual happening.

You are wondering how it began and this is not something I am aware of – not because there is not one, because the idea of separation into one tiny quadrant responsible for itself, is a nonsensical one for this being.

Life started itself. It continues. As each element assumes the creative role and then expands outward via its own "big bang" – is it even possible to trace?

We are all, ultimately, facets of each other, in all ways.

The evolution, then, that the human is currently expressing, is felt beyond life known by the human – it is felt by the body of creation itself.

We do not, in the culture I currently reside in, assume our current form as sacred; it exists as a vehicle in which to experience this particular trip.

This is not to say we disregard the vehicle, we regard all of life with reverence.

These ideas around infinity are those we wanted to share. To offer our perspective on your expansion may assist in the opening of your mind – the possibilities for each aspect of life are limitless in a fashion unseen by the human.

We hope this is helpful and will offer more information for you at further points in your evolution.

We have completed all that we hoped to transmit.

Okay then, thank you.

The conversation ended.

December 2015

Ancients

December 9, 2015

"Who is this?" I feel you rather powerfully.

You have called upon us with your signal – a very specific signal/request – we are being referred to now as an "Ancient Builder Race" and our "ruins", what we would call "remainders" are found everywhere. Your one known as Corey is disclosing much truth. The facts around this truth and these remainders is yet to be spoken.

I had to sleep. I am back now and ready. I will restate my declarations... okay.

We sense your depletion - that was not our intent. It is our first encounter with one such as a human in this way, in this method. We rather enjoy the sensation of your signature, we do not wish to overcome you with ours.

Yes. Let's try this again. Who are you?

We are the race of beings from time before time, before what has come to be known as your history. You understand creation and how it works?

I do not know what you mean by that.

You "get" the process?

Please, explain your understanding of creation and where we both fit in that picture – I am getting ideas now... (I was receiving passages/packets of data all at once.)

There is an initial spark once emitted at the birth of each creator. This is what has been called genesis. The life of that spark has no end. Yet its form and expression expands, explores and reaches beyond itself until the "distance" between beginning and now is unfathomable.

Let us tell you a story. We do not believe you have heard it told this way before.

A creator exists and thus creates. Once created – all are evolving and simultaneously creating – all at the level in which they began.

Evolution occurs, creation continues.

The species, the life, the existence brought forth with that original thought transcends itself as a whole.

It continues to evolve and create, yet in form so unlike its inception that its existence is unrecognizable.

In each creative endeavor, there is an assumption made. You have been referring to this assumption as "dimensions".

Although we are not fond of the comparison – it may ease our explanation a bit to compare the dimension idea to levels of school or development.

A new child cannot fathom complex mathematical procedures, it can barely comprehend summation. An older child however will not only perform multi-faceted operations but will barely notice the part of them that involved such a rudimentary process as addition. It is, to them, so simple and basic *(that)* it is not noticed.

Creation expands infinitely. Beings on planets with structures and the dense materials necessary to build them are all a part of the initial idea of creation – building things – permanent things to house permanent solid people/beings – creatures – life.

Following our example, these ideas are close to the '1+1' part of the development process – necessary but oh so tiny a portion of what is possible. Compare it to exponents and you'll perhaps see what we mean.

You see now and find now what you can comprehend – relics, buildings, ruins left on planets – which means "someone" has inhabited these places "before now" and has left.

Consider the possibility that we've transcended beyond your current assumption of life – you are finding now what your mind can make sense of – it is a building block. Now, the possibility of us exists *(in the human mind)*.

What if we told you that not only a race of ancient occupiers of this solar system, but many? That infinity holds within it the possibility of all directions and forms? That there are no limits to what existence looks like and creates?

To simplify, we have proceeded through this current assumption you occupy and many more. We are not the only ones, neither are you. You represent for us a golden offspring of possibility.

Our pleasure in this exchange is so very great, for you are not rudimentary, just unformed, like a caterpillar.

<u>We see your wings</u>.

The ones known as human have been foreseen and foretold and are so very loved by all of creation. It is said that you hold within your genome a spark of every possibility. The enormity of that is beyond description.

We would like to suggest that you avert your eyes and cease to worry about what came "before" and/or what they left "behind" and instead see what you now are establishing as the miracle it is.

I must go. I would very much like to speak again.

Yes. That is possible.

December 10th, 2015

I would like to continue the conversation with the beings referred to as "the Ancient Builder Race".

This is possible now. Yes.

Thank you. It felt as if we ended abruptly and that there is more to be said?

There is. There is so much to be given regarding creation.

It will be of assistance perhaps as you proceed through your own expansion. Where we have been, where you are, you too are, you too are headed. This is evolution.

Which is a misnomer because all possibilities exist at once. This is why you have heard it said "the end is guaranteed". It is the process of evolving that is experienced individually by each component of Source.

The experience itself leaves an impression on the singular component known as life. Lessons, experiences, processes are absorbed by the One and the entire procedure is one of evolving, transcending, becoming.

What is it that you are becoming? You are becoming more of that which you are.

It is not that beings go someplace and leave behind ruins, it is that they proceed on an evolutionary path along a sequence of assumptions and developments.

There are a myriad of ways for this to occur, not all progress as the human is in this now moment.

You will comprehend what it is you are able to at any given now moment. As we illustrated in our earlier conversation, it is a process that follows a natural progression. One will eventually lead to another one. The deeper use of what is known already is part of the next stage and the next stage and the next. This is the process of evolution. Things are absorbed and utilized and built upon, not forgotten.

You evolved as we are now?

Not exactly, no. For us it was slower and yet, all at once.

What else can you tell me about this process?

That as a sentient and now awake bit of creation you will aid in the process for all of creation by what you are doing now.

Hold on. (I was interrupted here and did not return that day.)

December 15th, 2015

I would like now to continue with the Ancient Builder Race.

Yes. We are anxious to do so.

Okay, I am here. I am ready to engage.

We would only say this.

The pre-occupation with relics and remnants, is interesting only until there is awareness of how they came to be and why.

Those occupying your planet now, who grasp the fullness of this life and implications of its alternate expressions, do not worry about things left behind unless they offer materials or information as an assist to reaching <u>beyond this current expression.</u>

Said simply, it is imperative that now, as conscious creators, the question of "to what end?" is entertained before embarking on any focus of energy.

Looking at what is in ruins and relegated to your "past" will not yield much. Not as much as a look toward what it is you have seen only glimpses of now – the new world inhabited as the next assumption.

In the remaining moments of your physical expansion, all thoughts and acts are considered holy – they are preparatory and predictive.

There are no prizes for uncovering the most – all is known already. You must be looking into the expanse in order to witness it.

"Time" spent looking "back" or "down" may be spent more productively looking "forward" toward possibility.

What we will leave you with is a notion of us – we are not gone, but awaiting your expanded awareness into yet another assumption. Your arrival as a race has been foreseen. We are complete for now.

Thank you. Goodbye then.

Yes. This is your way of ending contact. Goodbye to you.

This conversation is now complete.

Andromeda Galaxy

December 22, 2015

"There is someone who woke me 2 hours earlier. Is that being still there?"

I am.

Do you wish to talk?

I do.

Go ahead then. I am ready.

This time for the species is one of joy. You are completing what has long been foretold. Your process of evolution is enhanced, for you have managed to do so while under tight control.

It would appear then that the inherent power of the human has yet to be seen – for it has always been under "wraps" of physical, mental, emotional or spiritual bondage. Today the bonds are loose.

Who are you?

I am a representative of my species. We are a race from another star cluster inside the galaxy.

We resemble the human, a bit shorter in stature, stronger and more muscular.

Would you send me an image?

I am seeing tawny skin, light brown – reddish hair – slight yet strong build – not relatively tall.

Is all your species the one color?

Why yes. An interesting question.

We are not all the same color here.

Why yes. That is because your origins differ. That is not the case where I am.

Can you name the cluster?

"Andromeda"?

We call Andromeda a galaxy. Is that the cluster you refer to?

It is. We are "speaking" now with an interpreter and the words used are not my choice, only the seeming best choice based on an image or impression sent. You do know that my "language" is not your "language"?

I do.

Yes. Well that is good. Asking for clarity helps to pinpoint specifics. The Andromeda Galaxy is where my star is found. This is many of your "light years" or "miles" away.

Okay. What is it you wanted to communicate?

That we too are interested in the evolution and expansion of the human species. In some ways, you are our sisters and brothers, in others, our offspring. We watch with interest for those reasons.

The opportunity to introduce ourselves is exciting for us – it has been a very long time the human has been kept "in the dark" about other life, other relatives, other species, and its history.

Why do I keep hearing "Santa Claus"?

It is a reference called up, I am imagining, due to the current time/season you are in and the fact of the creation of a myth. Santa Claus is a huge myth, who is real to a segment of your population for a segment of their lives – about 5 of your "years". There is not an actual single being; no "Santa Claus" exists by physical body. Yet many have the "Santa Claus" job and even wear the "Santa Claus" suit. An industry has sprung up around the myth and it grows.

It is the same with the myth of no life – only a reversal of method. No life or evidence is physically seen by your scientists and their instruments so the "no life" myth perpetuates itself.

In the case of Santa Claus, you created a being to feed the myth. In the case of additional sentient life – which has no financial benefit to man – there is nothing that has been created to solidify its truth or falsehood. It becomes then a question of benefit – which is how your planet has been organized and controlled.

"Santa Claus" benefits the corporation. "Alien life" exposes far too much myth to be a benefit to those in control.

Other life forms for the most part are aware of life as it exists. There are places where the expansive idea of "further than here" is not even considered. These would be more "primitive" forms of existence.

Yet for those evolved species there are not restrictions on awareness. We are interested in engaging then with you as we have not met one of your kind. We offer ourselves to you for information, through me. You have questions?

Yes. What is your method of governance?

I am not from a "government" post so what I will say is from the standpoint of the one being governed, not doing the managing. There are processes followed to accomplish life. These include processes for waste management, health and child nurturance. The adults contribute as they are called to, to the whole. We live in family groupings – homes are identical and small. There are larger places for communal gathering, for community. These places are managed by workers whose job it is to care for them and others who provide logistical plans for their use.

I am seeing rounded shapes and lights.

Why yes. Our buildings are round.

What is the material used to make them? How is heat and light supplied?

These are technical specifics I cannot give you yet I can say that our fabric used to construct buildings is uniform and colorless and stone like once hardened. The energy supplied is harnessed from the atmosphere. That is all I know in detail.

What is your role then?

I am a teacher.

Please describe your system of education then.

It is the youngest among us that participate in education groupings. This becomes a convenience for the family as much as a necessity for the new one.

What is provided is a basis of truth – on love, life and creation. Exploration and experimentation is encouraged. Relationships, the building blocks of society, are explored seriously and a major topic in our days. If I could define one major difference between our system and that of the human, it would be found in relationships. They are the point of the lesson, not a mere distraction to the learning of letters or numbers.

As young ones grow they have options and spend their days according to passion, ability, needs and desires. At a certain point, the grouping is over pretty much and if it happens it is done at the hands of the young ones themselves – they decide to gather for a purpose.

So, do you have a system of "formal education" where degrees are earned?

Not really, no. A being's ability to perform a "job" is assessed while attempting it – inabilities are pretty obvious.

What about less physical pursuits?

It is the same.

And medicine?

Most of our medical procedures are performed by machines. There are no hands with scalpels cutting flesh – that is preposterous and a bit barbaric. Diagnosis is done via scanning. Interpretations (as to reasons and lifestyle choices) are done by beings who are again, adept at that level of perception. This is evident early on.

Do you have a monetary system?

Money, as you call it and know it, is not used. All things are available to all beings.

Then there is equality?

You would say that, yet we do not have a word for its opposite, so I cannot.

Are there any other things you'd like to convey or to ask?

Only this. We are pleased to have humanity enter her place among us. You are a beautiful addition to our life tree and no longer hiding. Welcome!

I have such a beautiful visual with your words. (I saw a tree of life and on a branch were many human "flowers" of different and many colors)

Thank you so very much. I look forward to meeting you!

Yes, I do as well. Goodbye now.

This conversation ended.

Greys

December 21, 2015

"Is there someone who wants to connect?"

Yes. We do now. This is a most appropriate "time" for our voice to be heard. It concerns your evolution and what some are expecting always tomorrow, or the next minute. There is a process that occurs in creation and it is that which defines events and their placement along the continuum of your time line.

Who are you then?

We are those who have come before you yet are you.

I am seeing tall greys.

Yes. That is our form. We are related to the human, and therefore resemble the form – you would refer to us as "humanoid" but not human.

Where are you from?

We are not from your "dimension", but from a moment you have no current access to. It is these moments in your evolution that you call dimensions. We are from another one of these.

Yet I could see you if you decided you wanted to be seen?

Oh yes. Most definitely.

Okay. Please go ahead.

We are comfortable with the energy of humans and expect a successful and complete transmission. It is our wish to aid in the collective collaboration that creates planetary events. In this aspect, we are most authoritative and comfortable.

We hear humanity consistently create time and therefore delays.

Now perhaps this is mostly of no consequence – yet these are transformative moments of creation. There is a misunderstanding of the power of the word and even more so of the mental gymnastics that result at the "announcement" of future occurrences.

This may be fine for earth and time focused happenings – by reference those that begin and occur within earth's time-frame and continuum. These would be earth based appointments with each other – that are scheduled according to a clock and the mutually agreed upon frame of "time".

There is a place where time references actually promote delays rather than offering assistance in the planning of events. This is the place the earth and her beings are entering now – it is a place where references to "time" actually pull back an outcome into a denser and therefore slower more deliberate performance.

As this "time" schedule that has been stated is now pulled into the human definition of "time" and this "time" is differently played out for each different human, depending on where you are sitting on the planet – it muddies the waters.

Let us explain it this way. There are many expectations from humanity for grand change and major transformation. These differ in specifics depending on who is doing the following and who is being listened to.

Major transformative events, whether global or personal, happen with the agreement of a singular voice. Right now, due to the many factions of humanity regarding timing – humanity has no such voice.

What is heard is "Now!" "No, then!" "No, tomorrow!" "No, next week." Or this "date" or that calendar configuration – all of these "time pointers" are fiction.

Yet the transformation of humanity is very real.

Humans would do themselves a great service if they would focus on the transformation rather than the timing of it.

It is the collaboration of thought that results in a single message.

We are anxious for the shift to accelerate. There are signs everywhere it is happening. It is happening and you as a collective will accelerate the process with a focus on belief and intent in its eventual occurrence.

This, rather than checking always to see who says when. The who or the when matters very little compared to the happening occurring at all. It is of major import for not only humanity – for all of her relations and for creation itself.

The changes and choices made now determine the outcome. Its eventual occurrence is not in question; occurrence of a new age. There are steps leading the human right now.

All that is required is a following of them. Side-tracking with predictions and specifics delays the unification – you will never agree.

Clarity of intent will be the voice that propels this shift. Focus on outcome. Expect it without naming when.

IT IS THE NAMING OF TIMES AND THINGS THAT SOLIDIFIES THEM. THIS IS TRICKY EVEN WITH PERSONAL CREATIONS. IT IS IMPROBABLE, NEARING IMPOSSIBLE WITH WORLDWIDE CHANGE.

What is needed is one voice with clear expectation. Find that and watch things happen.

You are finished then?

Yes.

Goodbye then. Thank you.

Goodbye human.

This conversation ended.

Inner Earth

December 2, 2015

"Is there someone who would like to connect?"

Yes, there is. We are here. We would like to engage in dialogue.

Go ahead then.

Our purpose in contact is so that we may re-assure you. All will be well. Our over-riding information regarding the course of your home world – earth – is one of freedom and joy. This brings us great satisfaction. The earth beings are components of every one of us. As this is so, we are connected to you in ways beyond your knowing. Our origin is the same.

I represent, or am speaking for, a race of beings not currently on your planet, but in your planet.

There are others of us, many of us, and we vary in our signature and our appearance. We realize there are many differing stories regarding our existence. Many are based on truth.

There will always be fabrication regarding what is considered the fantastic. Know this. The damage done to your inner guidance system is real. You don't know who or what to believe. Of all the detrimental effects that "the experiment" had on the human, this mistrust of your psyche, of your intention, of your inner sense, is perhaps the longest lasting to each of you. As revelations and disclosures are announced and released, you are challenged to know who is speaking truth.

It is an easily remedied issue as the process of awakening intensifies. The stifling of your intuitive sense recedes as your internal power grows. You will feel the truth, or better said, you will feel what stories resonate as actual portrayals of this life you are participating in.

Having introduced that, it opens a doorway for a discussion of the fantastic – things that are also true yet have been deliberately withheld from you. These things will require an open mind and a great deal of humor – you will want to allow for mistakes and not retain bitterness about the manipulation. Everyone has not been "in on it" or perpetrating it.

I see you are distracted –

Yes. I will have to complete this later.

I never finished this conversation.

A Later Dimension

December 15, 2015

"Can I speak to the one who woke me up 2 nights ago?"

You can.

Great. Who is this and what is the reason for waking me up?

The reason is to alert you.

Alert me to what?

Alert you to the fact of my, of our many, existence. We want to engage with you and you are not regularly available.

It is not just myself, but a contingent. The only "time" you are receptive to being disturbed is while you sleep. Your awake time is filled with others and activities and there is no disruption while that is going on.

So, you woke me to talk?

Yes. We feel we are running out of opportunities to reach you and because of that, we alerted you to our presence. We desire discussion.

What is it you want to discuss?

The coming shift in frequency and its resulting effect on life forms – of which you currently embody.

Who are you?

I specifically am one who comes now from another time/space/reality. The realm I currently inhabit is not even imagined by those in your current realm. Yet it is from here that many of you came.

You understand, or better said, are aware of this internally and because this is so, are receptive to the information.

What I came to remind you of is what you signed up for in the current transformation. It has been for the rest of us a gradual frequency shift and vibratory increase.

There have been none before now, before you, before the human – who've stepped from complete polarity/slavery density into an ascended state of awareness.

You know that the term ascended has nothing to do with going up. It is therefore a confusing term. Ascended (in this context) means a moving forward, a speeding up, a letting go – of form.

This does not mean that I have no form, nor that you won't. Yet there is a reason your kind has come to expect formlessness. This is due to the fact that you cannot see with your physical sight the form that I am or the place that I inhabit.

Dreaming is the time for sight. In dreaming, and by this I refer to <u>sleep dreaming</u>, your physicality is not considered. You are free.

In truth, all is dreaming. Yet for the sake of this transmission we will stick to the physical sleep dream only.

It is then that sight is enabled.

I have to go. (I was at a coffee shop and needed to leave for work)

Yes. We will continue?

Yes, in a bit.

(A bit later that same day)

I am able to continue now.

Yes. We will then.

The body of the human will participate in the current and upcoming expansion. Actually, the life forms of all kinds which surround you now will participate if they choose to do so.

Will some choose not to?

Yes, this is what we expect. The expansion and experience of each life is self-chosen. There are more than a few on your place of resonance whom are there to observe, not participate. Although they will be affected, they will not be "going" anywhere. This may not be the majority, and again, everything is undetermined until the now moment of the shift, yet it appears to be a significant number.

For those who participate, this change will distribute its effect down to every particle of their being. It is a monumental alteration of the operating physical. Nothing will be the same.

You all wonder about current maladies and diseases and their condition after the shift. Let us tell it this way – all of you exists in each vibratory expression – yet, and this is an important point – the current "you" expresses health and disease according to and in concert with current expectations for a life form of this density.

Once you change, all bets are off and this new form that is still you will not express exactly the same.

We would suggest you enjoy your current expression to whatever extreme you are capable of believing. Do not hold back.

All the while, imagine health and vitality.

For this imagination, THAT IS SO MUCH A VITAL PART OF WHAT YOU ARE NOW, IS THE ONLY THING WE ARE SURE WILL ACCOMPANY YOU.

WHAT YOUR IMAGININGS LOOK LIKE ONCE THE NEW FORM IS ADOPTED WILL BE NEW FOR US ALL.

THIS HAS NEVER BEEN DONE.

We are finished. That is all for now.

Thank you.

The conversation ended.

No longer in form

December 29, 2015

"Is there someone who wants to connect?"

Yes.

Go ahead then. I am available.

We would like to engage you in a discussion about what is transpiring for you and for all beings on the earth-sphere. It is of most relevance.

Please do. And introduce yourself while doing so.

This is not a subject we are accustomed to discussing. In fact, it is not something we primarily do – discuss things.

Our communication methods are complete comprehension – mind to mind. It is evident while engaging that concepts are only as fully absorbed as the being or entity is able to absorb them.

All levels of interest and comprehension are clear to the parties involved at the level of clarity possible.

Who are you? How would I identify you?

I am one who is not in form at this "time" – reaching to you from the "ethers" or other realms as you would or may describe it.

Please clarify.

I am of an original form that no longer is found in your "dimension". You would not see me or others of my kind.

I am finding the communication a bit stilted – hold on while I again center myself please.

Of course.

Okay, I am back. Please go ahead.

What it is we want to pass on to you is this idea of life that is held in the minds of your race. It is the idea of growth that is so intrinsic to you level of focus with each other.

I do not get your meaning.

What we wish to transmit to you is possibly new thought around the process of life. It may be of assistance, we feel, in your assessment of this now moment for the human cycle.

Certainly, you are at a pivotal point. This point has taken many revolutions around the sun to reach. Each of these turns in and of themselves were and are pivotal.

The human is fond of the big moment, the grand finish, the happy ending. This, (in all places except perhaps physical life), where the beginning is revered while the ending is denied any form of reverence – it is not seen as positive in any light & is cause for sadness.

What we'd like to introduce here is an idea that all moments in every form and cycle of life be revered.

What is so wonderful about the human is his/her enthusiasm and exuberance. What this conversation is introducing is a concept of excitement for every stage, all ages and each evolutionary point. This is indeed possible in races of beings not held back or controlled by forces beyond their awareness. It is always a trick to accomplish in races so bent on survival that downtrodden is their primary emotion.

There are races and places celebrating it all – birth, death, every moment of growth contributing to both and all evolutionary points on the scale. These are races who only know their own power retained and have awareness of the cycle of life. There is wisdom contained in the seed, beauty in the flower and nourishment in the decaying plant. All are crucial for life; all are imperative to completing the cycle and feed each other continuously. It is a never-ending journey.

Once the complete story is told, there is an appreciation for the richness of each component and the necessity of each contribution. This reverence is held in the stories themselves, as well as the voices sharing them.

In this way, new and experienced beings appreciate all stages. Seen as a cycle, there is then no fear of any stage – it is understood to be a cyclical journey and repetitive.

Life is celebrated and observed from the backdrop of an ancient landscape where the witnessing of the complete evolutionary path exists in the knowledge shared again and again.

The human has heard that he is a young race. What this means is that his evolutionary cycle is yet to be witnessed in fullness – it has yet to complete itself.

All of creation enjoys so much the enthusiasm of the human and watches eagerly each stage. Do not imagine this eagerness is only present in this now moment. For all moments are exciting, as the human chooses to define his path with passion and purpose and heroism.

Know that many of your human traits are unique to your race and not seen everywhere. Predominant among them is his passion. You are a passionate being in every circumstance.

It is this passion we see capitalized on by those in control and yet as well as the driving emotion breaking the chains.

We wanted to offer a cheer of love and enthusiasm as you proceed to further your evolution and also to say "embrace each moment about to transpire, for even in the midst of chaos, man is emerging transformed and transcended. This is a guarantee."

That is all.

Thank you. Goodbye then.

Yes. For this conversation, we say goodbye.

This conversation ended.

Rock-like Beings

December 5, 2015

"Who is here?" It is an unusual sensation I feel with your arrival – definite, concise, and immediate. I was tempted to relate it to the wavy, dizzy sensation I've been experiencing lately, and when I did that, it was brought to a halt, almost abruptly. Yet a sense of dizziness lingers."

Yes, well –

Hold a moment please. ... Okay, I'm back.

Yes, well once you become more acclimated to our vibratory level, the dizziness or sense of movement subsides. We notice this, and just now we have "helped" that to happen instantaneously – hence your feeling of an abrupt halt.

Yes, and we are here and desire contact. Our purpose is the same as it has been always – to assist in the evolution of the human.

There are some who question what it is that any of you are getting out of this contact. In other words – why are you talking to me? What motivates you?

What an interesting query – born of both suspicion and realism. We see that you do not share this emotion, which is both interesting and one of the reasons for us reaching out to you at this time and in this way. You are allowing the contact to come in without judgment as to what the result of the interaction will be.

As an answer to this question let us say that we receive expansion ourselves. The contact with you is expansive and loving and unusual. We gain new perspective from it.

As well know that all of this was agreed at the beginning. It is done by prior arrangement. How things look today may not be seen prior to now, but that they happen at all was planned at the outset.

There are many who've agreed to assist, on and off your planet. This, because we are but one single life form, expressed exponentially. Your evolution is ours as well. So what we "get" out of this is fulfillment and a more rapid expansion.

What is it you'd like to transmit now? I don't hear anything?

We are contemplating. The disclosure process has been put out there in a larger way, as was part of the plan, yet it changes the game a bit. Our initial point in contact was to introduce other life forms so that acceptance will be rapid when physical gatherings occur.

You have not told me who you are or described your appearance yet – that is always a help to my readers.

Yes, correct. It is not easy to put into your consciousness ideas that you have not been exposed to in your reality. We are not your typical being. Most of us would not even be considered as sentient or capable of thought, emotions, and decisions. We are more like rocks. Our structure is dense, slow moving – our life span is many thousands of your "years".

Why then does your energy create a feeling of dizziness?

The difference in speed is what determines the comfort level of their combination. We do not move in the same wavelength. As stated, the human would question our sentience.

Would you describe yourself further?

There is an ebb and flow to what is our life span. We are part of the structure you would call the ground and land and hills. Think about the rocks sprinkled on the planet you occupy – also sentient by the way.

The rocks or the planet?

Both. We do not appear as rocks, but rock like in solidity and compactness. Our colors are bright –

I see green, red, yellowish, blue – yet not distinct form.

Yes – life exists in forms unimagined. I cannot put the picture in your awareness of what you have no relative images for.

Would you try? What is your movement like? How do you loco-mote? What I see is a sort of flat, swirl of what I am supposing is vibrantly colored rock – if that makes sense.

It will have to do. What we want to transmit is our ideas about life and the process of longevity and change. What is an interminable length of "time" to a human is a "nano-second" to us.

What this extrapolates into is patience and a view of each decision that includes its result.

The span of "time" incorporated is the equivalent of a human lifetime. This allows for very solid decisions regarding all that we do around each offspring and invention and process.

You have offspring?

Of course, we do! How would we continue if not for "future" generations?

They are not created in the same fashion as humans and again, this is not a process I can put into your head. It is mutual manifestation based on decisions by the beings involved.

Please go ahead. I really have no questions that would even relate.

Yes...

I feel a new stage of dizziness suddenly and sense more of you – "younger" of you – joining the group.

Yes. We are gathering a crowd. I believe the best purpose for this interaction would be to transmit our standards for decisions – decisions to go ahead with an activity.

Okay, please do.

We continue doing something or follow a current plan only if there is a compelling reason to do so. This compelling reason has to be beneficial to the organism.

By organism is referred to our life form. Life form is not singular to us – it is all of us – it is us. Beneficial includes an extremely wide range of characteristics – yet regardless of what they constitute – they must give benefit.

Here, benefit means the organism's life span is extended. Period. We exist to further the experience of living, and anything that does not prolong that experience, instead shortening it, is rejected.

Now the choices have been witnessed over many thousands of "years" and as you can imagine, some take longer than others to expose their effect.

What this means is that at the outset there will or may be few obvious things to explain why a choice has been made. Yet that does not matter, as the information used to make the choice always has resulted in aiding the lifespan of the organism. Trust is put into that condition and questions are not expressed. In this way, wisdom is attained and shared. We live in Unity always.

I sense many questions.

I have them yes, but I would rather you continue.

Yes, I sense a conflicting emotional response – both fascination and confusion.

We are not a group of life forms you would consider contacting for communication. We are not like you in any fashion. Yet we are life and as such part of creation. We therefore expand as you do.

Our expansion will affect our comprehension of what is possible. It is one thing to know the human exists and quite another to encounter her energy. It is so light as to be almost invisible to us.

Realize that this surprises us – that one so miniscule and fluttery could have any affect at all on our own life form. Yet we know that it does.

Being connected to all life forms is a knowing we have always had. The young race of humanity is entertaining for us. We appreciate what you have added to our knowing. We will digest it now and leave you here. We thank you and have enjoyed the contact.

I as well. Thank you.

You are welcome.

Sirian

December 26, 2015

"Is there someone who wishes to connect?"

Yes, there is Sophia, on this day, we do.

Please introduce yourself then and go ahead.

We are Sirian. You've spoken in the past to others of our kind. We choose now an audience to assist in the restructuring of your life and society after the physical destruction.

We know that you are unprepared and unclear on what will need to happen. We can share our experiences as we have too experienced a cataclysm of drastic proportions and had to re-structure.

Explain please.

Yes, well the planet went through a physical cleanse, what you might call catastrophe. This was not deemed so (catastrophic) at the time for us as we were expecting it and ready in whatever fashion we needed to be.

It will be the same for you. The change that has been prophesied is not an end; it is a cleansing before a beginning. The earth itself must prepare herself for the upcoming inhalation of new frequencies. This by ridding herself of old ones – of frequencies that do not support an age of love and an influx of the light carrying it.

If your people understood the entire process of evolution and ascension they would rejoice – for the "catastrophic" will yield powerful, plentiful fruit.

What can be done first off is emotional preparation. Things are going to die, to end, to stop. Others are going to begin, to flourish, to move in to replace the empty ones. There is no void in creation.

Emotionally prepared then, you can move on to think of what physical needs will require for 2 weeks' time. Prepare in the supply categories of:

Food

Medicine

Shelter

Transportation

Heat and light

Water

Communication

Necessities are what we refer to here. In some, but not all cases, you will stay where you are and be asked to share with those who have not prepared.

In some, but not all cases, you will be physically removed in a moment's time so that you are not destroyed. You will not remain "off planet" and may not remember anything about the lift off – all this done to keep you in safety.

In some, but not all cases, you'll choose this moment as your exit. This, (as are all choices in creation), is personally decided.

It is most helpful for those of you seeing the earth through her shift to remember that every participation level was personally chosen right up until the minute it occurred, and there was and is nothing you could have done to alter the course of another being.

Life is eternal, which is the biggest take away as this physical alteration transpires. With an attitude of acceptance and assistance you will then proceed through this shift with the greatest amount of success and relative healing possible.

Remember that this is a necessary physical alteration. You reside in a physical existence. Things will not be effectively altered without physical alteration.

What did your race do to overcome the fear that must have been present?

We cradled those who needed comfort in love. These were not coddled, but held in love so that they themselves were then able to work through whatever they needed to in order to process the change. Some departed, many did not. We did not judge their choice. All of creation has a role in the shift, some more actively participating than others.

We did not hide information. There was a great deal of misinformation as well yet there was NO ONE COMPLETELY IN THE DARK. WHEN THE PHYSICAL EVENT OCCURRED – NO ONE WAS SHOCKED.

Some panicked, yet there was so much stability and compassion surrounding them that their panic was reduced and in many instances, eliminated.

The thing we wanted to give, through this contact, is our story of what could be called a successful journey through a similar cataclysmic transformation.

On the other side of the destruction there was unification, re-building for the sake of the whole, peace and a feeling of comradery and purpose and truth that was prevalent.

Our race is millennia beyond the catastrophe yet we hold it in our collective memory as a reminder of what has value, of what is important or relatively more important than small and petty considerations of differences.

Life wins in every case and where I come from it is the most valuable asset shared. We came to understand love not as a romantic ideal but a physical act between sovereign beings and life forms.

We hold as sacred the heart, which is the place from which love springs.

Ideas of separation do not reside in the heart, but are imagined by ego and created in the brain.

After our shift, what became clearest of all was which process held truth. It is held always in the process of loving, which is the basis of existence itself.

We are excited for humanity to share in this knowing on a global scale and join us on the evolutionary path to freedom and the cycle of creation.

We hope our meaning and message will help those able to hear it.

Yes. It does and will. Thank you for reaching out in this way.

You are welcome. We are pleased with the contact. *(I wrote here a note to self – "cat ears?")*

This conversation ended.

Stick Beings

December 16, 2015

Notes included with its original publication, which was February 2016 –

"You will hear below another way of thinking about unity. <u>In fact, oneness is truth.</u> It is our own perspective that creates the alternative; isolation and the possibility of control by someone other than self. This comes in the midst of the current greater conversation around "Disclosure Now" and the many predictions for massive upheaval these next 2 months.

These are things we've all chosen, whether out loud or internally, with our decisions and beliefs. Intend sovereignty and abundance for all. It is having a powerful effect, and more focus will only amplify things. Every ripple moves the pond.

We know for a fact that you tube and the internet are seen by a host of on and off world beings. Speak out, in whatever way you have at your disposal. We are one & it is time."

Here is the conversation...

"Is there someone who wants to connect?"

There is Sophia.

Go ahead please, I am available.

Okay, we will first introduce ourselves.

Please do.

We are not as you have seen, and/or even imagined in your picturing of a being with whom you are talking. We embody a form that is more geared for flight than walking.

There are wings. We are quite small and would hardly be noticed if we arrived in mass in your yard; more the size of a large insect. We see the image you hold in your mind of a very tiny humanoid and tell you we are smaller still and not humanoid. *(I was thinking of the Sirius Alien. Sophia)*

Our eyes are large. We communicate with gestures and mind to mind speak. This is what we are engaged with now, in this conversation with you, but a bit different.

(I had to leave for a moment...) I am back. Are you able to send me an image?

I am seeing mostly wings, frilly. Are you Mantis beings?

We are not. Our form is more stick like, our heads and eyes are different. We do not have legs as the mantis do.

(So, I drew this little figure here. It has squiggly lines on either side of the wings, a stick in the middle with two large circle-eyes at the top. No real tail, the stick/line in the middle ends/meets the bottom of the wings. – Sophia)

Okay. Let's move on. What are you here to discuss?

We are here for the specific purpose of unity. Not as a thing to do or practice or become – (but) as a component of life. Unity is as necessary to your survival, to our survival, (excuse us) as *(is)* your/our heart. You have a saying: "No man is an island" and this would be truth.

I am not a man, and the name for me has not been spoken. (Here is a reference to the fact that this race has not been "named" by us. Sophia). Yet no "being" is an island. The saying applies.

It was determined that we would reach you to offer our perspective on unity as a driving component of existence – not instead as a quaint idea for greeting cards and non-profiting endeavors.

Unity becomes then the invisible part – vital, unseen and its contribution unrecognized.

In our species, we cannot move singularly. We are fragile, sticks with wings. The force of just one of us is not enough to move through the air – to locomote. We require cooperation and collaboration to proceed in any direction.

Left alone, we are like a scrap of frilly lace – pushed about by whatever breeze shows up.

Yet we do not fathom "alone". Ours is a race unified at the outset and fully mindful of the implications.

We hear one song and gladly contribute our notes when they will harmonize or are necessary. There are no questions unanswered by the whole of us.

Ours is a mutual dependence.

None of us predominates. New directions are examined and shared, then considered by the group. Each of us emits a unique note and we are always heard.

What we don't have is any concept of pretending or ignoring or selfish – we are each appreciated, unified and depended upon, for service to the whole.

We cannot and do not move alone. We do not suffer from any notion of hiding or separation. We don't ever see ourselves behind something that could create such a barrier.

We have introduced ours as another way to be – individual yet ONE – which is true for the human as well. We see the human imagine different agendas. Yet what is different than life? It is the attribute universally held.

Your need for air and love is not different in any country or age. Your need for shelter or health or clothing or sustenance; these are identical.

At birth, the need for each other is most evident. "Failure to Thrive" becomes lethal for new ones of you *(who are)* not held.

Yet it is not just the new ones who don't move without help – it is the human at any stage.

Your legs become able to hold your weight, yet *your heart cannot create love it cannot see reflected (Italics mine. Sophia)*. This is the fragile section of the human instrument – the one in need of support always. Babies know this and burst into tears without it; kittens too.

It is the adult who forgets the necessary unity for survival. It is the adult to whom we speak.

Do not assume because you are able to walk alone, unlike us, that you are able to live in isolation. Your relationship with life determines how far you will get. All of life is as much you, as *(is)* your fingertips.

You move, you speak, you are as one. This is the message for you now.

There is no shame in dependence. It is a fact of unity – of life – of you.

That is all.

Okay. Thank you.

You are welcome Sophia.

This conversation ended. Wow.

Notes/Where to find me

Blog　　　　　　　　　http://www.sophialove.org/my-blog (w/ RSS feed)

Sovereignty Series　　　http://www.sophialove.org/sovereignty.html

Newsletter　　　　　　http://www.sophialove.org/subscribe-here.html

Facebook　　　　　　　@IAMSophiaLove

You-tube　　　　　　　www.youtube.com/user/sophialovequest

Sound-cloud　　　　　　soundcloud.com/sophialove

Website　　　　　　　　www.sophialove.org

Twitter　　　　　　　　HTTPS://TWITTER.COM/SOPHIALOVE_EDU

Amazon Author Page　　(you'll find my first book, "The Guardian", there)

　　　　　　　　　　　　amazon.com/author/sophialove

So, that completes this first volume of "Inclusion". There will be others. These contacts are expanding my appreciation for the word "life". It contains so much more than we realize, as do you. It is an honor to proceed on this journey together.

Thank you!

We are the Ones We've Been Waiting for.

With so much love,

~Sophia

The end.
(or is it the beginning?)

©2011-2017 Sophia Love. All Rights Reserved.